GHOST BOMBERS

THE MOONLIGHT WAR OF NSG 9

uftwaffe Night Attack Operations from Anzio to the Alps

Dedication

Den ehemaligen Angehörigen der NSG 9 und
ihren Familien gewidmet.
Für ihre Freundschaft und Geduld danke ich
ihnen aufrichtig.

First published in 2001 by Classic Publications Limited, Friars Gate Farm, Mardens Hill, Crowborough,
East Sussex TN6 1XH England

ISBN 1-903223-15-6

Cover design and book layout by CW Design

Origination by Colourwise Limited, England

Printed in Italy by Milanostampa Interlitho S.P.A.

GHOST BOMBERS

THE MOONLIGHT WAR OF NSG 9
uftwaffe Night Attack Operations from Anzio to the Alps

Nick Beale

Colour Artwork
Tom Tullis

CLASSIC
PUBLICATIONS

The Author

Nick Beale's interest in Second World War aviation was sparked off early in his life by his father's and uncles' stories and souvenirs of growing up in wartime. After years of reading other writers' books, he started conducting his own research in 1985, contributing articles to magazines before, in 1988, embarking with Italian authors Ferdinando D'Amico and Gabriele Valentini on what would become *Air War Italy 1944-45: The Axis Air Forces from the Liberation of Rome to the Surrender* (Airlife, 1996). Beginning in 1990, he was one of the first authors to use ULTRA material — decyphered German signals — in reconstructing the Luftwaffe's activities. Since 1985, he has also been a contributor of record/concert reviews to *fRoots*, the monthly world music magazine. His day job, which allows him to afford the researching and reviewing, is in local government. Nick lives with his partner, Linda, in the south west of England. They divide their time between Exeter, London and Paris but not in the right proportions.

Acknowledgements

This book would never have got off the ground without the help and patience of the NSG 9 veterans I have been able to meet or who have been kind enough to correspond with me, despite the grammatical disaster areas of my written and spoken German. First was Hans Nawroth both in his role as an informal archivist of NSG 9 and as my introduction to his comrades. A special "thank you" then to Hans and his wife Hanni.

The others are: Dirk Bunsen, Alfons Eck, Willy Ferling, Franz Fischer, Harry Fischer, Horst Greßler, Volkmar von Grone, Bruno Grüning, Werner Hensel, Herbert Kehrer, Alfred Kunzmann, Heinrich Leinberger, Werner Lotsch, Eduard Reither, Rudi Sablottny, Helmut Schäfer and Paul-Ernst Zwarg.

Sadly, Eduard Reither died on 18 August 2000, aged 84, shortly after the manuscript of this book was completed.

My thanks also for their generosity, hospitality and friendship to family members Irmgard Bunsen, Marga Eck, Christa Ferling, Toni and Erika Fink, Bernd Gräßer, Bernd and Christine Kehrer, Doris Liebscher, Isolde Hensel, the late Dr. Mathilde Holtz, Gerhard and Sigrid Leinberger, Rosa Lotsch, Gina Reither, Katarina Sablottny.

Help also came from: 1./NSG 4 veteran Alfred Partzsch; USAAF veterans Clark Eddy, Haylon R. Wood and Delbert "Deb" Wylder; RAF veteran Neil Galloway; Bob Rees, son of the late F/O Stewart Rees (RAAF).

Aviation researchers and authors: Ulf Balke, Winfried Bock, Steve Coates, Eddie J. Creek, James V. Crow, Ferdinando D'Amico, Larry De Zeng, Robert Forsyth, Tom Ivie, James H. Kitchens III, Antonio Maraziti, Christian Möller, Martin Pegg, Barry Smith, J. Richard Smith, Gabriele Valentini, Dave Wadman, Manfred Zundel.

Hans Moonen, of the "Propaganda Leaflets of World War 2" website (www.cobweb.nl/jmoonen/)

The Editor of The Fremantle Herald.

The staff of the Imperial War Museum and the Public Record Office; *D.ssa* Fiorella De Sanctis of the Archivio Storico Fiat; the USAF Historical Research Agency; the Bundesarchiv–Militärarchiv, Freiburg.

Apple Computers, without which…

Thanks above all to my partner, Linda Pardoe.

Nick Beale
Exeter, April 2001

CONTENTS

Foreword

by Johannes Nawroth, former *Bordfunker* with 3./NSG 9

I am pleased to be able to fulfil the author's request to provide some words of introduction to this book. Any question as to the book's sense and purpose would best be answered with the words: "a commemoration of the fallen, a reminder for the survivors, a warning for future generations."

Until now there was sadly no account of NSG 9, which was in action from early 1944 to the cessation of hostilities in Italy at the end of April 1945. The German Military Archives have very few documents from this era. One is very grateful to the author that despite this he has managed to put this account together. Much of this was only possible for the first time through the inspection of English and American war archives. It ought to be mentioned that it is a laborious and time-consuming job to write such a book about NSG 9 more than 55 years after the events described. Through its objective presentation this book will show the senselessness of the engagements and of war in general.

Author's Preface

The *Nachtschlachtflieger*, the night ground attack arm of the *Luftwaffe*, intrigued me from the first brief mentions I read in books and were one of the earliest lines I followed up when I finally started to do research of my own. This was not the world of bemedalled fighter aces that still preoccupies so much of aviation literature; some *Nachtschlacht* units began and ended their war flying biplanes only one quarter as fast as the jet aircraft by then in *Luftwaffe* service. Nevertheless, from ad hoc beginnings the *Nachtschlacht* branch took in more and more experienced aircrew as flying schools closed down and the daylight *Schlachtgeschwader* converted to single-seater machines. With better aircraft came bigger bombloads and (in the West and Italy) electronic assistance to deliver them accurately. NSG 9 progressed in the space of little more than a year from the slow Caproni 314 with 320kg of bombs to the powerful Fw 190F-9, capable of carrying a warload almost three times as great. Clearly investment in night attack was thought worthwhile.

I started to learn something of NSG 9's story while working with my good friends Ferdinando D'Amico and Gabriele Valentini on what eventually became *Air War Italy 1944–45*. Conscious that most of the available archive material offered an official rather than a personal perspective, we had made appeals via German aviation magazines for veterans' stories but had found none from NSG 9. It was 1993 and our manuscript had been with the publishers for several months when researcher Steve Coates showed me a five-year old copy of *Berliner Flugheft*, the newsletter of a group of Berlin aviation enthusiasts. An article by one Manfred Zundel reported on NSG 9's first reunion and asked anyone with information about the unit to write to Johannes Nawroth.

I sent letters to both him and Zundel and some time later a reply came from Hans Nawroth, a former *Bordfunker* with 3./NSG 9. He had moved house recently and thrown out a lot of papers I would love to have seen. Nevertheless, a productive correspondence ensued and we managed to include some of Hans's experiences in *Air War* when it was finally published.

With Hans's help and friendship, I was able to contact around 20 other NSG 9 veterans and have been attending their reunions each year since 1996. Suddenly I was meeting people who to me had previously been just names on historical documents and some of whom I had believed missing or dead since 1944. I soon learned that in many respects I had barely scratched the surface of their story and embarked on compiling a simple chronology for the unit's former members, thinking that it wouldn't take all that long but gradually my ideas shifted to writing a full scale book. Five years later…

Ghost Bombers has been written from scratch, reassessing what I thought I already knew as well as utilising the masses of new information I have accumulated, above all from the ever helpful and tolerant veterans of NSG 9 and their relatives. Their assistance and my own continuing researches have permitted the filling of innumerable gaps and the correction of many former errors. Wherever possible throughout this book, I have tried to tell the story in the words of those who were actually there.

Nick Beale

Abbreviations and Glossary

AA		Anti-aircraft
AB	*Abwurfbehälter*	Cluster-bomb canister (droppable)
A/c		Aircraft
AI		Airborne Interception (radar)
ALG		Advanced Landing Ground
Amis	*Amerikaner*	Americans/Yanks
ANR	*Aeronautica Nazionale Repubblicana*	Air Force of the Italian Social Republic
ATI		Air Technical Intelligence
B4		German 87-octane aircraft fuel
Bandit		Enemy aircraft
BG		Bombardment Group (US)
Bogey		Unidentified aircraft (usually suspected as hostile)
	Bordfunker	Wireless Operator
	Bordschütze	Air Gunner
Br. C	*Brandbombe Cylindrisch*	Incendiary bomb, cylindrical
BS		Bombardment Squadron (US)
CO		Commanding Officer
CSDIC		Combined Services Detailed Interrogation Centre
DAF		Desert Air Force (British Empire and Dominions element of MATAF, **q.v.**)
DF		Direction finding
	Düppel	Anti-radar foil strips (equivalent to Allied "Window")
E/a		Enemy aircraft
EK	*Eisernes Kreuz*	Iron Cross (Class I & II)
	Enigma	German cipher machine
ETA		Estimated Time of Arrival
FAG	*Fernaufklärungsgruppe*	Long-range reconnaissance Gruppe
FBG		Fighter-Bomber Group (US)
FBK	*Flughafenbetriebskompanie*	Airfield Servicing Company
	Feindflug	Operational flight
FG		Fighter Group (US)
FIU		Field Intelligence Unit
FJ	*Fallschirmjäger*	Paratroops
Flivo	*Fliegerverbindungsoffizier*	Luftwaffe Liaison Officer attached to army unit
Fl.H.Ber.	*Flughafenbereich*	Airfield Region
	Flugkapitän	Civilian pilot's rank
FS		Fighter Squadron (US)
FSU		Field Signals Unit
FuG	*Funkgerät*	Radio/radar device
Funknav. Trupp	*Funknavigationstrupp*	Radio Navigation Section
FW		Fighter Wing (US)
GCI		Ground Controlled Interception
G.d.S.	*General der Schlachtflieger*	General of the Ground Attack Forces
GMT		Greenwich Mean Time
Gr.	*Gruppe* (German), *Gruppo* (Italian)	
Gr.C	*Gruppo Caccia*	Fighter *Gruppo*
HE		High explosive
Ia		Operations Officer (Luftwaffe)
IAS		Indicated Air Speed
Ic		Intelligence Officer (Luftwaffe)
IFF		Identification Friend or Foe
i.G.	*im Generalstab*	General Staff Officer
	Infanterie Division	Infantry Division
	Jäger Division	Light Infantry Division
JG	Jagdgeschwader	Fighter Geschwader
	Kasino	Officers' Mess
Kdo.	*Kommando*	(1) Detachment; (2) Command Echelon
KG	*Kampfgeschwader*	Bomber *Geschwader*
Koflug	*Kommando Flughafenbereich*	Regional Airfield Command
Komm. Gen.	*Kommandierender General*	General Officer Commanding
Kogen	[as above]	

KTB	*Kriegstagebuch*	War Diary
Lfl.	*Luftflotte*	Air Fleet
LG	*Lehrgeschwader*	Demonstration Geschwader
L/G		Landing Ground
LN Rgt.	*Luftnachrichtenregiment*	Air Force Signals Regiment
Ln. Zug (mot.)	*Luftnachrichtenzug (motorisiert)*	Air Signals Platoon (motorised)
MAAF		Mediterranean Allied Air Forces
MASAF		Mediterranean Allied Strategic Air Forces (part of MAAF)
MATAF		Mediterranean Allied Tactical Air Forces (part of MAAF)
MG	*Maschinengewehr*	Machine-gun
	Mittelitalien	Central Italy
MM	*Matricola Militare*	Serial Number (Italian military aircraft)
MO		Medical Officer
M/T		Motor Transport
NAG (or NAGr.)	*Nahaufklärungsgruppe*	Tactical Reconnaissance Gruppe
NCO		Non-Commissioned Officer
NSFO	*Nationalsozialistischer-Führungsoffizier*	National Socialist Leadership Officer
NSG (or NSGr.)	*Nachtschlachtgruppe*	Night Harassment Gruppe

Note: although Gr. may be the official abbreviation for a *Gruppe*, the veterans call their unit NSG 9 and so this book follows suit.

Ob.	*Oberbefehlshaber*	Supreme Commander
Ob.d.L	*Oberbefehlshaber der Luftwaffe*	Supreme Commander of the Luftwaffe
	Oberitalien	Upper Italy
Ob.SW	*Oberbefehlshaber Südwest*	Supreme Comander South West
ORB		Operations Record Book
OKL	*Oberkommando der Luftwaffe*	Luftwaffe Supreme Command
OKW	*Oberkommando der Wehrmacht*	Supreme Command of the Armed Forces
	Personalverlustmeldung	Personnel casualty report
	Panzer Grenadier	Mechanised infantry
PR		Photo-reconnaissance
PRG		Photo Reconnaissance Group
PoW		Prisoner of War (English abbreviation)
P/W		Prisoner of War (American abbreviation)
	Panzer	Tank, armour
RAAF		Royal Australian Air Force
RCAF		Royal Canadian Air Force
RCM		Radio Counter Measures
Revi	*Reflexvisier*	Reflector gunsight
RK	*Ritterkreuz*	Knight's Cross
r.p.g.		Rounds per gun
R/T		Radio Telephony (i.e. voice communication)
RV		Rendezvous
SAAF		South African Air Force
SD	*Sprengbombe Dickwand*	Thick-walled (semi armour-piercing or fragmentation) bomb
SD	*Sicherheitsdienst*	Security Service (of the SS)
SG	*Schlachtgeschwader*	Ground attack *Geschwader*
Sigint		Signals Intelligence
Sqn		Squadron (RAF and Dominions)
St.	*Staffel*	
TG	*Transportfliegergeschwader*	Transport *Geschwader*
TO	*Technischer Offizier*	Technical Officer
TRS		Tactical Reconnaissance Squadron
ULTRA		Allied security classification for decrypted Enigma (**q.v.**) traffic
U/s		Unserviceable
	Versuchsverband	Trials Unit (Luftwaffe)
	Volkssturm	German equivalent to British Home Guard
WNr.	*Werk Nummer*	Production serial number
Y		Allied radio monitoring (hence Y-Service)
z.b.V.	*zur besonderen Verwendung*	Special purpose/duties

Italian Province Names

As with American states, each place name in Italy carries a suffix in brackets to identify the province in which it lies. This is an aid to location, especially in the numerous instances where a name recurs many times over in different parts of the country. The province codes used in this book are:

AN	Ancona	FI	Firenze	PC	Piacenza	RO	Rovigo
AR	Arezzo	FO	Forlì	PD	Padova	RM	Roma
BA	Bari	GR	Grosseto	PG	Perugia	SI	Siena
BL	Belluno	IS	Isernia	PI	Pisa	TO	Torino
BO	Bologna	LI	Livorno	PR	Parma	TR	Terni
BS	Brescia	MC	Macerata	PS	Pesaro	VE	Venezia
BZ	Bolzano	MN	Mantova	RA	Ravenna	VI	Vicenza
CN	Cuneo	MO	Modena	RE	Reggio Emilia	VR	Verona
FE	Ferrara	NO	Novara	RI	Rieti	VT	Viterbo

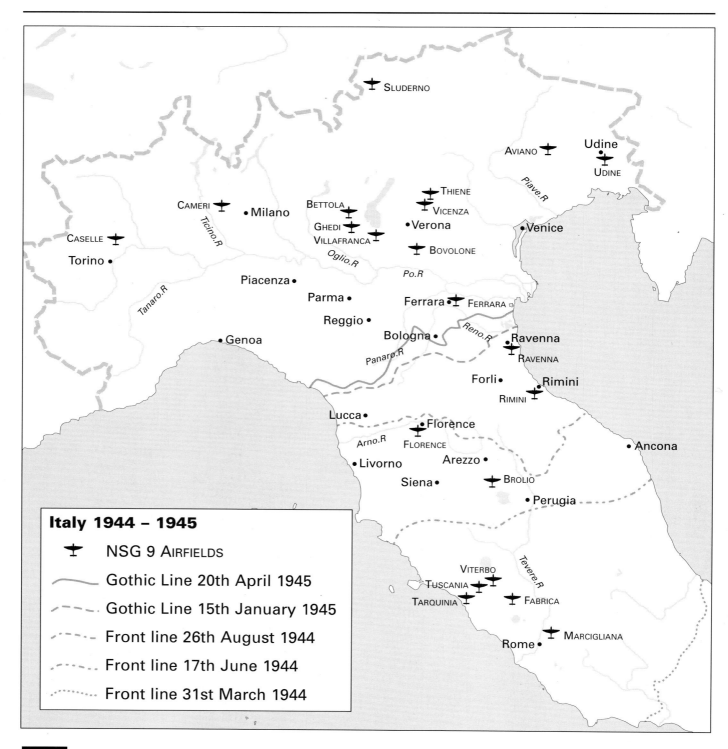

Italy 1944 – 1945

✈ NSG 9 Airfields

— Gothic Line 20th April 1945

– – Gothic Line 15th January 1945

–·– Front line 26th August 1944

–··– Front line 17th June 1944

······ Front line 31st March 1944

"From improvisation to weapon"

*T*he above headline by German war correspondent Gerhard Rauchwetter aptly sums up the development of the *Luftwaffe's* night attack units, the *Nachtschlachtflieger*, who progressed in their 2½ year existence from ad hoc raiding with obsolete types like the Arado 66 to radar guided bombing with the Focke-Wulf 190.

During the winter of 1941–42 the Red Air Force began to deploy light aircraft such as the Po-2 and N-5 as night bombers. Dubbed "sewing machines" by German soldiers, on account of their engine noise, they reportedly operated from frozen lakes and rivers to drop their small but irksome payloads on strongpoints and runways. These attacks continued on a larger scale during the German summer offensives of 1942. Obviously the Soviets could not expect decisive results but all damage to the onrushing enemy was welcome. If nothing else, even small bombs deprived his troops of that most valued resource, sleep.

By the Autumn, the *Luftwaffe* in the East was forming *Behelfskampfstaffeln* (auxiliary bomber squadrons), soon renamed *Störkampfstaffeln* (harassment bomber squadrons), with whatever light planes were to hand and improvising night flying equipment and bomb racks in the field. Not content with imitating Soviet tactics, at times they used captured bombs as well. Crews were found from, inter alia, transport and liaison units and men medically precluded from higher performance flying. These units lived a nomadic life, thrown in wherever the need was greatest, and of necessity developed a high degree of self-sufficiency. Pilots' intimate knowledge of their operational areas, rapid response from bases close to the front and surprise through low altitude gliding approaches combined to give results that the *Luftwaffe* found highly satisfactory. Not only regular troops but also Soviet partisans became their targets.

By 1943 the *Staffeln* had been banded into *Störkampfgruppen* and Herbert Kehrer describes how 2./*Störkampfgruppe Luftwaffenkommando Ost*, the unit that would eventually become 3./NSG 9:

> …was put together in early November 1942 in Görlitz [now Zgorzelec, Poland]. We were 15 pilots, all lacking the blind flying ticket. I came from Aalborg (Denmark) where I'd been flying transports for a year and a half. We received the Go 145, a training aircraft on which we practised night flying in Görlitz and then flew on the central sector in Russia (Vitebsk, Bryansk, Orel, Kursk). Our assignment was to fly far into the hinterland and cause a commotion by dropping single bombs. In early March 1944 we got the Ju 87 with which we could also intervene by day in the vicinity of the front.

A captured Soviet Po-2 attracts attention from troops of 3. SS Infanterie Division 'Totenkopf' somewhere on the Eastern Front. Dubbed 'sewing machines' by the Germans on account of their engine noise, the nocturnal use of these aircraft proved extremely successful and out of all proportion to the effort involved. Although the material effects were not great, nightly harassment of the already exhausted German troops deprived them of badly needed rest and their fighting ablity the next day was severely weakened. So effective were these nocturnal nuisance raids that the Luftwaffe imitated them and created their own night harassment units.

LEFT: *Early days: Ar 66 D3+OK of 2./Störkampfgruppe Lufflotte 6 in flight over the Eastern Front, 1943.*

ABOVE: *An Ar 66 of 2./Störkampfgruppe Luftflotte 6 is refuelled while D3+LK and two other Arados wait their turn. According to Obgfr. Harry Fischer, these particular aircraft belonged to the Nachtschwarm Oberleutnant Haimböck which he joined late in 1943.*

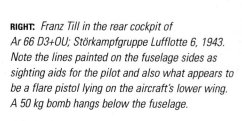

RIGHT: *Franz Till in the rear cockpit of Ar 66 D3+OU; Störkampfgruppe Lufflotte 6, 1943. Note the lines painted on the fuselage sides as sighting aids for the pilot and also what appears to be a flare pistol lying on the aircraft's lower wing. A 50 kg bomb hangs below the fuselage.*

LEFT: *8 May 1943: Franz Till crashed in this He 46 (believed to be BB+CU, WNr. 1247) of 1./Störkampfgruppe Luftwaffenkommando Ost at Orel.*

RIGHT: *Obergefreiter Harry Fischer's Ar 66, D3+UK of the Nachtschwarm Oblt. Haimböck (note the yellow Eastern Front tail band).*

BELOW: *Members of 1. Störkampfstaffel Ost in Borisov, 1943.*
Sitting: Oblt. Haimböck, Major ?, Werner Hensel, Box.
Standing: Wolfgang Schäfer, Krämer, Ebeling, Katzenberger, Büchner.

Harry Fischer was another who made the transition from transport pilot to *Störflieger*.

> I'm a trained paratrooper, transport glider pilot [and I was sent] for re-equipment at Mogilev just a few days before our *Staffel* met its fate in the Velikye Luki pocket. From then on I was always together with *Hptm*. Reither, Werner Hensel and Horst Rau.

In a meeting chaired by *Generalfeldmarschall* Milch at the RLM on 10 September 1943, *Oberstlt*. Ernst Kupfer, discussed the units he would superintend in his new post of *General der Nahkampfflieger*[1]. When it came to the value of the *Störkampfstaffeln* he was able to describe from personal experience (while serving with *Stukageschwader 2*) how effective their Russian counterparts, the "sewing machines", were.

He pointed out that although the idea of using obsolete aircraft in the front line was often ridiculed, during the past winter and in July's offensive at Kursk, those on the forward airfields had learned what anxiety such machines could stir up just by flying about and dropping a few bombs. Throughout the night, the men were afraid and it simply was not true that one could get used to it. Everyone lived with the fear that the next bomb might fall on him and even those exploding some way off always seemed nearer than they were. That was why, Kupfer emphasised, the *Luftwaffe* should "carry on this business"; such aircraft were an ever-present nuisance, making a deep impression on the troops:

> We have achieved excellent results on the Eastern Front with this method of air warfare. Operations were flown with any old aircraft that was available, such as the Arado 66 and the Fw *Weihe*. These aircraft, which would otherwise have been useless, were put to a very practical use without the pilots possessing much flying experience on the types and, what's more … These machines fly so slowly that nobody can hit them, so we have enjoyed light losses and good results.

Milch concurred, recalling that Rommel had experienced something similar from RAF Wellingtons near El Alamein, attesting to their tremendous effect on morale, droning around all night and fraying the nerves of commanders and soldiers alike.

Kupfer's conclusion was that that every effort must be made to employ these old aircraft operationally, with any not needed for training being assigned to the *Störkampfstaffeln*. It was a type of warfare that could, he thought, be further developed, especially since it was so easily accomplished.

Unteroffizier. Dirk Bunsen, led to expect a posting to the *Störflieger* in early 1944, knew their kind of flying by reputation:

> …this business with the Ar 66: night instrument flying with an observer who alternately drops bombs and grenades from his sack onto Ivan's positions. If a searchlight crew thinks it a good idea to illuminate the bird, the second man [i.e. the

Three men who would later serve with NSG 9, Franz Till, Rudi Sablottny and Karl Gabauer, watch as a flock of sheep straggle along the cobbled road of a town in the East.
The photographer's shadow falls on the pavement.

ABOVE: "...the cold of Russia": an ammunition supply convoy in Polozk, November 1943.

ABOVE: Although it has been fitted with exhaust shrouds and had its undersides painted black for night operations, this Ar 66 is still highly conspicuous thanks to its underwing Balkenkreuze, yellow fuselage band and wing tips.

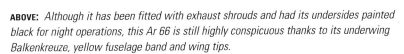

ABOVE: Early 1943: a barely camouflaged Ar 66 at what look to be extremely rudimentary dispersals at Prosk.

LEFT: The men belong to 1. Störkampfstaffel Ost. The mural of a swooping Ju 87 is dated "43" and the artist is "AKA"; the location is probably Borisov. Around the table are Uffz. Werner Hensel (later to serve with NSG 9), Fw. Büchner, Katzenberger, Lt. Haimböck and Major ?

observer] showers them with pleasant greetings from his machine-gun. Essentially you can only count on affecting morale of course. Then it's just a matter of finding your own airfield again, at the precise moment when they light the flare path.

In the reorganisation of the close support arm in autumn 1943, the *Störkampfgruppen* were renamed *Nachtschlachtgruppen* (literally "night battle groups", functionally "night ground attack groups"): NSG 1, 2, 3, 4, 5, 6, 10, 11 and 12 were serving on the Russian front; NSG 7 was established to fight the Yugoslav partisans; NSG 8 would form later, to operate over Finland; in Italy there would be NSG 9.

CAPRONI Ca.314	
Wing span:	54ft 8in (16.7m)
Weights:	10,032lb (4,560kg) empty; 14,560lb (6,618kg) maximum
Power plant:	2 x Isotta-Fraschini Delta RC. 350 developing 700hp each at 11,500ft (3,500m)
Max speed:	215mph (408km/h) at 13,780ft (4,175m)
Climb:	14min 41 sec to 13,000ft
Ceiling:	27,000ft (8,182m)
Range:	750 miles (1,200km)
Armament:	1 x 12.7mm MG fixed in each wing root; 1 x 12.7mm MG in dorsal turret; 1 x 7.7mm MG in ventral position; 700lb (320kg) bombload.

In his post-war recollections, *General der Flieger* Max von Pohl wrote that *Luftflotte 2's* commanding officer, *Generalfeldmarschall* Wolfram *Freiherr* von Richthofen, was offered pilots for a night attack unit if he could supply the aircraft and ground echelons himself. In September 1943 the Western Allies had landed in mainland Italy and the country had broken from the Axis. German forces had been swift in seizing the territory of their erstwhile ally, securing in the process a windfall of some thousands of aircraft of the *Regia Aeronautica*. The Caproni Ca.314, first flown in March 1941, was a twin-engined reconnaissance/light bomber with a crew of three. It was the latest in a series stemming from the pre-war Ca. 309, designed to "police" Italy's colonies and, as such, these machines were apparently judged suitable for the analogous task of fighting partisans. Around 400 of the type had been built. Initially there was no thought of sending NSG 9 against the Allies because the *General der Schlachtflieger's* inspectorate thought Italy's mountainous terrain would pose navigational problems and lead to numerous losses.

The picture reaching the Allied intelligence services at this time was not entirely straightforward. They were to learn from an Italian airman who had left Pola (now Pula, Croatia) on 13 October that:

8km north east of Pola is the airfield of Altura [di Pola], used… entirely by Germans. About 30 Ju 52 were there and a few Caproni 113. The latter aircraft were used for strafing the partisans.

The identity of that formation is unknown: the nearest known night attack unit, *Störkampfstaffel Kroatien*, was recording losses only of the He 46. However, decrypted radio traffic revealed that on 23 November KG 76 had ordered the dispatching of mechanics to Udine in north eastern Italy to assist in setting up 3./NSG 7. Four days later, the Luftwaffe signalled from Berlin its intention to set up *Nachtschlachtstaffeln* using seized Italian Ca.313 and 314 aircraft.

On 10 December, in connection with the establishment and re-equipping of *Nachtschlachtstaffeln* and NSG 7, Berlin ordered arrangements to be made to assist *Fliegerführer* (*Flifü*) Croatia with technical equipment and supplies, including machine-gun ammunition for the Caproni 314. For his part, the *Flifü* was to detach an officer to *Luftflotte 2*, who would put his operational experience at the disposal of the CO of "I./NSG 9" in Udine.

To the author's knowledge, this was the Allies' first intimation of NSG 9's existence and RAF Intelligence considered it possible that it was a renamed 3./NSG 7 which, as we have seen, they understood to have been forming in Udine during late November. Since a decrypted order of battle from as late as 25 May mentions only the *Stab, 1.* and *2. Staffeln* of NSG 7 and the first explicit mention of a third that the author has found comes on 20 July 1944, that assessment may well have been correct. What is known is that 1./NSG 9 was formally established on 30 November 1943 with the unit identification code E8.

---

1. "General of the Close Support Fliers." On Göring's instructions the title was later changed to *General der Schlachtflieger*.

"Sunny Italy seemed very attractive"

I n September or October 1943, ten experienced crews were detached from NSG 3 on the northern sector of the Russian Front and posted to SG 111 at Stubendorf, Upper Silesia[1] to convert on to the Ca.314. The commander of this training unit was *Major* Andreas Zahn, the *Kapitän* of its 1. *Staffel* was *Oblt*. Wagner and its Chief Flying Instructor, *Oblt*. Wilmar.

Volkmar von Grone remembers that by the Autumn of that year he was rated by his superiors as an experienced, successful pilot and had just regained his *Leutnant's* rank following an earlier clash with authority:

> My *Kommandeur*… asked me if I was prepared, along with a few comrades from my current outfit whom I myself could nominate, to take over the cadre of a new *Nachtschlacht* unit to be set up in Italy, then equipped with the Ju 87… Naturally I replied in the affirmative, since the prospect of swapping the cold of Russia for sunny Italy seemed very attractive.

Meanwhile during October, the assembly of a ground echelon for NSG 9 had begun in Mantua, many of the men then being sent on courses elsewhere in Italy before transferring to Caselle-Torino (Turin) in the north west on 26 January. After their training, the aircrew had arrived in Udine (according to *Oblt*. Rolf Begemann) on 20 December. Horst Greßler adds that Udine was the unit's HQ and that he spent only a short time there before moving on to Caselle, where Ca.314s were being ferried in from Linz and Wiener Neustadt in Austria, which ties in with information from ULTRA concerning the presence of "captured aircraft of NSG 111" at Linz-Hörsching on 3 December. Command of NSG 9 was given to *Hauptmann* Rupert Frost, a pioneer *Nachtschlachtflieger* who had been appointed *Kapitän* of 1. *Behelfskampfstaffel Luftwaffenkommando Don* on 1 November 1942, leading this and its successors with distinction. The officers and pilots of his new unit were:

Staffelführer	*Hptm*. Rupert Frost
Offizier z.b.V.	*Lt*. Rolf Begemann
T.O.	*Oblt*. August Müller
Pilots:	*Fw*. Johann Deffner, Horst Greßler, Volkmar von Grone and Artur Heiland
	Uffze. Müller[2], Kaspar Stuber and Werner Waißnor
	Gefre. Johann Horn, Ewald Kapahnke, Richard Schwobe and Franz Spörr

Once in Italy, von Grone and a few similarly-experienced pilots spent some time evaluating the operational potential of both the Caproni and the Fiat CR.42 biplane fighter:

> … the Caproni 314 was a big worry to us because we lost some good crews in crashes. I repeatedly had bad experiences with this type, especially on a winter flight to Vienna. The landing gear wouldn't come down and after numerous aerobatic attempts I had to land on one wheel.
>
> The landing passed off gently since, using the rudder, I was able to keep my lame duck on her one leg along an adjoining snowed-in strip until her speed had fallen enough that I could do the last bit as a sleigh ride. That showed right away that the captured Italian planes weren't a practicable alternative to our relatively slow but dependable Ju 87.

Campoformido, January 1944: in the shadow of their Ca.314, Fw. Volkmar von Grone (right) and a fellow crewman strap on their parachutes prior to a flight. For von Grone, flying the Caproni was "a big worry…"

ABOVE: *Italy's surrender in September 1943 gave the Luftwaffe a windfall of thousands of ex-Regia Aeronautica aircraft. NSG 9 was assigned the Caproni Ca.314 light bomber but found it completely unsuited for night operations.*

ABOVE: *A 1./NSG 9 Ca.314 taxying. It has acquired a Luftwaffe fuselage Balkenkreuz and Mediterranean Theatre white band but although its original Italian tail markings have been thinly overpainted the German Hakenkreuz has not yet been applied.*

ABOVE: *Although of poor quality, this photograph shows the rudimentary nature of the Ca.314's instrumentation, part of the reason it was unfit for night operations.*

ABOVE: *Campoformido-Udine, January 1944: a Ca.314 of 1./NSG 9 runs up its engines. This machine has no white fuselage band and the darker paint inboard of the underwing Balkenkreuz is noteworthy.*

BELOW: *Another of 1./NSG 9's Capronis runs up its engines.*

There was another problem built into Italian aircraft. *Unteroffizier* Alfred Kunzmann recalls that:

> [They] had a disastrous attribute leading to fatal misunderstandings among the pilots. On every German machine you gave it more gas by pushing the throttle forward. With the Italian ones it was the other way round. The tragic consequence: there were several fatal accidents during conversion.

SG 111 recorded the loss of two Capronis during the winter of 1943–44:

> 07.11.43: Ca.314, MM. 12315, 100% destroyed in crash at Zobten[3] (burned on impact). Pilot, *Fw.* Walter Härtel, and flight engineer, *Uffz.* Siegfried Albrecht, both killed.
>
> 06.01.44: Ca.314, MM. 12188, 80% damage in crash attributed to pilot error (aircraft burned on impact). Pilot, *Obgfr.* Rudolf Buhrle; flight engineer, *Uffz.* Heinz Heinrich; gunner, *Obgfr.* Rolf Krause, all killed.

On the last day of 1943, 1./NSG 9 had twelve Ca.314s on strength, none of them serviceable. At 13.55 on 10 January, Ca.314 MM. 12740, E8+EH crashed during a practice flight at Campoformido-Udine, killing *Uffz.* Johann Horn (pilot)[4], *Uffz.* Karl Dopatka (observer), *Gefr.* Friedrich Wendler (gunner) and *Obgfr.* Heinz Hopp (wireless operator). The Caproni was nevertheless tried out in attacks against partisans in the Alps north west of Torino, the "three-country triangle", but found completely unfit for the purpose. It had bad blind- and night-flying characteristics, especially in the hands of novice crews, and its weaponry, radio and instrumentation all required changes. While surviving German daily operations reports list a number of anti-partisan raids in the Udine-Gorizia region and one south west of Torino during February 1944, these are not attributed to a specific unit and so it is not possible to pin down NSG 9's early trial missions (certainly the variegated machines of *Flugbereitschaft Luftflotte 2* were also used for the same purpose). The Caproni was never used by NSG 9 over the front lines.

Growing impatient with the slow progress NSG 9 was making, Richthofen directed that the *Staffel* equip itself instead with the Fiat CR.42 *Falco* single-seater. The CR.42 had first flown in 1939 and was destined to be the world's last production biplane fighter. Although of the outgoing generation of fighters it was exported to Belgium, Hungary, Sweden and Finland and fought for Italy over the Mediterranean theatre, Africa and England. Unable to hold its own as an air superiority fighter, it was latterly employed for night fighting and fighter-bomber duties. Having taken over Italy, the Germans thought the type might yet have a future in the night attack role and ordered 200 from Fiat. In this new incarnation it was fitted with flame dampers, armour for the pilot's seat, air filter, ultra-violet instrument lighting and other detail changes to meet *Luftwaffe* standards. It was armed with a pair of 12.7mm machine-guns and underwing ETC 50 racks permitting the carriage of 70 kg bombs (although 50kg weapons were the normal load). Loaded, the aircraft could achieve about 210km/h (133mph) which was considered adequate but the combination of increased weight, narrow-track landing gear and "aggressive" compressed air brakes led to problems when making night landings on forward airstrips. On the other hand this was a highly agile type, one RAF combat report describing tactics that involved "hard weaves, losing height and altering speed. Diving target was able to pull up very quickly, causing Beaufighter to tend to overshoot."

On 20 January 1944, 1./NSG 9 had 13 Capronis (7 of them serviceable) and this was also the date when, according to Begemann, training began at Caselle for night operations with the Ju 87. On the 28th the establishment of 2./NSG 9 was ordered "with immediate effect", which was, as we shall see, connected with the arrival of these new aircraft. The Allies however still lacked a clear picture of what was afoot. On the 21st, their radio interception service monitored eight Fiat CR.42s leaving the Torino–Airasca area from 11.40–11.44 for Bergamo-South; on the 28th:

> 1 Ca.314 of I./KG 50 arrived VICENZA from AVIANO at 13hrs., and continued to CENTOCELLE, arriving there at 1655.

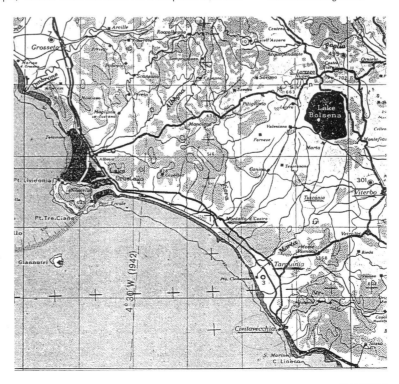

This extract from an American pilot's map has potential targets in the area north west of Rome underlined: NSG 9's airfields at Viterbo and Tuscania among them.

FIAT CR.42 FALCO

Wing Span:	31ft 10 in (9.7m)
Weights:	3,763lb (1,710kg) empty;
	5,042lb (2,292kg) normal load
Power plant:	one Fiat A 74 RC 38 radial
	developing 840hp
Max speed:	266mph (425km/h) at
	13,120ft (4,000m)
Climb:	5min 26sec to
	13,120ft (4,000m)
Ceiling:	33,000ft (10,000m)
Range:	488 miles (780km) at
	214mph (345km/h) at
	19,685ft (6,000m)
Armament:	2 x 12.7mm MG with 400 r.p.g
	fixed above the engine;
	2 x 50kg bombs on wing racks

Note: *in service with NSG 9, the addition of flame dampers and other equipment would have raised the aircraft's weight while reducing its speed and climb.*

This is significant to our story because the short-lived KG 50 had been the previous user of the E8 unit code. MAAF Signals Intelligence were evidently in two minds about this attribution because, summing up January's findings, they wrote of the "E8 Communications Unit", including aircraft with the codes: E8+AH, E8+FH, E8+GK and E8+ZK.

Meanwhile, on the 22nd, an Anglo-American force had made a surprise amphibious landing in corps strength, behind German lines at Anzio-Nettuno (Roma) and it was feared that this beach head could, if not rapidly thrown back, threaten both Rome and supply lines to the German troops on the southern front. This new threat lent additional urgency to 1./NSG 9's reaching operational status and at the beginning of February, *Hptm.* Robert Hegenbarth who had been in charge of conversion to the CR.42 was apparently moved aside and Frost took over. Hegenbarth's practice, recalled by a subordinate, of flying home at weekends to Klagenfurt, Austria in the unit's Fieseler *Storch* may not have gone down too well in the circumstances. *General* von Pohl's memoirs even blame "the *Staffelführer* in charge" for choosing the unsuitable Caproni but, as mentioned above, the order to utilise that type had emanated from Berlin. Veterans no longer remember the ins and outs of this episode and the author has not been able to establish exactly what did happen. The first of NSG 9's Fiats to go to war carried the markings of Frost's *1. Staffel* but Hegenbarth was still commanding 2./9 when its CR.42s went in their turn to Anzio.

On 6 February, JG 77's Technical Officer was inquiring where "I./NSG 9" could collect electrical release gear for 50kg bombs and two days later orders were issued for Viterbo (VT) airfield to be supplied by the 10th of that month with Italian 50kg bombs sufficient for six operations by a *Kette* of CR.42s carrying two bombs per aircraft per operation. Commenting on that intelligence, Britain's Government Code and Cipher School remarked that "Ca.314 aircraft recently heard on W/T with markings E8 and *Staffel* letter may also belong to I./NSG 9."

On the 6th, at least two CR.42s were active, "6284" at 10.45 and another at 13.15 while next day, Fi 156 "E9+YH" of "I./KG 50" took off at 12.58 and landed at 15.35. On the 9th, Ca.314s E8+AH, BH and FH were all overheard by Allied Field Signals Units. On 10 February, Ca.314 E8+KH was up at 10.07 and PH three minutes later. Other codes detected during February were E8+DH, E8+NH, E8+YH, E8+GK and E8+ZK. According to Signals Intelligence's monthly summary, the aircraft complement consisted of six SAIMAN 202s, one Ca.309, a Ca.314 and a Fi 156, all thought to be based at Centocelle North (Roma). Yet again MAAF had produced an evaluation at odds with what German documents, then of course inaccessible, now tell us. It is possible that "Centocelle" was a misreading of "Caselle",

Fi 156C, E8+YH of 1./NSG 9, seen at Caselle in late January or February 1944. The all-black characters "YH" are just discernible on the original print, the full code is known from Allied Signals Intelligence reports.

where we know NSG 9 to have been and similarly the aircraft inventory would make better sense were "SAIMAN 202" to be read as "CR.42." Fiats were certainly on the strength by this time and it seems strange that they should go unremarked. The SAIMAN was a small liaison aircraft, its combat potential lower even than the Caproni, and the author is aware of corroboration for only one serving with NSG 9: E8+ZK, which featured in an ULTRA intercept late in July. The Ca.309 was a predecessor of the 314 and could conceivably have been on strength; E8+YH was the unit's Fi 156 communications machine (the earlier report of "E9+YH" was probably no more than a transcription error). The *Luftwaffe's* own records tell us that on 10 February, 1./NSG 9 reported a strength of 14(3) Ca.314s whereas on the 29th it had 25(10) aircraft, a mixture of the Ca.314, CR.42 and Ju 87.

On 29 February, apparently unaware that colleagues back in England had identified NSG 9, F/L J. Robertson of MAAF Intelligence signalled the RAF's radio monitoring organisation in Italy as follows:

> **To:** No. 276 Wing for D.I.3
> **From:** HQ MAAF Intelligence Section
> **AI.366** **29th February SECRET**
>
> KG 50 almost certainly dissolved. Therefore Italian aircraft with prefix E8 probably belong to unidentified communications unit.
>
> **Priority:** IMPORTANT

A "windfall" from the Italian surrender of 1943, the two-seat SAIMAN 202 communications aircraft was used by many Luftwaffe units in Italy. Although the Allies believed that no fewer than six were serving with NSG 9 in February 1944, only one was subsequently detected, 2. Staffel's E8+ZK. The example shown here carries the green/white/red Tricolore of the Italian Aeronautica Nazionale Repubblicana.

---

1. Horst Greßler told the author that his conversion training took place in Lamsdorf, Upper Silesia (now Lambinowice, Poland).

2. It is not certain whether this was Benno or Heinz Müller: both were *Unteroffizier* pilots during NSG 9's early months.

3. Now Sobótka, Poland.

4. Horn, along with *Obgfr.* Walter Gockeln, had been injured in the crash of a He 46 (WNr. 1161) at Schari on 19 July 1943, while serving with *1. Störkampfstaffel Luftflotte 1* on the Eastern Front.

1./NSG 9 groundcrew (Gerhard Fischer, centre) in Caselle, February 1944. The Ju 87D-3 is still in standard green/blue camouflage and lacks exhaust flame dampers and wheel covers, all of which suggests it is a recent arrival in Italy.

"Several fires observed"

During March, Allied Signals Intelligence detected its first Italian-based Ju 87s of 1944. The five machines in question (6Q+NH, OH, FP, ND and DY) bore the markings of SG 151, were supposedly at Villafranca di Verona and Centocelle and not operational. The same source reported that the E8 code was carried by two SAI. 202s, a pair of CR.42s and a Fi 156 "probably based at Centocelle North." All this is hard to reconcile with other evidence and so it helps once again to read "Centocelle" as "Caselle." For its part, SG 151 was a training unit although as the war went on individual *Staffeln* were increasingly committed to combat. It, or at least some of its former aircraft, may perhaps have been playing a part in the build-up of NSG 9.

A rare ULTRA intercept of *Luftflotte* 2's order of battle showed that on 7 March 1./NSG 9 had 7(2) aircraft (type unspecified) while the 2. *Staffel* had 12(2) CR.42s; the unit as a whole had 19 pilots, nine of whom were ready for operations. Allied radio monitoring the same day detected Fi 156 E8+YH of a "Field Communications Unit" leaving an airfield in the Siena–Lucca area at midday, bound for Padua. Not revealed however was that after the preparations detected a month earlier, NSG 9 was about to go into action. By this time the Germans' February counter-offensive at Anzio-Nettuno had failed, ushering in a long and bloody stalemate; the Allies in the contemporaneous Second Battle of Cassino had not dislodged the defenders and the Third Battle was about to end the same way.

On the 10th, *Unteroffizier* Kurt Pallas of 2./NSG 9 was killed in a flying accident at Ciriè, the location of NSG 9's own supply unit, a short distance north west of Caselle at the mouth of the Val d'Aosta. His CR.42, MM. 90831, was completely destroyed. At 13.12 the same day, CR.42s E8+EH, E8+FH, E8+JH, E8+SH, E8+VH, E8+AH and E8+GH left Caselle for Bologna, then between 13.38 and 14.15 the following afternoon they flew out of this intermediate destination for – as the decrypted signal had it – "Piavono."[1] Horst Greßler:

> In March came the deployment of six CR.42s to the forward airfield of Fabrica di Roma, south east of Viterbo in the vicinity of Lake Vico. From here attacks were flown against Frascati–Anzio–Nettuno, the beach head of US VI Corps, as well as in the Liri Valley and along the Via Casilina.

Greßler is as certain that six aircraft were involved as ULTRA was that there were seven. In this he has the support of *Gen.* von Pohl:

LEFT: *Six pilots of 2./NSG 9, sun themselves in front of a hangar, possibly at Caselle. Fw. Horst Greßler is on the left, Fw. Horst Rau, Uffz. Schmieduch Gefr. Franz Spörr, Gefr. Ewald Kapahnke (?) and an unidentified Unteroffizier.*

RIGHT: *Three pilots and a dog of 1./NSG 9 sit unconcernedly on 50 kg bombs at Caselle, February 1944. From left: Fw. Volkmar von Grone, Uffz. Werner Waißnor (KIA, 27 July 1944) and Gefr. Richard Schwobe (MIA, 23 July 1944).*

LEFT: *Groundcrew of 1./NSG 9. From left: Grampe, Günther Helbig, Fw. Engelmaier, Heinisch (above) and Gruber. The CR.42 behind them shows to advantage its flame dampers and white spinner. This aircraft lacks even the cut-down wheel farings typical of NSG 9's Fiats.*

Trial CR.42 operations were flown over the front lines following deployment of six aircraft to an airfield on the shores of Lago di Bolsena (Viterbo?) during early March. Operations were flown only during moonlit periods since crews were inexperienced, the Fiat biplanes carried no radio aids to navigation and were based further from their targets than was usual for this type of unit.

However, according to *Maj.* Frost's postwar testimony:

> At the beginning of March 1944 operations began with seven CR.42, all flown by pilots with long *Nachtschlacht* experience in the East. They were based at Canino and Tuscania… Operations during the first period of moonlight were successful and there were no losses although AA fire was heavy. Targets were artillery emplacements and road traffic near the front. The harbour was only attacked in cloudy weather because of strong AA and searchlight defences.
>
> A second *Staffel* was set up, based at Viterbo, with less experienced pilots but they suffered losses due to the hilly terrain. Losses grew and so, in the moonless periods of March and April, the Ju 87 was introduced.

There is further documentary evidence in the form of menu lists dated 10 March 1944 and captured when the Allies occupied Rome. These showed that Frost had requested rations from *Flugplatzkommando* 430 in Guidonia for 10 flying personnel and 31 technicians of 1./NSG 9. Since Guidonia lies just to the north east of the Italian capital, it seems clear that these provisions were for the contingent that had set off for the front that day

Apart from the conflict over numbers, there are differences over the bases concerned. In February Viterbo was being stocked with bombs for a three-aircraft deployment which apparently never took place, while in the summer the wreck of CR.42 MM. 90843, "EH+FH" was found there by the advancing Allies. If "EH" was a false transcription of "E8" (and we know E8+FH had deployed to the south), this supports Viterbo's claim to be the field to which 1./NSG 9 brought forward its Fiats in March. For his part, Frost seems to have telescoped the events of the Spring: Canino and Fabrica were certainly used by 2./NSG 9 later on (with Civita Castellana (VT) available as an alternate to the latter, according to Greßler), while Tuscania was a base for Ju 87s.

Information about Viterbo and its satellite was obtained from two pilots of SG 4 and one from JG 77 shot down at this period. Viterbo Main was still in use:

> …although it had been heavily damaged by Allied bombing some time ago. The remains of wrecked aircraft had not been recovered or bomb craters filled in as these served to camouflage activity on the airfield.

> …a single small runway [1,000m x 60m] only is in use, which frequently gives rise to considerable congestion.

Meanwhile, the satellite field offered a 1,000m x 300m landing area.

What is known of NSG 9's operational debut derives mainly from the daily reports made by *Oberst* Bloedorn of *Luftflotte 2* to the Italian Air Ministry:

11/12 March   For the first time five *Nachtschlacht* aircraft (five CR.42s) have been used in action against enemy artillery operating from the beach head. A loud explosion was heard but due to low clouds it was not possible to observe the results. The attack was interrupted by bad weather…

On that last point, Horst Greßler recalls that the cloud base lay at 600m that night. During the afternoon of the 12th, *Luftflotte* 2 issued orders for the coming night: the serviceable elements of 1./NSG 9 were to be operationally subordinate to *Nahkampfführer*[2] *Luftflotte* 2. Operations would take place against targets in the beach-head, weather permitting. As for what transpired:

> Thirteen *Nachtschlacht* aircraft operated against enemy artillery positions in the beach head. Good placement of hits on both gun sites and anti-aircraft sites. Machine-gun nests were strafed. Several fires observed…

LEFT: *Posing by this CR.42 which has the red spinner of 2./NSG 9 are, from left: Gefr. Franz Spörr, Fw. Horst Rau, Uffz. Schmeiduch, Fw. Horst Greßler and (on his shoulders), Gefr. Ewald Kapahnke.*

ABOVE: *Pilots of 2./NSG 9, from left: Uffz. Schmeiduch, Gefr. Franz Spörr (KIFA, 28.11.44), Gefr. Ewald Kapahnke (KIA, 03.07.44), Fw. Horst Rau and Fw. Horst Greßler (WIA, 02.06.44) with one of the Staffel's CR.42s. Point to note are the Gruppe's "E8" code and the way the underside camouflage paint has partly obscured the fuselage Balkenkreuz.*

LEFT: *Seen at Caselle undergoing a periodic inspection, a Ju 87D-3 of 1./NSG 9. Although it has the white spinner tip seen on the Staffel's Fiats, this aircraft still retains its dive brakes and has yet to receive NSG 9's distinctive camouflage. The ground crewman on the left is named Gruber.*

Given the small force actually available, the "13 aircraft" probably represented multiple sorties by each Fiat. On the 14th, bureaucratic formalities were apparently completed when 1./NSG 9 was added to the distribution list of *Fliegerführer Luftflotte 2*. Rather more significantly, at 14.00 that day a report was sent by *Oberbefehlshaber Südwest* on the operations of the previous night: batteries firing in the Padiglione Woods north of Anzio had been bombed and strafed by *Nachtschlacht* aircraft. This ULTRA decrypt, incidentally, goes beyond Bloedorn's daily report which speaks only of bomber operations. There were to be two more nights' operations in this opening round:

14/15 March   *Nachtschlacht* aircraft attacked enemy artillery positions in the wood north of Anzio. Some results were obtained as the guns suspended their fire. Guns and mortars were strafed with effect.

16/17 March   *Nachtschlacht* aircraft attacked enemy artillery positions and anti-aircraft sites in the wood north of Anzio and on both sides of the Aprilia-Anzio road. Good placement of hits. Strafing of light AA sites, machine-gun nests and trenches.

This CR.42 still lacks both the extended exhaust shrouds and the camouflage found necessary in NSG 9's moonlight war.

On the 20th, the strengths of the *Gruppe's* two *Staffeln* were above their twenty-aircraft establishment, with 22(19) and 25(7) respectively. On the 24th, the elements still in Caselle flew an operation against nearby partisans:

> An area occupied by enemy partisans east south east of Torino and pockets of resistance have been attacked with bombs and strafed. Several houses set on fire.

Unteroffizier Benno Müller of 2./NSG 9 crashed in his CR.42 (MM. 90845) at the mountain village of Perrero during this mission, his death attributed to an accident[3]. Thus blooded, 2./NSG 9 began to deploy to the southern front, staging, like *1. Staffel* before them, through Bologna, from where at 15.55 on the 28th, CR.42s E8+PK and E8+KK took off for Canino.

---

1. The Allies were unable precisely to locate Piavono but believed it lay within *Flughafenbereich 9/VII*. Another oddity of this second intercept was that aircraft E8+GH appeared to have been replaced by E8+CH. While a typographical error is the most likely explanation, it is impossible to know now which letter was the right one.

2. Tactical Combat Leader, also referred to as *Fliegerführer*.

3. The date was typed on the casualty report as 24 March but amended by hand to the 27th. Since ULTRA confirms an operation against guerillas west of Torino on the former date, whereas on the latter it was the partisans of Slovenia who were under attack, I have opted for the 24th. The amendment may simply reflect that the unfortunate Müller lived for three days after the crash.

"So romantically lit"

H: Have you done any night-flying?

S: We never did anything else.

H: But… with Stukas?

S: Oh, they're excellent for that.

(Covertly recorded conversation between prisoners *Obgfr.* Hoffmann of
40. *Lw. Nachrichten Rgt.* and *Fw.* Kaspar Stuber of 1./NSG 9 on 12 December 1944)

T o date, NSG 9 had not made any great impact on the Allies, if MAAF situation reports are any guide. As accounts of the Anzio campaign make all too clear, conditions within the beach head were so dreadful that attacks by a handful of (unseen) biplanes with small bombs are unlikely to have stood out from the general torment. At Cassino and on the Garigliano front too, the opposing armies battered one another but appeared to be going nowhere.

The early days of April witnessed the first appearance of the *Gruppe*'s Ju 87s over the front. The Ju 87D would, as it was supplanted by the Fw 190 in the ranks of the daylight *Schlachtgeschwader,* become the mainstay not only of NSG 9 but most other *Nachtschlacht* units. Attaining about 250km/h when fully loaded, it was slow — and far less agile than the *Falco* — but strong, reliable and able to withstand battle damage. Against the Fiat's normal 100kg, it typically carried 750kg payloads (with a maximum of 1,000kg). The Junkers had good blind flying characteristics and a sturdy wide track undercarriage, making for safer night landings; its second crewman could assist with both navigation and defence.

Diary of NSG 9 Operations, April 1944
Daily Reports to Italian Air Ministry by Oberst Bloedorn

Night 3/4th Nachtschlacht aircraft attacked artillery positions in the Nettuno area. Bad weather precluded the observation of results.

Night 7/8th Nachtschlacht attack on artillery and AA positions in the southern part of the beach head with incendiary and fragmentation bombs. Several small fires seen in the southern part of a wood. Twenty-two aircraft employed: no claims and no losses.

Night 10/11th Special operation against the beach-head together with bombers [known from other sources to include 38 Ju 88s of LG 1 plus others from KG 76]… Nachtschlacht aircraft operating north of Anzio against land targets with 9/10 cloud, bad visibility and strong enemy reaction. All bombs released on targets. Ground observers confirmed several fires with explosions and smoke.

Night 12/13th Nachtschlacht aircraft not operating due to bad weather over our own airfields.

Night 14/15th Nachtschlacht aircraft not operating due to bad weather over our own airfields.

Night 15/16th Thirteen Nachtschlacht aircraft operating against land targets in the Anzio-Nettuno area. Several small fires observed.

Night 28/29th [After Ju 88s had bombed] Nachtschlacht aircraft successfully attacked dumps and artillery positions in the beach-head, causing several large fires and some small ones.

Night 30/31st Nachtschlacht aircraft attacked artillery positions and AA sites in the beach-head. Good placement of hits on targets. Two large fires and several small ones started.

Self-defence would be needed as Allied night fighters increasingly came to grips with the new threat presented by the *Nachtschlachtflieger*. After the war, German staff officers gave their captors this assessment:

> …the heavily-armoured though slow Ju 87 could frequently regain home territory even after having received strikes from light AA, but fell an easy prey to the predatory night fighter.

It did not perhaps seem so easy from the Allied pilots' perspective; the tactics appropriate to shooting down a Ju 88 bomber or reconnaissance plane did not always apply and new ones had to be evolved. From 03.00 on 4 April, F/O N.A. Branch and F/S Balchin of No. 600 Squadron RAF tried repeatedly to intercept a Ju 87 flying at 90-100mph and strafing the beach-head. They were unable to manage it because their Beaufighter was too fast. This was the first recorded encounter between an NSG 9 Ju 87 and a Bristol Beaufighter. This robust British-built night fighter was to be the *Gruppe's* main aerial adversary for the rest of 1944 and in the vast majority of instances it would be flown by a 600 Sqn crew.[1] For some unaccountable reason however, NSG 9's veterans are apt to refer to all Allied night fighters they encountered as "Lightnings", an aircraft which (so far as the author is aware) was never once used against them in the air.

In addition to what was set out in the Germans' daily reports (see above) on the night of the 8th/9th, what the Allies characterised as "harassing aircraft" attacked shipping off Anzio and gun positions within the bridgehead itself. This prompted RAF Intelligence to observe that such aircraft, used by night during the Tunisian campaign and in Yugoslavia, had later been incorporated into *Nachtschlacht* units. On the 10th, NSG 9's total of CR.42s and Ju 87s had increased to 46(17) and reported movements of Ju 87s with factory markings suggest that new aircraft were continuing to arrive.

On the 15/16th, there was evidence that the *Gruppe* had been given new targets when at 04.15 F/L G.B.S. Coleman DFC· and F/O N. Frumar (RAAF) made contact with a Ju 87 over Cassino, only to lose it again. That night a Ju 87 is reported to have crashed in the Anzio-Nettuno beach head but no confirmation or details are forthcoming from either German or Allied sources.

The 19th of April saw a Ju 87 arrive at Udine from Graz, Austria at 16.50, while at 14.00 next day two "CANT 313" (by which was probably meant Caproni 313s) in four-letter markings landed at an airfield in the Venice-Udine region from the "Milan-Turin-Genoa area." The latter in ULTRA decrypts seems almost invariably to have referred to Caselle and the departure of Capronis from NSG 9's inventory is borne out by the strengths reported on the 20th: 1./NSG 9 had 23(11) Ju 87s while *2. Staffel* now had 20(6) CR.42s. An incomplete return five days later placed both *Staffeln* at Caselle with four and nine serviceable aircraft respectively.

NSG 9's efforts over the front seem to have been valued by the ground troops. On the 24th, 3. *Panzergrenadier Division*, in the line at Anzio, requested the *Luftwaffe*'s help

JUNKERS Ju 87D-5

Wing Span:	49ft 2.5in (15m) [Ju 87D-3: 45ft 3.5in/13.8m]
Weights:	8,687lb (3,940kg) empty; 14,553lb (6,600kg) max. loaded
Power plant:	one Junkers Jumo 211J inline, developing 1,400hp
Max speed:	248mph (400km/h) at 15,745ft (4,800m)
Ceiling:	24,248ft (7,300m)
Range:	510 miles (815km)
Armament:	2 x 2cm MG 151 cannon (fixed forward) [Ju 87D-3: 2 x MG 17 7.9mm machine-guns] and 1 x MG 81Z twin 7.9mm machine-gun in a GSL K-81 turret (rear-firing); 2 x 50kg or 70kg bombs on each wing rack and one 250kg or 500kg on fuselage rack [typical loads in NSG 9].

At dispersal, 13.20 hours. This Ju 87D-5, coded [KH?] +XH, still carries its conspicuous white Italian Theatre fuselage band but has yet to receive night camouflage.

to suppress Allied artillery during an operation to be carried out between 18.30 and midnight, only to be told that as yet there was insufficient moonlight for the *Nachtschlacht* units. Three days later, however, 14 Ju 87s of 1./NSG 9 left Caselle. They were: E8+AH, BH, CH, DH, EH, GH, HH, JH, KH, LH, OH, RH, SH and TH and by now those who decrypted this information knew enough to comment "marking possibly NSG 9." They apparently staged through Bologna, spending about an hour on the ground there before flying on to Tuscania (VT) that evening.

Although he places it in January, when no Ju 87s were operational with the *Gruppe*, Volkmar von Grone may be referring to this deployment when he writes:

LEFT: *On 27 April 1944, fourteen Ju 87s of 1./NSG 9 deployed to their operational base at Tuscania.*
This understandably rare photo of a daylight formation of 1./NSG 9 aircraft in Spring 1944 may show that flight.

> …with an enlarged *Staffel* of 14 aircraft, the transfer took place to a forward airfield near Viterbo, north of Rome. Our task was to attack targets in the harbour area of the enemy bridgehead of Anzio-Nettuno and behind the enemy front at Monte Cassino. In flying terms, the moonlit journeys to and from the target areas of that period were often ones of unprecedented charm. The approach flight along the Ligurian coast and over the mouth of the Tiber, heading for the Alban Hills, historic Rome with the silver moonlight pouring over the dome of St Peter's Cathedral, is for me an unforgettable sight and impression. Not all these operations were so romantically lit…

The tactics the Ju 87 crews adopted were adhered to for the rest of the war and were believed to be very successful, at least in the early stages. The aircraft would fly from its base at minimum altitude to a point just short of the target, climb to diving height and make its attack. The climb, at a rate of only 100m (330ft) per minute, was the most vulnerable time, when night fighters often made contact. The evasive action favoured by experienced crews was a falling corkscrew turn; trying to escape by simply diving seldom worked whereas the corkscrew complicated pursuit and allowed the Ju 87 to depart the scene in almost any direction and at any point in the descent that its pilot chose. Crews might also jettison their bombs

BELOW: *Probably the best known of all NSG 9's aircraft, Ju 87D-5 E8+CH is serviced in broad daylight, with no attempt at concealment. A "CH" was among the first Junkers the Gruppe sent to Anzio in April 1944 and the "Caesar-Heinrich" of Fw. Pieper was badly damaged by AA fire during the Loreto raid of 5/6 July.*

THIS PAGE: *Ju 87D-3, WNr. 2600 (callsign BJ+_O) is towed and manhandled by over a dozen men into concealment beneath trees. Manpower on this scale would become harder to find as groundcrew were "combed out" for infantry service. In operational paintwork and coded E8+GK, WNr. 2600 was found at Bovolone in 1945 by a Technical Intelligence team.*

Two photographs of the same group. "With comrades, by our new machine. Italy, 20 April 1944." **ABOVE:** The Ju 87 carries a white "S" on its port wheel cover and the extreme tip of the spinner is also white. The aircraft is fully fitted and camouflaged for night operations but retains its dive brakes. A parachute hangs on the starboard wing bomb rack. **BELOW:** Fw. Günther Gräßer (second from left), three fellow airmen and two groundcrew, all from 1./NSG 9, and Ju 87D-5, E8+SH.

RIGHT: *When 1./NSG 9 deployed to Tuscania in April 1944, its technical personnel were accommodated in these tents. The occupants' efforts at camouflage are somewhat compromised by the prominent line of white washing hung out to dry.*

BELOW: *Technical personnel of 1./NSG 9 in Tuscania, April 1944. At left is Obgfr. Herbert Westerheide, a driver killed by Allied strafing on 4 May 1944, 3km west of Tuscania, while en route to a railway station in Rome. Third from left is Emil Hach.*

ABOVE: *Home of 1./NSG 9's technical personnel at Tuscania, April 1944. Far right: Emil Hach.*

LEFT: *1./NSG 9 technical crew at Tuscania in April 1944. From left: Emil Hach, Willi Uzkurreit, Kreher, Sperling(?), Max Merz. First-aid kit in foreground.*

as they dived and an explosion on the ground right where their "victim" was expected to crash may have prompted some of the RAF victory claims as yet unmatched to German losses. The flight home from the target made practical use of the coastal scenery that so impressed von Grone. Tuscania and Canino (VT) had been selected as forward airfields both because they were hard to spot from the air and for their proximity to the sea. Crews would fly low along the coast until they saw a visual beacon, then turn inland for their base.

The night of the 28/29th, brought NSG 9's first casualties in combat against the Allies when a Ju 87D-5 (WNr. 141024, E8+FH) was shot down at Nettuno, killing *Uffz.* Heinz Müller and *Gefr.* Werner Teichert. Examination of the wreck suggested to the RAF that it had been hit by AA fire and burned out when attempting a forced landing. Incidentally, readers will note that ULTRA was not all-seeing, since no E8+FH is mentioned in the above list of those deploying to the front.

From 23.00-23.30 on the 30th, S/L O.H. Archer and F/O Barrington were vectored on to two bogeys north of Cassino. These proved to be Ju 87s which the Beaufighter was unable to intercept on account of their low speed and violent evasive action. As Volkmar von Grone puts it:

> The piper would soon have to be paid once the enemy night fighters focused on us. Night flights brought more and more losses and we had constantly to think up new tricks to elude the enemy's powerful air superiority.

Not all the Ju 87s were at the front on 30 April, for ULTRA revealed that at 12.30 one with a "white marking" had landed in Caselle from Bergamo. The 2./NSG 9 had 16(2) CR.42s on strength that day and its status on the order of battle was "re-equipping" but this process had suffered a setback on the 25th. Again we hear from von Grone:

> Meanwhile, I had been appointed the *Gruppe's* Technical Officer and so I was responsible amongst other things for the technical state of the operational aircraft. For this reason, when required we ferried our machines to the FIAT aircraft works in Torino for a complete overhaul...
>
> One bright day we were able to watch as a formation of at least 100 enemy bombers headed for Torino and unloaded its bombs on to the ... factory. As TO, I was immediately given the job of flying to the works airfield in a Fieseler *Storch* to find out what had happened to our aircraft that were there for overhaul. I grabbed two men as escort and landed shortly afterward between the bomb craters on the totally destroyed grounds of the adjoining FIAT works.
>
> There was no one to be seen and so we marched off on our own initiative and forced our way into the abandoned assembly halls where we suspected our aeroplanes were. Boundless chaos awaited us there and observation convinced us that there was nothing we could salvage.
>
> On the way back to our airfield, we encountered a totally despairing, weeping man who identified himself as the chief pilot of the FIAT works. He was firmly convinced that the destruction of his life's work was entirely attributable to sabotage and treason. We tried to console him [and] in the end he led us to the airfield perimeter where stood two undamaged civilian aircraft, one single-engined and one twin. He asked us if we'd like to have the two of them, which I of course accepted with pleasure. After conferring with my *Kommandeur*, the two planes were ... taken over as so-called liaison aircraft.

Two MG 151/20 wing cannon boosted substantially the Ju 87D-5's firepower as a ground strafer. This aircraft has received muzzle flash dampers for its guns and flame dampers for the exhausts but still lacks night camouflage.

---

1. To avoid repetition during the remainder of this book, Beaufighter crews' units will only be cited if other than No. 600 Squadron.

LEFT: The scene outside the factory is chaotic. The apparently intact CR.42 at left has standard crosses and appears to be coded either +EK or LK (no unit code is visible). Interestingly for a 2./NSG 9 aircraft, the spinner looks as if it could be white.

RIGHT: CR.42 E8+JK of 2./NSG 9 damaged in the raid on the Fiat works. Note the extensively toned down camouflage and the flame dampers for night operations.

LEFT: E8+FK of 2./NSG 9, another victim of the 25 April raid. The white numbers roughly painted on this aircraft and E8+JK were probably for the convenience of factory workers, rather than a unit marking.

ABOVE: *"… the destruction of his life's work"* An Italian civilian surveys the wreckage of at least half a dozen of NSG 9's CR.42s after the raid on the Fiat works on 25 April 1944. Note the non-standard, oversized Hakenkreuz on two of the aircraft and what appear to be the red spinners of 2. Staffel.

ABOVE: *"…there was nothing we could salvage."* CR.42s wrecked by the Allied air raid on the Fiat works in Torino, 25 April 1944.

BELOW: The burnt-out aircraft at left offers one of the clearest views we have of the red spinner marking of 2./NSG 9. In the background, the lower fuselage side of +JK has been sprayed with a broad "snake" of a darker colour to improve its night camouflage.

"Too slow and manoeuvrable"

"20–30 Ju 87's and most probably CR.42's operating over the battle area at points of Allied penetration, without causing significant damage."

(RAF Intelligence assessment)

"Their bombs rewarded his lorry columns for rolling brazenly along the Via Casilina [with] their lights on full … tracer bullets struck the road where Americans, New Zealanders and Frenchmen scattered to seek cover in the ditches."

(German War Correspondent)

On the morning of 2 May, ULTRA confirmed to the Allies that NSG 9 was using the airields of Tuscania and Marcigliana. *Nahkampfkorps Süd*, the *Luftwaffe's* unified command for *Flak* and tactical airpower in Southern Italy, announced that *Nachtschlacht* operations would take place that night in the area Le Pastinelle - Cervaro [FR], about 5km east of Cassino, at 20.15 and 23.15. In addition to these, the *Gruppe's* first raids on the Liri Valley front, six Ju 87s attacked the beach head at 22.00, Allied situation reports recording that they bombed their own troops and that the defending AA claimed three destroyed. 1./NSG 9's *Fhr.* Heinz Zwierkowski and *Gefr.* Gerhard Beier were killed when their Ju 87D-5 (WNr. 141022) came down 2km south south west of their base at Tuscania and was completely destroyed. Surviving records give no indication of the cause nor whether they were on the outward or return leg of their mission. Similarly opaque are the circumstances in which a *1. Staffel* air-gunner, *Gefr.* Horst Filß, came to be wounded 3km north of Tarquinia on the same night. The casualty report also indicates that he became a prisoner of war and, although the given location was well within German lines, states that his "further whereabouts are unknown." What is more, notification of the degree of damage to his Ju 87, WNr. 131604, was "to follow."

Diary of NSG 9 Operations, May 1944
Reports to Italian Air Ministry by Oberst Bloedorn

Night 2/3rd *Nachtschlacht* aircraft, notwithstanding the presence of night fighters and the dropping of bombs over their base, attacked road traffic in the Cassino area for the first time with good placement of hits. After the bombers… they also attacked artillery positions in the beach head, causing big fires and explosions.

Nights 3/4th and 4/5th No operations due to bad weather.

Night 5/6th *Nachtschlacht* aircraft attacked road traffic in the Cassino area with good placement of hits.

Nights 6/7th and 7/8th No operations due to bad weather.

Night 8/9th *Nachtschlacht* aircraft attacked road traffic in the Cassino area and artillery positions in the beach head. Good placement of hits. Fires started in the Cassino area.

Night 9/10th *Nachtschlacht* aircraft continued attacks against road traffic in the Cassino area and artillery positions in the beach head. Enemy artillery ceased firing.

LEFT: Horst Greßler's motorcycle carries the emblem of NSG 9 on its petrol tank.

On the 4th, *Generalfeldmarschall* von Richthofen set off on a tour of inspection of the front, including a visit to 1./NSG 9 at Tuscania and apparently recorded in his diary his satisfaction with what he saw there. Also on the 4th, three of 1./NSG 9's ground echelon were killed in a strafing attack 3km west of the airfield: they were *Dr.* Walter Stremmel; *Stabsgefr.* Karl Rudolf, a cook; and driver *Obgfr.* Herbert Westerheide. A prisoner taken in July claimed that NSG 9 had never been bombed at any airfield except Tuscania and that:

> Here flak shot down two enemy fighters … whereas they lost no aircraft on the ground. This in spite of the fact that Allied planes flew over the various localities almost daily but dispersal and camouflage were so good that they were not seen. An air raid warning was given about 15 minutes prior to the arrival of enemy planes.

At 15.00, orders were given to 1./NSG 9 that at 01.00 next morning it was to attack shipping off Anzio, otherwise instructions (the nature of which was unrevealed to those who decrypted the message) were the same as for the night of 3/4 May. As we have seen, bad weather put paid to these plans and, on the afternoon of the 6th, *Luftflotte 2* signalled its intentions during the coming night to carry out the shipping attack postponed from the previous two nights. Whether this was a case of third time lucky is not known since the daily report only mentions a mission to Cassino and a Ju 87D-5, WNr. 141004, crashed to destruction 3km north of Palestrina (about 25km east of Rome). Again, the cause of the deaths of *Fw.* Johann Deffner and *Gefr.* Gerhard Kaczorowski went unrecorded.

Whatever the *Luftwaffe* may have told the Italian Air Ministry (see "Diary of NSG 9 Operations" above), after dark on 7 May attention turned again to the Cassino front, Ju 87s attacking near Venafro (IS) according to MAAF. Next night, two Junkers were reported as dropping a bomb and one flare north of Venafro airfield before strafing it. Although No. 600 Sqn. scrambled a Beaufighter in response, it was unable to find the raiders. On the 9th, another Beaufighter did sight a Ju 87 but could not maintain contact.

During 10 May, three Ju 87s in factory markings passed through Vicenza (the usual first stop for aircraft arriving in Italy from München-Riem) en route to Caselle. Strength returns for that date showed the following:

1./NSG 9	16(12)	Ju 87, CR.42
2./NSG 9	15(9)	Ju 87, CR.42 (re-equipping)

BELOW: The engine cowling of this night camouflaged Ju 87D-5 is replaced after servicing at a field dispersal. Note how the "meander" camouflage extends over the spinner. Also, the dive brakes have been removed.

Next day, Allied reconnaissance aircraft reported 10-15 Ju 87s at "Viterbo II" and at 18.00 operational orders were sent to NSG 9: the coming night's task was (according to an incomplete intercept) to attack targets including the beach head prior to 01.40. For the night of 12/13 May all aircraft were to be committed to a twofold operation from Tuscania. Their targets were to be observed gun positions in the beach head with times over target set for 00.10 and 02.40; artillery fire would be put down before these operations, from 23.25–23.55 and 01.55–02.25.

What the Germans had not been expecting was that the Allies would, on the night of the 11th, launch Operation DIADEM, a huge offensive to breach the Gustav Line. At 22.30, the *94. Infanterie Division* reported that its sector had been under artillery bombardment for 90 minutes and that it had already repulsed one Allied attack and asked whether support from *Nachtschlacht* aircraft was possible — an indicaton of the value placed on NSG 9's interventions.

ABOVE: *Major Rupert Frost (front seat), NSG 9's Kommandeur, returning from the funeral on 6 May 1944 of three of his men killed in a strafing attack two days earlier. The vehicle bears the badge of NSG 9, a ghost carrying a bomb. This crest was never applied to the unit's aircraft, however.*

At 22.00 on 12 May, the *Kommandierender General der Deutschen Luftwaffe in Mittelitalien*[1] announced his intentions for the 13th, including "...night ground attack aircraft: according to special order, according to situation." This again shows that reading German signals did not necessarily allow the Allies to know the enemy's every move. The early hours of the 14th brought what was probably NSG 9's first aerial encounter with the USAAF when, at 03.25, a Beaufighter of the 415th Night Fighter Squadron was vectored on to a Ju 87 but lost contact. Fifty minutes later, a Beaufighter from No. 600 Sqn was guided toward another Ju 87 north of Cassino but this one too was able to evade. This abortive interception may have led to a victory of sorts, for *Gefr.* Lothar Strube, an air-gunner from 1./NSG 9 bailed out over the Cassino battle zone without orders from his pilot and was posted missing. From the same *Staffel* and in the same area, *Obgfr.* Heinz Schönauer and *Obgfr.* Georg Schmidt were badly wounded, presumably by anti-aircraft fire.

Early on the 15th, F/L Coleman and F/O Frumar gained radar and visual contact on a violently manoeuvring Ju 87 near Cassino. They reported:

> Mk VIII AI ...(00.20-05.15) Patrolled from Marcianise for GCI BLUNDER. Taken over by MIMIC at 04.00. Contact dead ahead 2 miles, target slightly above doing 130 IAS over mountainous country. Contact held while bandit jinked violently. Visual obtained at 1,000ft and target identified as Ju 87B. Target then dived steeply among mountains. As it did so, Beaufighter fired short burst with unobserved results (04.15 hours). Beaufighter did not dive in pursuit, being already very low.

The moonlight on which NSG 9 depended was now all but gone and that evening *Komm. Gen. Mittelitalien* announced that 1./NSG 9 was to leave the front for Caselle. The *Oberkommando der Luftwaffe* confirmed that air transport capacity was assured for the transfer (presumably of ground crews and equipment) and early next morning, Ju 87s E8+RH, HH, BH, CH, DH and GH left Tuscania and were down at Bologna by 06.30.

RIGHT: *"In camp, May 1944": this photos from the album of 1./NSG 9's Günther Gräßer shows life at the field landing ground of Tuscania. The dog seems to be enjoying the great outdoors.*

During the second half of May, Ju 87 practice flights were heard in the Milan-Torino area and radio traffic was intercepted from aircraft E8+AH. On the 20th, 2./NSG 9 recorded a strength of 15(12) CR.42s and its status was listed as "in action." Since the moon was dark and the *Staffel* at its rear base, this probably referred to its readiness rather than its present employment. Two days later, 2./NSG 9 suffered a blow when, in what *Ofhr.* Klaus Wolff-Rothermel described as a "strange accident", CR.42 MM. 90881 crashed at Caselle, killing the *Staffelkapitän*, *Oblt*. Rolf Martini. The Italian researcher, Ferdinando D'Amico, has established that Martini was engaged in a practice combat with FIAT test-pilot, Valentino Cus. On 25 May, 2. *Staffel* reported 15(11) Fiats on strength. On the morning of the 24th, five CR.42s had taken off from an airfield in the Bergamo-Vicenza area for Osoppo and groups of three would leave Torino for the same destination on both the 29th and 30th. These may have been deliveries from the FIAT works to NSG 7 in the Balkans.

While Monte Cassino had finally been evacuated on the 18th, until now the Germans had at least been able to contain the beach head at Anzio-Nettuno although not to eliminate it. On 23 May however, the Allies had begun their

breakout, linking up two days later with advance elements of the US II Corps coming up from the south east. Now there was only one front, it was highly fluid and for the rest of the summer NSG 9's role would be the harassment of armies on the move rather than troops in place. As yet however there was too little moonlight for operations and not until the 28th was 1./NSG 9 again committed to the battle, Ju 87s E8+VH, QH, DH, NH, OH, BH and UH leaving Bologna for Tuscania at 18.45 local time.

Early next evening, *Komm. Gen. Mittelitalien* announced his intention for *Nachtschlacht* aircraft to operate that night while the moon was up, giving W/Os D. Kerr and G.H. Wheeler an eventful but ultimately fruitless patrol, the diarist of No. 600 Squadron noting:

> …targets were too slow and manoeuvrable for Beaufighter which tried the
> overshoot procedure and succeeded in obtaining a brief visual on Ju 87 going into
> bank of mist but pilot could not get guns to bear at speed of 100 IAS.

Patrolling between 22.25 and 03.30 under the direction of VIRTUE Ground Control, Kerr and Wheeler were, in the words of their combat report:

> Vectored on to slow flying aircraft at 23.45. Contact 12 miles north east of ANZIO. After 6
> miles chase closed to 500ft, 100 IAS flaps down. Target dived and contact disappeared but
> another picked up immediately. Closed to minimum range and overshot. Did overshoot
> procedure twice and again closed to minimum range. Brief visual before target, believed Ju
> 87, went into bank of mist … target dived, contact lost in ground returns. Third contact
> obtained and lost. Another at 01.30, also lost.

During the afternoon of the 30th, CR.42s E8+KK, RK, UK, PK and GK left Caselle for Bologna, en route for Fabrica di Roma. MAAF reported that at 03.00 "10-12 enemy aircraft" had made low level attacks on the Anzio area while *Luftflotte 2's* situation report for the night spoke of:

> …concentrated attack by 51 bombers [i.e. Ju 88s] on Cisterna and alternate targets Littoria, Nettuno and Via Appia, no losses. *Nachtschlacht* aircraft: attack by 17 Ju 87s against Aprilia and also motor transport columns and batteries firing in same area, no losses.

The next day's communiqué from the *Oberkommando der Wehrmacht* was the first to refer to NSG 9:

> Bomber and *Nachtschlacht* aircraft attacked targets in the Cisterna area as well as enemy columns and battery positions in the Aprilia area with good effect.

Of the *Gruppe's* part in the breakout battles of late May–early June, War Correspondent Rudolf Bruening wrote:

ABOVE: *Three of NSG 9's Ju 87s await action. In the foreground, "A" has no flash dampers on its MG 151/20 wing cannon and does not seem to be carrying a centreline weapon. On its wing racks are four blunt-nosed AB 23 containers for small anti-personnel bombs and the "tiger striped" underside camouflage is clearly visible. Behind it, the second aircraft is being attended to by several ground crew.*

LEFT: *Its engine and cannon shrouded against the damp night air, this Ju 87D-5 sits at dispersal on the edge of a meadow. Points to note are the absence of dive brakes and the streaks of camouflage on the undersurfaces. The cylinder on the centreline rack is a transport container for cargo and the crew's belongings. A rifle lies against the port wheel cover.*

When the enemy's offensive on the [River] Garigliano began, they were at him on the first night. Their bombs rewarded his lorry columns for rolling brazenly along the Via Casilina to the front, their lights on full. Before the enemy knew what was happening to him, the aircraft, flying singly, had already brought their machine-guns to bear on the lines of lights. The tracer bullets struck the road where Americans, New Zealanders and Frenchmen scattered to seek cover in the ditches. Everywhere light AA quickly came to life, the red shells like strings of pearls in the target area. At times like these … the manoeuvrability of his aircraft is the flyer's best weapon. With the agile Ju he can also evade the night fighters that fly standing patrols over the forward areas…

The *Nachtschlachtflieger* have already been in action over the Italian front for some while. For a long time the grenadiers in their foxholes round Aprilia and Cisterna didn't know what the humming overhead during moonlit nights meant. From the red curtain over Anzio they could divine that German aircraft were attacking but they did not know what sort they were. The droning of aircraft flying at no great altitude did not sound powerful enough for a bomber.

When the reverberating sky has stilled on both sides of the lines, when the light of fires marks fresh conflagrations, then for the troops the attack is over. Other considerations occupy them once more. For the *Nachtschlachtflieger* however, the mission is only over when the aircraft is parked at its dispersal. Hostile night fighters are not only over the front, they pursue the German aeroplanes to their airfields. They would very much like to curtail the Germans' flight, to establish exactly where they are based. The British often fly standing patrols and look out for every light signal that might come from a German aircraft. A *Nachtschlacht* aircraft was set upon by three night fighters at the moment of touchdown. However, they were hindered in their attack by the abrupt reaction of the *Flak* defences and their shots went wide.

Nachtschlachtflugzeuge im Ringen der Italienfront
Mit Bomben und Bordwaffen gegen den feindlichen Nachschub

Mit ihrer Maschine, die vor Jahresfrist niemand gern in der Nacht flog, ueberqueren die Nachtschlachtflieger hundert, zweihundert und noch mehr Kilometer. Als die Feindoffensive am Garigliano begann, waren sie in der ersten Kampfesnacht bereits am Feind. Ihre Bomben galten feindlichen Fahrzeugkolonnen, die unverfroren mit aufgeblendetem Licht auf der Via Casilina der Front zurollten. Ehe der Gegner wusste, wie ihm geschah, hatten die einzeln fliegenden Flugzeuge bereits ihre Maschinengewehre auf die Lichterreihen gerichtet. Die Leuchtspurgarben zischten auf die Strasse, wo Amerikaner, Neuseelaender und Franzosen deckungsuchend in die Strassengraben spritzten. Die leichte Flak wurde allen-

RIGHT: *"Nachtschlacht aircraft in the struggle on the Italian Front": a war artist's impression of a Ju 87 pulling up into the moonlit sky after attacking a column of Allied trucks. War Correspondent Rudolf Bruening's magazine article on NSG 9's part in the Anzio breakout battles appeared on 12 June 1944.*

One has often had the impression that the enemy suspected the position of a German airfield. Day after day the fighter bombers orbit several times in the vicinity. Perhaps they are looking for the field, perhaps they are only covering the roads. The *campagna* is broad, the extensive pastures could be one big landing field and the battlegrounds of the night lose themselves by day in the uniformity of the countryside.

The *Wehrmacht* communiqué has mentioned the operations of the *Nachtschlacht* aircraft three times in recent weeks, according due recognition to the efforts of the men who have become the grenadiers' nocturnal helpers. What does it mean for instance to bomb and strafe Artena (near Valmontone), which clings to a mountainside like a swallow's nest? The *Monti Lepini* are close and high. What concentration the decisive seconds call for, what practice the mastery of aircraft with which navigation by night must succeed under differing, difficult conditions! And nevertheless, whenever the weather is favourable, the *Nachtschlachtflieger* are off. Battery emplacements near Aprilia, columns at the Cisterna crossroads, mountain villages on the most threatened sectors of the front and troop concentrations in all parts of the contested Southern Front were their targets. In the grey light of dawn, they are already home. The crews make their way to their tents and sleep their restful sleep while the sun is in the sky and warms the broad grasslands again. The airfield lies deserted, only a small flag and a telephone betray it to the observant seeker and even these are covered with hay so that the whole field lies under a cloak of invisibility that will only reveal its secret with the coming night.

By 31 May, the *Gruppe's* strength had grown, albeit still falling short of its paper establishment of 20 aircraft per *Staffel*:

1./NSG 9	19(8)	Ju87
2./NSG 9	18(15)	Cr.42

Komm. Gen. Mittelitalien's intentions that morning again included *Nachtschlacht* operations. Although the night's targets had yet to be selected, more aircraft were heading south. ULTRA showed two CR.42s, tentatively identified as "EP+IK" and "EP+AK" landing on an unknown airfield at 15.00 having started from Caselle. A Ju 87, markings "E8+A (slight indications K)", took the same route, time unspecfied. In hindsight this was more probably E8+AH since 2./NSG 9 had no Ju 87s and a Junkers in these markings had, as we have seen, featured in recent radio traffic from the North.

On 1 June, OKW issued this report of the previous night's operations:

> *Nachtschlacht* aircraft attacked the town of Aprilia as well as enemy batteries and columns in the same area with good effect.

---

1. General Commanding the German *Lutwaffe* in Central Italy, *General der Flieger* Maximilian von Pohl.

"Despite massive loss of blood"

T he Allied rupture of the Gustav Line and the breach of containment at the Anzio bridgehead had left the German Tenth and Fourteenth Armies in desperate trouble, especially the former since its lines of communication seemed about to be severed. In the event, US General Mark Clark saw the city of Rome as his objective rather than the destruction of enemy forces, a move which did not win him universal approbation either at the time or in the eyes of historians. The Germans were in full retreat but showing their characteristic ability to salvage men, equipment and some kind of order from even the most desperate situations. For NSG 9, help was on its way from the Eastern Front. On the morning of 1 June, 2./NSG 2 left Lida in Byelorussia (now Belarus), staging through Warsaw and Breslau (now Wroclaw, Poland) to Prague/Rusin where the *Staffel* spent the night, having covered 900km that day. As Herbert Kehrer recalls, "We were all glad to get away from Russia." A prisoner's claim that it had been intended to transfer the entire *Gruppe* is corroborated by captured *Luftflotte* 2 orders of 11 June that "up to five" *Nachtschlachtstaffeln* would be operating in the next full-moon period.

ABOVE: *Russia, 22 May 1944. On one of their last missions in the East, Toni Fink and Hans Nawroth of 2./NSG 2 set off from Budslav for a dawn attack on woods west of Mongoliya. Their Ju 87D-3 is D3+HK, white 8.*

RIGHT: *Spring 1944. An airman shaded by a Ju 87D-3 of NSG 2. The aircraft carries a yellow Eastern Front tail band; its spinner has a white or yellow tip and beneath the wing the letters G and A have been overpainted. The "D3" unit code is in white and there is a coloured letter (possibly a D) after the fuselage cross. No flame dampers are fitted.*

BELOW: *2./NSG 2's two-day journey to Italy, set out in the Flugbuch of Harry Fischer: Lida (Belarus) – Warsaw – Breslau – Prague – Pilsen – München – Vicenza – Torino.*

Lfd. Nr. des Fluges	Führer	Begleiter	Muster	Zu-lassungs-Nr.	Zweck des Fluges	Abflug Ort	Flug Tag	Tageszeit	Landung Ort	Tag	Tageszeit	Flugdauer	Kilometer	Bemerkungen
515	Fischer	Uffz. Thöne	Ju 87	23+HK	Verlegung	Lida	1.6.44	11⁴⁰	Warschau/Okec		13²⁵	105'	370	
516	"	"	"	"	"	Warschau/Ok.	"	14¹⁰	Breslau/Schöng.		15³⁰	80'	300	
517	"	"	"	"	"	Breslau/Schöng.	"	17¹⁰	Prag/Rusin		18²⁵	75'	230	
518	"	"	"	"	"	Prag/Rusin	2.6.44	8¹⁵	Pilsen		8⁵⁰	35'	90	
519	"	"	"	"	"	Pilsen	"	12⁴⁰	München/Riem		13⁵⁰	70'	270	
520	"	"	"	"	"	München/Riem	"	15⁵⁰	Vizenza		17⁴⁰	110'	450	
521	"	"	"	"	"	Vizenza	"	18⁴⁰	Turin		20¹⁵	95'	350	

Diary of NSG 9 Operations, June 1944
Aeronautica Nazionale Repubblicana
"Situazione Aeronautica — Aeri da Combattimento Notturno"

Night 1st/2nd   Operations against vehicle columns, lorry assemblies, artillery positions at Artena, Giulianello, Cori and nearby areas. Explosions and fires observed. Attacks performed with bombs and machine-guns.

Night 2nd/3rd   Concentrated attack by all aircraft against Valmontone and vehicle columns on nearby roads. Fires observed on and near the roads. Some AA batteries silenced. One CR.42 missing.

Night 3rd/4th   Attacks on traffic on Via Casilina between Valmontone and Colonna. Bombs dropped on targets, then machine-gun attacks. Burning and exploding vehicles observed.

Night 4/5th   Attacks on Colonna, Grottaferrata and Frascati. Large fire observed at Grottaferrata. Large explosion observed near the east end of Frascati. Low altitude attack on vehicle columns at Colonna and near the front line.

Night 5/6th   Attacks on vehicles and supply convoys in the area Frascati - Grottaferrata - Marino. Strong AA fire observed. Good positioning of bomb hits on targets. Fires observed at Torre Gaia and Torre Nuova.

Night 6/7th   No information on aircraft activity could be reported due to communications problems.

Night 7/8th   No operation owing to need to restore combat readiness.

Night 8/9th   No information reported.

Night 9/10th   Attack on supply vehicle traffic on coastal roads south of Civitavecchia and south of Viterbo with bombs and machine-guns. Strong AA reaction. Large explosion observed in the area of Viterbo.

Nights 10/11th
– 11/12th   No operations due to bad weather.

Night 12/13th   Bomb and machine-gun attacks on vehicles at Montefiascone and on the road Montefiascone - Viterbo. Anti-aircraft positions also attacked. Several fires observed.

Night 13/14th   Attacks on enemy positions in the areas of Viterbo and Orbetello. Attacks against supply vehicles on the coastal road. Fires observed NNE of Orbetello, enemy positions hit effectively. Machine-gun attacks against vehicle columns and single vehicles on the coastal road and on the road NE of Orbetello.

Night 14/15th   No activity reported.

Night 15/16th   No operations due to redeployment of unit to other bases.

Night 16/17th   No activity reported.

Nights 17/18th
– 19/20th   No activity reported. Bad weather reported.

Nights 20/21st
– 28/29th   No activity reported.

Night 29/30th   Attacks on vehicle columns and batteries in the area Perugia - Chiusi - Orvieto. Explosions and fires observed

Night 30th/1st   Attacks on vehicle columns in the area Buonconvento - Ansa dell'Ombriene (west of Lake Trasimeno). Results could not be assessed due to heavy fog.

ABOVE: *Fw. Horst Greßler in the cockpit of CR.42 E8+BK of 2./NSG 9. Greßler was shot down and badly wounded during an attack on the Anzio beach head on the night of 1/2 June 1944. He was the first NSG 9 pilot to fall victim to an Allied night fighter.*

Meanwhile in Italy on the first night of June, there was a half moon, the skies were clear and cloudless and targets hit included Allied artillery positions and traffic in the area of Artena, Giulianello and Cori. The OKW daily communiqué summed up NSG 9's operations thus:

> *Nachtschlacht* aircraft bombed and strafed enemy batteries and columns in the Artena area as well as the town itself.

Horst Greßler has good cause to remember that night:

> After the conclusion of the third defensive battle round Rome we were again flying operations in the battle zone. During the night of 1/2 June we were flying attacks on the US 7th Fleet at Anzio-Nettuno from the landing ground at Fabrica di Roma, about 20km east south east of Viterbo. On the return flight, near Lake Vico, I was chased by a Beaufighter at around 1400m and, after around 10-15 minutes, fired upon. You know what happened then…

Flying Officers Stewart W. Rees (RAAF) and D.C. Bartlett had been aloft since 22.30 and their sortie report gives their perspective on what ensued:

> 23.05, 10,000ft., Anzio area: taken over by GCI "PROJECT"…
> 23.30, 10,000ft., North of Rome: contact and visual on a Baltimore.
> 00.01, 10,000ft., South of Rome: given vector 270 degrees on to bandit travelling south at 8,000ft. Contact obtained at 4 miles' range, below and to port. Target taking evasive action, losing height and changing course. Contact was lost when target entered Anzio flak area.
> 00.15, 6,000ft., PROJECT gave vector and contact was regained at 4 mile range, below and to starboard on target at 5,000ft. Bandit was now on a northerly course and weaving. After 15 minutes' chase, target altering course, speed and height as Beaufighter closed at speed of 110-120 IAS. Beaufighter finally with wheels down and 30 degrees of flap closed in to 700ft. and below and identified bandit as CR.42, now at 4,000ft. Bandit continued to lose height and vary speed. Beaufighter dropped back and closed rapidly…

They were now dead astern of the Fiat and down moon:

> 00.30, 3,290ft, Lake Vico: …from 150ft. fired one short burst. E/A blew up in mass of flames and burning pieces were seen to fall in Lake Vico.

Horst Greßler was on the receiving end of 40 cannon shells and 120 machine-gun rounds:

> …my CR.42 took a load of hits, it's quite possible that some pieces were blown off, and I thought, "Now you're going to crash." I only managed to get away thanks to the CR.42's manoeuvrability, regaining control at 200m. Despite massive loss of blood and [the aircraft's] transformed flying characteristics, I was able to bring the severely

RIGHT: *F/O Stewart Rees taxies Beaufighter VIf "M" toward the camera. This is probably the same aircraft (s/n MM905) in which he shot down Fw. Horst Greßler on the night of 1 June 1944 for No. 600 Squadron's first victory against NSG 9.*

YEAR 1944		AIRCRAFT		Pilot, or 1st Pilot	2nd Pilot, Pupil or Passenger	DUTY (Including Results and Remarks)
Month	Date	Type	No.			
—	—	—	—	—	—	—— Totals Brought Forward
JUNE	1	BEAU VI	M	SELF	F/O BARTLETT	ANZIO TO MARCIANISE
JUNE	1	BEAU VI	F	SELF	F/O WILMER	R.I. EXERCISES.
JUNE	1	BEAU VI	M	SELF	F/O BARTLETT	N.F.T.
JUNE	1	BEAU VI	M	SELF	F/O BARTLETT	PATROL (ANZIO) ONE FIAT C.R. 42 DESTROYED

damaged machine the last 10km at low level from Lake Vico to [our] base at Fabrica di Roma. I made an emergency landing and passed out from blood loss, the machine caught fire and exploded.

His was the first NSG 9 aircraft to be shot down by a night fighter. As for Greßler himself:

I'd been shot through the left shoulder and had several glass splinters in my face. I was given emergency treatment by the *Staffel's* MO and at first light taken to the clearing station at Montefiascone [VT]. Because this was near a bridge, fighter-bomber raids continually rattled the window panes. The next night an SS lorry drove to Perugia - with me in it!

From the hospital in Perugia I went a few weeks later to Bologna, then from Gardone on Lake Garda to Baden-Baden. After surgery on 2 August, I was put in plaster, pronounced healed and discharged into convalescence. With only a field dressing and after two weeks' leave, I landed back in Italy.

GCI had followed the interception and now saw Greßler's blip fade from their scopes. Rees and Bartlett set off after another target coming south and climbing. When it reached 10,000ft, it dived to starboard and levelled out at 5,000ft before turning south and climbing again. The Beaufighter was above it and from 1,500ft range was able to get a visual on what was identified as another CR.42. At this point the enemy aircraft dived violently to port down to 2,000ft — the Beaufighter following at 300 IAS — entering the Anzio *Flak* zone from the landward side. Rees was forced to break off when the guns opened up, GCI lost the Fiat and there was no further contact.

Later on the morning of the 2nd, 2./NSG 2 continued its journey via Pilsen to München-Riem and thence over the Alps to Vicenza and on to Caselle: 1,160km and five hours and 10 minutes flying time in all. Allied Intelligence was soon aware that something was going on as ULTRA revealed the following:

17.00: Ju 87s VR+OC, CE+JW, SF+NV up from Bergamo/Vicenza area for an airfield in the Milan-Turin-Genoa area.

16.35-16.40: Ju 87s D3+AK, JK, EK, RK, HK, LK, MK, PK, DK, RK, OK, QK, GK and BK left Vicenza.

18.00: Ju 87s white 1, 2, 4, 5, 7, 8, 10, 12, 13, 15, 16, 17, 18 and 19, arrived at an airfield in the Milan-Turin-Genoa area. Vicenza informed.

Commentaries issued with these intercepts noted that the latter two items referred to the same fourteen aircraft, that the D3 code was hitherto unknown and that "RK" was given twice in the German original. Aircraft of 2./NSG 2 carried not just the usual four character code but white numerals on their rudders corresponding with the alphabetical position of their individual identification letter. On that basis, one of the so-called RK's was in fact SK/white 19.

The OKW communiqué told the German public that on the night of 2/3 June:

Bomber and *Nachtschlacht* aircraft attacked enemy columns and assembly positions in the area of Valmontone with good results.

ULTRA offered the additional detail that the northern exits of the latter town had been a target. Valmontone's significance was that a German rearguard had been holding on there while Tenth and Fourteenth Armies escaped encirclement and it had fallen to the Allies during the day.

TOP LEFT: *F/O Stewart Rees's log book for 1 June 1944. After returning from an overnight stay in Anzio, there followed a radar exercise and a night flying test, the day's flying culminating in the destruction of the CR.42 of Fw. Horst Greßler of 2./NSG 9. The symbol of the fasci suggests that Rees was unaware that the Fiat belonged to a Luftwaffe unit.*

ABOVE: *Certificate awarding the Wound Badge in Black to Horst Greßler after he was shot down on the night of 1/2 June 1944.*

Squadron Leader Jim Bailey and "Shrimp" Wint (described by his pilot as "a frail Flight Sergeant from the Midlands of England") were there too:

> The night was clear with a good moon. I took the second patrol and had no sooner arrived over the beach-head than a raid started. The Germans had been using Ju 87s latterly, because these elderly dive-bombers flew so slowly that Beaufighters overshot them at night. In fact, as we flew up to Anzio, American voices in rich southern accents had come surprisingly to us on the radio out of the mountains and darkness promising a bottle of Bourbon whisky to the first Beaufighter crew able to fly slow enough to catch a Stuka. They never paid up.

Bailey's after-action report omits this unofficial incentive:

> 23.00, 8,000ft., Anzio area: patrolled with GCI "GONAT"…
>
> 23.30, 8,000ft., Rome area: vectored 15 degrees on to bogey north of flak area.
>
> 23.35, 4,500ft., Rome area: contact made at 2 miles range well to starboard, target crossing starboard to port slightly below and losing height gradually. Beaufighter closed at 130 IAS with wheels down and 20 degrees of flap. Visual obtained at 2,000ft on aircraft identified as Ju 87 slightly above and dead ahead. Beaufighter then turned to port and back to starboard to avoid overshooting. From 250 yards range fired short burst with 30 degrees deflection. Strikes on cockpit were observed and E/A dived.
>
> 23.40, 2,000ft., north of Colle Laziali: Beaufighter fired another burst but no strikes obtained. Ju 87 now dived into ground, exploded and was seen burning on the ground.

In his post war memoirs, Bailey would elaborate on the dry account he had set down on RAF Form 441A back in 1944:

> I … slowed down until the great gun-platform was wallowing in the air and then, as the Stuka crossed starboard to port, fired … One cannon shell exploded near the pilot's seat and the Stuka dived for the ground. I watched it in the milky air. Streams of tracer hurried past me as the gunner, in place of parachuting, fired back. [At the time Bailey had reported, "No return fire."] I saw it dive all the way down into the Alban Hills, where it exploded with a flash that lit the countryside. An aircraft falling away from you thus, when it is moonlight, resembles an object sinking through a well of water.

Unequivocal as these accounts are, no record survives of NSG 9 losing a Ju 87 nor any personnel that night, although the situation report to the Italian Air Ministry states that a CR.42 was missing.[1] Bailey and Wint went on to intercept another Junkers soon after, causing it to jettison its bombs over its own side of the lines and evade in a dive. Later in this same patrol, the Beaufighter shot down a Bf 110G-4 of II./NJG 6.

The night of 3/4 June saw NSG 9 bombing and strafing columns along the Via Casilina, the road into Rome, between Valmontone and Colonna (Roma), this being reported on the home front as follows:

> Last night, bomber and *Nachtschlacht* aircraft attacked enemy columns and
> assembly positions in area of Valmontone effectively.

For the next night the targets were Colonna, Grottaferrata and Frascati (Roma). A large fire was seen at the second of these towns and an explosion near the eastern end of the last.

At 15.08 on 5 June, Ju 87 E8+RH left Caselle for Bologna. That night the *Gruppe* was again attacking transport columns and artillery positions at Grottaferrata, Frascati and along the Via Casilina. However, a signal from *Komm. Gen. Mittelitalien* at 21.30 had stated that "if serviceability … can be re-established after transfer, ops in forward area, night 6/7th", things becoming clearer on the morning of the 6th when ULTRA revealed that the two operational *Staffeln* were withdrawing from Tuscania to Brolio (AR) and (rather vaguely) an "airfield in the Perugia/Pisa area." Away from the front, Ju 87 BD+YD landed at the unusual destination of Maniago from Vicenza at 17.30. According to an RAF log of *Luftwaffe* activity, three CR.42s and a pair of Ju 87s from NSG 9 arrived in Bologna on 8 June. The 2./NSG 9 had now begun converting to the Ju 87 and on the 9th, *Uffz.* Karl Oefele was killed in an accident while flying Ju 87D-3 WNr. 100090 at Caselle. The *Staffel* would go into action with its new aircraft before the month was out.

Meanwhile at the front, that night's target was traffic on the coastal road and south of Viterbo. There was bad weather on 10/11 June and so no night attack operations that night or the next. On the 12/13th however, NSG 9 was again able to bomb and strafe traffic and AA emplacements around Montefiascone and Viterbo, causing fires. Despite an announcement that no *Nachtschlacht* operations were intended on the 13th, the crews were sent against troop assembly areas and artillery positions in the Viterbo–Orbetello (GR) area that night. On the 15th came another signal that NSG 9 was not intended to operate, effectively marking the end of this particular deployment.

By now, NSG 9 was the sole *Luftwaffe* offensive force in Italy. When operations began in March, the night harassment aircraft had been augmenting the efforts of the ground attack Fw 190s of I. and II./SG 4 and the Ju 88 *Gruppen* of LG 1 and KG 76, as well as *Fliegerdivision 2's* bombers raiding Anzio from bases in southern France. The Focke-Wulfs had been pulled out of the line in May to restore their strength, never to return to action on the Italian front, while in June the medium bombers were withdrawn to fight the Normandy landings. From now on NSG 9's bombs and guns would be, one brief interlude aside, all the air support that German troops were going to get.

BOTTOM FAR LEFT:
"Nachtschlacht aircraft attack: effective support of the army — successful attacks in Frascati." In this report of 8 June 1944, the *Völkischer Beobachter*, official newspaper of the Nazi Party, brings news of NSG 9 to the home front. *"On Sunday (4 June) Nachtschlacht aircraft also attacked at Frascati in the battles before Rome where, with bombs and guns, they attacked enemy troops and screened the Army's disengagement … our Nachtschlächter – as the Nachtschlacht flyers are called for short in combat airman's German – stand at the side of their comrades from the Army with dashing, aggressive action in the heavy battles against the enemy masses."*

LEFT: By contrast, Anglo-American propaganda speaks of the *"Retreat of the Southern Army without air cover."* An RAF spokesman is quoted as saying on 12 June that, *"The German Luftwaffe has abandoned the Tenth and Fourteenth Armies…"*

RIGHT: *Described by a captured comrade as "an old hand", Uffz. Ernst Kienast of 1./NSG 9 pictured in Caselle, June 1944.*

The 2./NSG 2 was not yet operational, having first to adapt to the new conditions in which it was to fly. According to prisoners and veterans, aircraft were "painted brown" and fitted with a larger oil cooler and exhaust flame dampers. Hans Nawroth recalls that:

For us the country was as different from Russia as day is from night. Also, our pilots were trained in night flying in Caselle. We had been flying the Ju 87 in Russia for some time, however our operations were only by day.

Alfons Eck's impressions were similar:

As far as flying was concerned, Italy was a complete turnaround for all of us. We could fly only by night. Not being on the ground at the first glimmer of daylight definitely meant "curtains" for the aircraft and its crew.

Eck also recalls:

…the words with which our *Kommodore* in Italy greeted us: "We are a forlorn hope, I admit, but we will have to do our duty."

For another *Staffel* member, their "welcome" still rankled in the summer of 1950 when the former *Major* Frost was running a hotel reception desk rather than a *Nachtschlachtgruppe*:

I passed the hotel every day [but] I never looked Frost up… He begrudged us in 3. *Staffel* the recognition that we were really due. He [had] stated in front of the assembled men, "Gentlemen, how you flew in Russia is of no interest here. Here you must start from the beginning."

The *Staffel's* conversion to the Stuka had taken place in February and March 1944 and although 2./NSG 2 may not previously have flown this particular type at night, it seems clear that its predecessors such as the Ar 66C were largely confined to the hours of darkness. For these first weeks in Caselle, surviving log books contain little more than a sequence of brief circuits of the airfield until the 20th, when an operation was flown against partisans west of Torino. Even so, bad weather induced at least one aircraft, *Ofw.* Toni Fink and *Fw.* Hans Nawroth's D3+DK, to break off the mission. So far as is known, 2./NSG 2 saw no more action during June[2]. The continuing danger from the guerillas was underlined on the 24th when *Uffz.* Friedrich Schröder, an aircraft electrician with 2./NSG 9, disappeared along with his car on the road between Caselle village and the airfield. He was posted missing, presumed abducted.

RIGHT: *Airmen of 2./NSG 2 enjoy the Italian summer.*
From left to right:
Obgfr. Rolf Möhrke,
Uffz. Rafael Szyglowski,
Obgfr. Harry Fischer,
Fw. Oskar Hug,
Fw. Otto Brinkmann,
Obgfr. Josef Jantos,
unknown, unknown.

On the 21st, Allied reconnaissance had identified no fewer than 47 Ju 87s at Caselle. The following day, *Flughafenbereich 18/XI* had been informed that Caselle would for the time being continue as the base and re-equipping airfield for 1. and 2./NSG 9 and 2./NSG 2 and that the ground echelon there should be reinforced accordingly. Thiene (VI) would also be available to these *Staffeln* for the same purposes. Casabianca (TO) was intended to accommodate the *Gruppenstab* "and one further *Staffel*" of NSG 2 and, in addition to sending more men, was to be stocked with 7.5t of C3 fuel and 2,000 rounds of 2cm ammunition. *Hptm.* Huntjeur of the airfield command was to liaise with the Italian *Ten.Col.* Alderighi over the necessary facilities. The 1. and 2./NSG 9 were expected to be operational in Ravenna and Forlì from the 25th onward, while Rimini would also be used by "weak elements" and another airfield in the same area would be needed for 2./NSG 2 once technical re-equipment was complete. The deployment necessitated *Luftflotte* 2 bringing up an airfield servicing company to these bases and the erection of "heavy revolving beacons" on the Futa Pass and between Ravenna and Forlì as well as Morse beacons at the alternate landing grounds of Ferrara and Bologna.

When MAAF Field Intelligence looked over Viterbo Main aerodrome on 25 June they found not only the CR.42 mentioned earlier but three Ju 87s: E8+AH of 1./NSG 9, fitted with the *Peilgerät* IV direction finder but burnt out; WNr. 32739, badly looted; and callsign CP+EH on a dump, stripped and burned. The latter was camouflaged light blue on its undersides and had a green and brown mottle on its upper surfaces, the signature scheme of NSG 9, and this same paintwork was encountered on a set of Ju 87 wings found on the airfield. From this it appears that a detachment of 1./NSG 9 had been at Viterbo in the course of one of the *Staffel's* forward deployments in April, May or early June. One might speculate that these particular aircraft were caught by an air raid but unless the Lutwaffe's 1944 aircraft loss records resurface, there seems no way of knowing. Deciphered communications told of much activity on 28 June. Ju 87s were being delivered to Italy, KT+PM landing at an airfield "in the Bergamo-Vicenza area" at 07.50 from Bergamo-South (as the Germans characterised the base known to the Italians as either Orio al Serio or Bergamo-Seriate) while TF+GG, KT+PF, PQ+CR and DO+IR landed at Bergamo from Erding before moving on to Caselle that same morning. That evening, from 17.45, some 22 Ju 87s left Caselle. From 1. *Staffel* E8+AH, BH, CH, DH, EH, GH, HH, MH, OH, QH, UH and VH, were headed for "the Ancona/Piacenza area" (in fact Ravenna), while 2./NSG 9's E8+BK, CK, DK, EK, FK, GK, JK, KK, LK and MK set down at Forlì around 19.30. Also, from 28–30 June Hans Deutsch took the *Gruppenstab's* Fw 58 E8+ZB on a courier flight around several North Italian airfields.

For the penultimate night of the month, a two-wave attack was ordered, with the main area of concentration both sides of Lake Trasimeno where the Germans had been fighting a delaying action since the 20th along the aptly-named "Trasimene Line." The first wave was to take off at 19.45, hitting targets south west of the Lake and south of Perugia 45 minutes later. A follow-up would be launched against the same areas at 22.00, the outward and return legs for both strikes following a direct course.

ABOVE: *On 20 June 1944, bad weather forced Ofw. Toni Fink (pictured here) and his radio-operator, Fw. Johannes Nawroth, to break off a mission by 2./NSG 2 against partisans west of Torino.*

BELOW: *When they reached Viterbo in June 1944, the Allies found these wrecked and burned out CR.42s, formerly operated by NSG 9.*

The German 334. *Infanterie Division* had nominated targets in the Badia (PG) area but at 19.00, *Komm. Gen. Mittelitalien* sent word that as yet the moonlight was too weak for these to be engaged. Nineteen Ju 87s achieved 25 sorties against the road from Orvieto (TR) to Chiusi (SI) as well as artillery batteries south of the latter town. On the 30th only three sorties could be put up, attacking traffic columns in the Buonconvento (SI)–Ombrone Bend area. Volkmar von Grone and Heinrich Lenz flew on both nights against a railway and road south of the Lake. Their aircraft was E8+HK, which von Grone had taken on its acceptance flight on the 22nd and ferried to Forlì the following morning.

---

1   There is no other mention of this casualty and it may be a belated reference to Greßler's misfortune the previous night.

2   ULTRA did report that "bombers attacked localities occupied by guerrillas north west of Varese" by day on the 14th but the unit involved was not specified.

The other side

"In eight nights ten Stuka aircraft have been shot down by the City of London Squadron Bristol Beaufighter aircraft. The Ju 87 aircraft were attempting to bomb and strafe Allied troops in the Gothic Line battle area. These RAF Beaufighters, by their nightly patrols, are giving protection to our forward troops, who would otherwise be subject to attack by prowling Junkers."

(Australian press release, September 1944)

NSG 9 was the first *Luftwaffe* night attack unit to face a state of the art air defence system. A comprehensive Ground Controlled Interception (GCI) network and fast, heavily armed fighters carrying centimetre wavelength airborne interception (A.I.) radars helped Allied airmen inflict losses on a scale that came as a nasty surprise to veterans of the nocturnal war on the Eastern Front.

The overwhelming majority of NSG 9's combats with enemy aircraft involved Bristol Beaufighters of No. 600 (City of London) Squadron, Royal Auxiliary Air Force[1]. Formed as a day bomber unit on 14 October 1925, No. 600 converted to the fighter role in July 1934 with, successively, Hawker Hart and Demon biplanes before receiving the Bristol Blenheim in January 1939. The Squadron formed a special flight of three Blenheims in November of that year to test the first A.I. sets from Manston in Kent, this flight later becoming the nucleus of the Fighter Interception Unit. The rest of the Squadron continued operating in daylight, incurring heavy losses over the Low Countries during the *Blitzkrieg* of spring 1940 before being assigned wholly to night fighting duties.

The Blenheim's performance, impressive when the type entered service in 1937, barely sufficed to catch the bombers of 1940 and it carried an offensive armament (in its improvised fighter version) of just five 0.303in machine-guns. In September the Squadron began conversion to the new Bristol Beaufighter IF which could achieve 333mph at 15,600ft (compared to the Blenheim's 260mph at 12,000ft) and could climb over 4,000ft higher than its predecessor. On top of all this, it carried the unprecedented arsenal of four 20mm cannon and six 0.303in machine-guns and a radar of much better performance and reliability, the Mk. IV.

The Squadron remained in Britain until November 1942 when it was deployed to Maison Blanche in Algeria to counter the growing activities of *Luftwaffe* night bombers there. It moved to Malta the following June in preparation for the invasion of Sicily, to that island once the Axis armies were expelled and afterward to the Italian mainland. In March 1944, Wing Commander C.P. "Paddy" Green DSO, DFC (a 14-victory ace) handed over command of the Squadron to W/C Lawrence H. Styles DFC, who was to lead it until December when W/C A.H. Drummond took his place. In the Mediterranean the Squadron flew the Beaufighter VIf, still using the old A.I. Mk. IV radar at first but going over the more capable centimetric A.I. Mk. VIII during the spring of 1944 as the Germans' use of chaff and active jamming became ever more troublesome. The Beaufighter VI had more powerful engines and increased fuel tankage compared to the Mk. I but its performance was broadly similar, despite an increase in weight.

The Squadron converted to the De Havilland Mosquito Mk. XIX in January 1945. This type had a maximum speed of 372mph at 13,000ft, a ceiling of 28,000ft and was armed with four 20mm cannon; its radar was the American SCR 720 centimetric set, known as A.I. Mk. X in RAF service. The Beaufighter would have been hard pressed to counter NSG 9's Focke-Wulf 190s effectively and so the Mosquito's arrival was timely. By 1945 however, *Nachtschlacht* operations in Italy were severely curtailed and the *Gruppe's* run-ins with the Mosquito correspondingly few.

No. 600 Squadron claimed 31 of NSG 9's aircraft destroyed, plus one probable and five damaged. Within this total the top-scoring pilot was F/L Stewart W. Rees, RAAF of Fremantle, Western Australia (5-0-1). Rees, who had joined up on his 18th birthday in September 1941, was assigned to night fighting when he was found to be colour blind. He was posted to No. 600 on 22 February 1944 and began his score with the destruction of a Ju 88 on 14 May. He was awarded the DFC in December and left the Squadron in January 1945. He spent the rest of the war with training units in England, returning home in peacetime to work as a civil engineer. He was just 35 when he died in February 1959.

The Squadron's most successful Navigator/Radar Operator in actions against NSG 9 was F/O G. Beaumont with 6-0-2 Ju 87s to his credit. Of these, 4-0-1 were with F/L Denis A. Thompson and the remainder with Rees.

By the time it came up against NSG 9, No. 600 had adopted its own idiosyncratic marking system, abandoning the unit identification code "BQ" in favour of a figure "6" and a letter to identify the individual aircraft. From the scant photographic evidence, there was no one way of applying these markings to the aircraft; the characters could be together or separated by the fuselage roundel, and either the number or the letter could come first when reading left to right. Both Green and Styles flew Beaufighters coded "F".

After fighting over North Africa, Sicily, Salerno, Cassino, Anzio and on up the Italian peninsula, No. 600 disbanded in Aviano on 21 August 1945. The Squadron was reformed at Biggin Hill the following May, flying Spitfires and then Meteors in the day fighter role until it was again disbanded along with the rest of the Auxiliary Air Force in March 1957.

---

1. No. 255 Squadron was rarely employed to defend against NSG 9's raids but nevertheless distinguished itself by claiming the destruction of nine Ju 87s in only four nights' operations during July 1944.

ABOVE: *9 September 1944: two highly successful crews from No. 600 Squadron. Left to right: Flying Officer Stewart Rees of Fremantle, Western Australia and F/O D. C. Bartlett of Old Trafford, Manchester; F/O G. W. Judd of Spears Point, New South Wales and F/O J. R. Brewer of Norton, Sheffield (both former Post Office workers). In all, Rees claimed five NSG 9 aircraft shot down and one damaged, three of them with Bartlett. Judd and Brewer claimed four Ju 87s together. Because this photograph showed the fairing for Beaufighter's centimetric A.I. Mk. VIII radar, the back was stamped "Secret: not to be published or sent home."*

BELOW: *Flying Officers Bartlett, Brewer, Judd and Rees of No. 600 Squadron. Rees was the most successful Allied pilot against NSG 9, claiming 5-0-1 of their aircraft plus a Ju 88 (probably from II./LG 1) during his 10-month tour of operations in Italy.*

BELOW: *This picture from the album of the late F/L Stewart Rees, probably shows aircrew of 600 Squadron's "B" Flight. It also dispays to advantage the size of a Beaufighter, the extended radome of its centimetric radar and the rough ground of the dispersal area. Unlike their opponents, the RAF could confidently park their aircraft in the open in broad daylight, without any attempt at concealment; by this time they had little to fear from Luftwaffe bombing.*

LEFT: *The sign over the door says "600 SQDN OFFICER'S MESS" but at least two Flight Sergeants are present, the one at far right wearing navigator's wings.*

BELOW: *The victory tally of No. 600 (City of London) Squadron RAF, showing 131 kills, 19 of them Italian aircraft. Against NSG 9 the Squadron claimed 31 destroyed, one probable and five damaged.*

The Focke-Wulf Fw 58 in Nachtschlachtgruppe service

Fw 58 aircraft of 1./Störkampfgr. Lfl. 6 camouflaged for the Russian winter. In the foreground is CE+__ , the second aircraft is coded D3+AH and the third is +DH. The yellow tail band denoting service on the eastern front can be seen on the first two aircraft.

No photographs are known to survive of the two Fw 58 Weihe (Kite) liaison aircraft of Stab/NSG 9. The examples depicted here served with 1. and 3./NSG 2 and their forerunners in Russia during 1943, where the former Staffel used the type operationally, and give a good impression of the Weihe's distinctive appearance. NSG 9's machines, E8+CB and E8+ZB, vanished from the order of battle after 10 November 1944, probably because fuel could no longer be spared for them.

ABOVE: *The cockpit of a Focke-Wulf Fw 58. The pilot is thought be named Löffler.*

BELOW: *An Fw 58 of Störkampfgr. Lfl. 6 in Russia during the summer of 1943. The men are thought to be (from left): Erich Schäfer, Mullenschläder, unknown and Werner Sudbrach.*

ABOVE: *Summer 1943. From left Müllenschlader, an unknown ground crewman and Werner Sudbrach. Note the hastily applied paint on the aircraft.*

BELOW: *Vitebsk, Summer 1943. From left: a flight engineer, Erich Schäfer and Werner Sudbrach of 3./Störkampfgr. Lfl. 6 Sudbrach wears a mission clasp, Iron Cross First and Second Class, aircrew badge and two other insignia that cannot be identified in this photograph. He has his flying helmet slung from his belt, as well as a sidearm. The aircraft may be Fw 58 WNr. 3536, D3+GL, reported lost on 8 December 1943. Its upper surfaces appear to be camouflaged in a single shade of dark green, albeit repainted in places; the black "G" may be outlined in the 3. Staffel colour of yellow. The rear machine gun has been dismounted.*

ABOVE: *A roughly snow-camouflaged Fw 58 of NSG 2 in Bryansk, October or November 1943. The pilot is Haferländer and on the wing is his gunner, Scharwak.*

BELOW: *October 1943 in Prosk. in the foreground is Fw 58, +DL of 3./NSG 2 which appears to lack a unit code. The Ar 66 at left carries the individual letter P on its yellow fuselage band; its unit code (which is not legible) is in white, a characteristic of NSG 2 aircraft in the East. The Arado's crew positions are covered with a tarpaulin.*

"He ended up in Africa"

"…the night fighters ruined our enjoyment of Italy's beauty. After six weeks in action we had more losses than in a year and half in Russia."

(Herbert Kehrer)

*T*hroughout July, NSG 9's area of operations would be dictated by German defence of the line of the River Arno in the west and by the progress of the Allies — in particular General Wladislaw Anders' Polish Corps — up the Adriatic coast. The German theatre commander, *Generalfeldmarschall* Albert Kesselring, was bringing his two armies back to the Pisa–Rimini (or "Gothic") line according to plan. The Allied advance lost impetus throughout the month thanks both to the efforts of their opponents and the withdrawal of forces for the invasion of southern France set for August. The pursuit phase of the campaign was already giving way to another round of slog and bloody stagnation.

The 2./NSG 2 was finally committed to the front on the 1st, with Ju 87s D3+AK, EK, DK and QK leaving Caselle at 17.45 and landing in Rimini just under two hours later and it was at this airfield that their *Staffelkapitän*, *Hptm.* Eduard Reither, was to meet the Italian employee who after the war became his wife. The crews were billeted in a small coastal resort:

> We lived in Riccione, [in the] Hotel Vienna… The proprietor made us promise to take good care of the accommodation.

The remainder of the *Gruppe* was in action that night, mounting a total of 28 sorties against road traffic and artillery positions south and south east of Lake Trasimeno, including the Tiber Valley from Bastia-Umbra to Piccione (PG). From 2./NSG 9, *Obgfr.* Walter Büttner and *Uffz.* Eugen Pendel were killed when their Ju 87D-3 (WNr. 1244) crashed at Forlì airfield as it returned from its mission.

Issued at 11.30 on the 2nd (and decrypted in England 11 hours later), *Komm.Gen.'s* intentions included operations by NSG 9 from Forlì, Ravenna, Rimini and Firenze (Florence) against traffic west of Lake Trasimeno as far as the line Sinalunga (SI)–Monte Fulciano plus an attack on the town of Cecina

"Sunny Italy seemed very attractive" but within weeks all but two of these young men would be dead, injured or captive. On their first operational deployment, in July 1944, the crews of 2./NSG 2 had their quarters in the Hotel Vienna in the Adriatic resort of Riccione. Seated left to right: Gefr. Hans Wilk (KIA, 03.08.44), Obgfr. Josef Jantos (MIA, 04.09.44), Obgfr. Rolf Möhrke (KIA, 04.09.44), Uffz. Eduard Kimmel Obgfr. Paul Sonnenberg (PoW, 03.09.44), Obgfr. Franz Till (WIA, 26.07.44). Standing: Uffz. Rafael Szyglowski.

Diary of NSG 9 Operations, July 1944
Aeronautica Nazionale Repubblicana
"Situazione Aeronautica — Aeri da Combattimento Notturno"

Night 1st/2nd	Attacks on vehicle columns and artillery batteries south and SW of Lake Trasimeno, and on the coastal road south of Cecina. Bomb hits on targets, effective machine-gun attacks, fires observed.
Night 2nd/3rd	Attacks on vehicle columns and artillery batteries on two sides of Lake Trasimeno and on the coastal road of Cecina. Targets hit at Chiusi, Borghetto and Cecina, several large fires observed.
Night 3rd/4th	Attacks on vehicle traffic in the area of Loreto and Macerata, bombs dropped on enemy positions and vehicle columns, several fires observed.
Night 4/5th	No operations due to bad weather
Night 5/6th	Attacks on targets at Loreto and Porto Recanati and supply vehicles in the same areas. Good results from the attacks, large explosions and large, long-lasting fires observed at Loreto and Porto Recanati. Machine-gun attacks on supply traffic.
Night 6/7th	Attacks on supply lines and single vehicles south of Ancona. Also bomb attacks on Recanati, San Domenico and Osimo, long-lasting fires observed.
Night 7/8th	Attacks carried out despite poor visibility and strong AA defence, with bombs and machine-guns, against vehicles between Monteriggioni and Siena. Burning vehicles observed.
Night 8/9th	Operations against vehicles in the area of Pomarance, on the Siena-Monteriggioni road, NNE of Lake Trasimeno. Bomb hits well placed on targets, machine-gun attacks against moving vehicle columns, several fires observed.
Night 9/10th	No operations due to bad weather
Night 10/11th	Despite bad weather, attacks carried out on the road NW of Lake Trasimeno. Results cannot be reported due to bad visibility.
Night 11/12th	No operations due to bad weather
Night 12/13th	Enemy prisoners confirm the effectiveness of night aircraft attacks, in particular the machine-gun attacks of July 6/7th. No activity reported.
Night 13/14th	No activity reported.
Nights 14/15th – 25/26th	No activity reported.
Night 26/27th	Attack on Ancona and Livorno. Anti-aircraft positions and harbour facilities hit in Livorno
Night 27/28th	Chiaravalle and Vallone, South of River Arno and in the area Pisa - Pontedera. Fires and explosions observed.
Night 28/29th	No operations due to bad weather.
Night 29/30th	Attacks against supply convoys with lights on, on roads in the area Bucine - Arezzo. Fire in the west side of Arezzo, other targets hit on the road Passignano - Perugia.
Night 30th/31st	No operations due to bad weather.
Night 31/1st	No operations due to bad weather.

(LI) and road traffic in the surrounding area. The plan was to repeat the operation several times during the moonlight period. Three Spitfires strafing 1. *Staffel's* base at Ravenna at 19.45 caused no damage and the *Gruppe* put up 25 sorties. This first mission over Allied lines in Italy for 2./NSG 2 was Toni Fink's 499th flight: his D3+DK took off from Rimini at 23.05 to bomb Borghetto (PG) on Lake Trasimeno and the railway on the lake's western shore, landing an hour later.

Warrant Officer H. Ewing and F/S J.T. Chenery, patrolling around the lake, damaged one Ju 87 at 22.05 before it peeled off and was lost in the ground mist (Volkmar von Grone in E8+HK logged "fired on by night fighter" that night) and eight minutes later lost another in similar circumstances, being assured by their controller, "OK, we will get him on the way back." They then stalked another contact for 15 minutes before getting a visual at 22.42. This Ju 87 they bracketed with fire, setting both wings ablaze and sending it down to crash on the north bank of a river about 55 miles north east of Lake Trasimeno. Here again, corroboration from the German side is lacking. At 00.45 Allied aircraft bombed the Morse beacon 8km west of 1./NSG 9's Ravenna base, one bomb falling 100m away but failing to explode.

On the 3rd, German ground forces were notified that during the moonlight period (full moon would be on the 6th) Ju 87s would be taking off from Forlì, Ravenna and Rimini to attack Macerata (MC), with Loreto (AN) as alternative target. *Unteroffizier* Alfred Kunzmann was a gunner who flew around 40 combat missions, some of them with *Major* Frost as his pilot. Asked if he recalled any particularly important operation, Kunzmann replied:

> Yes, the massive onslaught on the place of pilgrimage, Loreto. The HQ of Anders' Polish Army was there. Routes in and out were over the Adriatic from Ravenna. We dropped incendiary and HE bombs. The operation was the most comprehensive that NSG 9 ever carried out.

There were casualties before the operation even got underway: E8+VH of 1./NSG 9 was being started up at 21.50 when its engine caught fire. The aircraft was already bombed-up and when the flames could not be put out it was abandoned, its destruction ensuing an hour later in the inevitable explosion. Then two of the *Staffel's* Ju 87D-5s collided on take-off from Florence: in WNr. 141010, *Uffz.* Ewald Kapahnke and *Gefr.* Wilhelm Happe were killed while the gunner of WNr. 140994, *Uffz.* Adolf Jaegers, also died. From 2./NSG 2, Herbert Kehrer and Alfons Eck took off in D3+QK at 22.25 but had to abort when about two-thirds of the way to their target and return to Rimini.

Toni Fink and Hans Nawroth took off in D3+DK at 22.30, bombed Loreto and were on the ground again at 23.30; rearmed, they were back in the air after 40 minutes, assigned the same target. The turnaround time before their final sortie of the night was a mere 25 minutes; they went back to Loreto and set down at Rimini once more at 02.35. In all *Luftflotte 2* achieved 32 Ju 87 sorties against the Loreto-Macerata area although Nawroth remembers an alarming incident between missions:

> It must have been the 4th or 5th of July. We were back from a mission. The machines were being serviced and refuelled. There were still one or two Jus coming back and all at once there was the explosion of small bombs — it must or could have been fragmentation bombs dropped by an enemy aircraft. The [hostile] machine must have found itself behind a Ju. A minor panic broke out, various Jus had already been turned round and were taxying out. There were people who jumped from their Jus without switching off the engine and other brave ones who got back into [these aircraft] and stopped them … This all came about because we'd never experienced anything like it in Russia and weren't so accustomed to the different conditions in Italy. The attack hadn't done us any damage though and we then carried out the rest of our operations for the night.

Late next afternoon, 2./NSG 9 was reinforced when Ju 87s E8+BK, HK and OK left Caselle, headed for Forlì. Another two aircraft seem to have been flown to Rimini for 2./NSG 2 but weather conditions prevented any raids being mounted on the night of 4/5 July.

The next night there were no such problems and a maximum effort was put up. *Oblt.* Rolf Begemann was a pilot and *Offizier zur Besonderen Verwendung* in 1./NSG 9 with 17 war flights to his name, all of them in Italy. He and his gunner, *Uffz.* Hermann Lehr, had already flown one mission that evening and at 21.35 their Ju 87D-5 (WNr. 140999, E8+OH) and eight other aircraft of 1. and 2./NSG 9 lifted off from Ravenna again. Each had an individual assignment, Lehr and Begemann's being to bomb and strafe traffic and troop concentrations on the main roads leading to Loreto. War Correspondent Wilhelm Zimmerman was on hand to convey 1. *Staffel's* part to the people back home:

Bold Warriors of the Night

Nachtschlachtflieger Operations in Central Italy

*T*he soft light of the moon pours out in golden abundance into the fading evening. The contours of hills and houses, trees and bushes start to blur. The levelled surface of the field landing strip spreads out wide before the eyes. Everything looks unreal, dreamy. The Ju 87 machines, which are only rolling out of their well camouflaged dispersals now that the daylight is fading, look like the shadows of giant birds.

In the command post of the *Nachtschlachtflieger* there is no sign of the magic that the dreaminess of this hour lays over everything. The pilots and air-gunners stand, drawn up attentively before the *Kommandeur*, *Major* F[rost]. The orders are unambiguous, clear and sober. With the serious professionalism that follows every briefing the final preparations for the mission are attended to. Everyone knows that this operation calls for the highest flying skill. The proximity of the front, the danger that night fighters or bombers will disrupt the take-off, preclude the illumination of the airfield in the way that a night operation warrants. There can be no lighting of obstructions on this landing ground; just a few lamps serve as a flare path; that is all. Since for the most part the crews have amassed their experience on night ops with harassment aircraft in Soviet Russia or purchased their skill with hard training, the brief illumination of the lamps is enough to get them clear of the field. They are already imprinted with an exact picture of the landscape, know every river, every road or the lakes that as reference points offer a clue to the watchful eye. They know what a night flight in a Ju 87 entails. As loyal helpers of their comrades fighting on the ground at Nettuno, Valmontone, in the Alban Hills, during the withdrawals north of Rome, on nearly every road, in numerous night operations, they have already attacked hostile AA and artillery positions with bombs and guns, assailed supply columns or enemy concentrations of all kinds. Ground mist and haze, the foes of these *Nachtschlachtflieger*, and strong enemy defences have often posed great difficulties but again and again on their return they have been able to report "mission accomplished." The two-man crew works well as a team; their watchful eyes know how to master the dangers and find the assigned targets.

Frequently, an enemy night fighter orbits the field, whenever the few lamps of the flare path flash on for a moment, but before he can open fire the machine is already aloft, flies toward the hills at low level, pulls up and, taking evasive action, makes for the target. This time an Adriatic coastal location where numerous enemy HQs have ensconced themselves immediately behind the front merits an attack on the road that runs by the town and is used by the enemy as a supply route to the front line.

Here and there are English or American parachute flares but the aircraft of *Major* F[rost]'s unit avoid them. The gunner peers watchfully into the moonlit night to report to the pilot every threatening shadow that emerges. The pilot sits calmly at the joystick and brings the machine to the designated place. *Uffz*. W[aißnor] wants to attack the town from the east so that the light from the golden disc hanging in the sky will reveal all the details of the countryside below him. Then suddenly he ducks beneath a cloud layer. "What a silhouette my 'Marie-Heinrich' must be making on that" goes through his mind. That would be something for the night fighters. Swiftly he turns away to approach the town from the south west. Enemy *Flak* almost had him, its lines of tracer pass right and left of the machine like red pearls. Through the [ventral] window he makes out the streets and houses of the town beneath him. In the instant that he sees a rewarding target pass the tape[1], he throttles back, holding his machine in check, waits a few moments more until it comes into his sight and pulls into a dive. The *Flak* fires like mad. *Uffz*. W[aißnor] doesn't let that bother him. As the plane pulls out he sees that his bombs have hit. Dark red flames ascend from the rapidly spreading inferno. *Uffz*. Sch[wobe] in "Anton-Heinrich" goes in again after the bombs have dropped. He goes after a *Flak* emplacement that has been putting up a dense curtain of fire round the town. As he dives on it, cannons firing, it goes silent. The gunners prefer to take cover! Calmly but keeping a sharp look-out, he pulls out over the sea, again coming under fire. It must be from torpedo boats whose wakes show as dark streaks in the water. As a precaution he fires recognition flares but the boats don't stop shooting – it's the enemy! With swift determination *Uffz*. Sch[wobe] dives on the torpedo boats and fires until he is out of ammunition. Despite the fierce defensive fire, nothing has happened to his plane. Calm and equable as ever, it flies on a homeward course.

Landing at base, *Uffz*. Sch[wobe] meets *Fw*. P[ieper]. This 38 year-old who shares the vitality and skill of all his younger comrades was just a hair's breadth away from not getting back. As he dived boldly and determinedly on his target, the hostile *Flak* latched on to him. Numerous hits in the fuselage, wings and flaps seriously troubled his "Caesar-Heinrich." Although his vision was obstructed because his cockpit glazing was sprayed with oil, the old and experienced airman from the Nordmark brought his Ju 87 safely home nonetheless.

Only a short time remains for the crews to make a combat report and to swap stories. In the shortest time, the serviceable aircraft are loaded up again and once more are off against the enemy. *Fw*. St[uber], a calm, strong man from München, this time dives his "Heinrich-Heinrich" on a vehicle column. He had clearly seen the glimmer of their lights before they were precipitately extinguished when the enemy apparently heard the sound of his engine. Several fires and explosions show him that he has got good hits. "But what's that?", he thinks as he sees a huge fireball, travelling at frantic speed, disappear behind the hill on which the town stands. Has a comrade been shot down? The flames that shoot up after impact settle the matter. He only gets confirmation when, despite the night fighter circling the field, he lands back at base. *Oblt*. B[egemann] and his gunner have sealed their mission with death. They speak only a few words about their *Oberleutnant*. Everyone knew him well. He always set a shining example of fighting spirit. Sadness for the fallen warriors wells up in the comrades' hearts. The death of good comrades does not make them despondent however. They fight on.

With courageous hearts again they fly against the enemy — once, twice, three times a night. Their successes were again recognised in an OKW communiqué for this date. This fills them all with great pride. The *Nachtschlachtflieger* are right in the front line. Their great flying skill, their aggressive spirit which they share with the grenadiers and paratroopers whose loyal front-line comrades they are; their fanatical desire for victory allow them never to fear the enemy who with superior commitments of men and materiel tries violently time and again to break through the German front in Central Italy.

For the *Nachtschlachtflieger,* the great battle in the South poses the utmost test of their courage, combat-readiness and unbending willpower. They fly continual operations. Whenever the weather and bright nights permit, they take off three, four and five times a night, even when enemy planes attack their bases. In half a year they flew well over 1,000 sorties. Thus they play a decisive role in the battle on the German Southern Front which they support through their attacks on supply routes, depots and troop concentrations. Artena and Valmontone, Colonna and Loreto, Ancona and Civitavecchia and Arezzo were the main targets of their attacks for which they were repeatedly mentioned in OKW communiqués. Since the start of the battle on the Adriatic Front they have been in action almost every night on the most difficult missions against the enemy torrent trying to gain a decision here by force which up until now has been warded off.

Amidst the obligatory Nazi death-worship and fantasies of resolute young heroes gladly embracing their own extinction for the Fatherland, Zimmerman offers a valuable account of one of NSG 9's heaviest attacks. While Desert Air Force — whose night fighters made no contacts that night — estimated that 40-plus Ju 87s had operated against the Polish Corps, in fact 70 sorties were flown. The other *Staffeln* seem also to have been heavily involved, Fink and Nawroth of 2./NSG 2 making four sorties to bomb the railway station at Porto Recanati (MC) while *Uffze*. Kurt Urban and Gottfried Lässig of 2./NSG 9 flew there three times from Forlì in E8+DK, reporting a major fire and explosion in the town.

Rolf Begemann did not fulfil his fiery Wagnerian destiny that night as Zimmerman had imagined[2]. He had been flying at about 1,000 metres, the time around midnight, when his engine was hit and caught fire. Having seen no anti-aircraft fire, he assumed a night fighter was responsible but none had had any success, while the AA gunners claimed two aircraft. Both he and his wireless operator bailed out at 800 metres and Begemann was taken prisoner but the 21-year-old Lehr was never found and was eventually declared legally dead. Although CSDIC interrogators learned a lot from Begemann, deliberately or otherwise he led them a merry dance on the subject of aircraft, claiming that the entire *Gruppe* flew the Ju 87D-3 while shipments of the D-5 from Germany were still awaited. According to him, two or three of NSG 9's machines had been fitted with a pair of Italian BREDA 12.7mm machine-guns over the engine, synchronised to fire through the propeller arc; a few even had underwing 3.7cm cannon in place of their 2cm guns and were used for attacks on targets such as tanks. Sadly, none of these exotica can be corroborated from other sources.

Another fall-out from the night of 5/6 July was the break-up the Fink/Nawroth crew. According to Nawroth, his pilot had deviated from his assignment to make a successful attack on an enemy column and been grounded by *Hptm.* Reither in consequence, although Fink's log book suggests this punishment lasted less than 48 hours.

On the 6th, CR.42s E8+WK, DK, RK, OK and FK, no longer on the strength of 2./NSG 9, left Caselle around 11.10, landing in Ghedi at midday. These biplanes were probably bound for service in the *Reich* or with one of the Balkan *Nachtschlachtgruppen*.

OKW Daily Communiqués

<u>**6 July 1944**</u> On the Adriatic coast sector [last night], *Nachtschlacht* aircraft caused major fires and explosions in enemy supply depots.

<u>**7 July 1944**</u> Last night, *Nachtschlacht* aircraft attacked enemy supply traffic on the Adriatic coast with good effect.

Targets for the Ju 87s on the night of 6/7 July were as before although only 44 sorties could be achieved, while the Allies noted that the "Poles report little damage and no casualties." This time however, Beaufighters from No. 255 Squadron had been sent up from Foggia on defensive patrol. Flying Officers Bruce Bretherton and T.E. Johnson had been subjected to heavy AA fire both sides of the lines before they were vectored after a bogey 6 miles south of Ancona. Apparently they were spotted because it tried to escape to the north before the Beaufighter closed in to 500ft, identified it as a Ju 87 and shot it down in flames north of Ancona. Back on patrol, they destroyed another which crashed on a hill just outside the town. The third Junkers they intercepted went down almost vertically and pouring smoke after three short bursts from 300ft range to hit the ground, this time to the west of the port.

ABOVE: *This photograph of F/Os Bruce Bretherton (right) and T.E. Johnson marked their shooting down three Ju 87s over Ancona on the night of 6/7 July 1944, during No. 255 Squadron's brief but highly successful deployment against NSG 9. Bretherton was from Melbourne, Australia and Johnson from Haywards Heath, England.*

Flight Sergeant T.C. Griffiths and Sgt E.R. Kimberley were the next crew on the scene and had prosecuted several unproductive vectors before they got a contact at 3 miles which they soon lost. Their next spotted them and peeled off into a dive which they followed before opening fire from 400yds, registering strikes in the undersides of both its wings. Pieces flew off which they thought were the dive brakes as the Ju 87's speed suddenly increased to an indicated 270 mph. The Beaufighter was forced to break off for fear of collision and the Junkers was last seen spiralling down at great speed before it was lost to sight. Their victim came from 2./NSG 2. *Oberfeldwebel* Wilhelm Böwing and his *Bordfunker* on this occasion, *Fw.* Hans Nawroth, had lingered over the target area, circling three times to relish the spectacle of an ammunition depot hit by *Lt.* Müller and *Obgfr.* Rudi Sablottny:

> ...an intoxicating sight... the way everything kept exploding... and then it happened: an English night fighter opened fire ... the pilot said the controls were hit and he could no longer hold the Ju. We dived, then... recovered and then another dive. Suddenly the Ju was flying straight and by this time we were at 300m at most. As the pilot kept telling me to

jump, I did so from low level. I struck my hip on the stabiliser, turned myself round and pulled the rip cord and… was soon on the ground. However the pilot had been able to fly the Ju 87 back to Rimini…

Nawroth, with injuries to his left hand and knee, landed in a steep-sided valley and counted himself lucky not to have hit the rocky slopes. His flying overalls were covered in blood and, having no idea which side of the lines he was on, he set about hiding his parachute. Hearing shouts of "Hallo!" his first thought was that American soldiers were coming for him. Baying dogs added to his alarm and he drew his pistol but as the searchers drew nearer he could make out in the moonlight that they were Germans looking for him:

In the early morning I was transported to a casualty clearing station, then to hospital in Forlì and after that by hospital ship from Cesenatico to Venice and from there to Merano.

The next 255 Squadron crew up on patrol was S/L J. McLaren and F/O A.W. Tozer who obtained radar and visual contact on a Ju 87 before opening fire from 300ft away. The first burst struck the fuselage and started a fire in the Germans' cockpit. After two more bursts, two parachutes were seen before the aircraft hit the ground and exploded.

Squaring the night's claims and losses is difficult, in part because there appear to be no records surviving for 2./NSG 2 at this period. Apart from the damage to Böwing's plane, two losses are known: both from 2./NSG 9, during their return flights but still in the target area, all four airmen being slightly wounded. The Ju 87D-3 (WNr. 100355) of *Uffz.* Erich Ackermann and *Uffz.* Hermann Kasper was destroyed while that of *Lt.* Fritz Itzstein and *Gefr.* Wilhelm Rumbolz (WNr. 100382, E8+NK) belly landed at Falconara with 40% damage. Although officially repairable, it was never recovered and was later examined by an Allied Field Intelligence Unit.

Although a decrypted report from the morning of 7 July still placed 1./NSG 9 at Ravenna, 2./NSG 9 at Forlì and 2./NSG 2 at Rimini, radio traffic intercepted that evening betrayed the transfer of five of 2./NSG 2's aircraft to Florence. Surviving logbooks show that among them were D3+DK, FK and QK and that a mission was launched ten minutes after midnight. In all the *Gruppe* put up 19 aircraft in 25 sorties, attacks taking place across the western half of the peninsula. Toni Fink and *Obgfr.* Paul Sonnenberg in D3+DK bombed a road junction south of Pomarance (PI); sorties went in against road traffic between Monteriggioni and Siena while further east, at Umbertide (PG):

An undetermined number of e/a bombed troops … causing 56 casualties at 2300/0130 hours. 7/10 Ju 87s dive bombed Polcorps troops.

BELOW: *Photographed while staging through Bologna, Uffz. Erwin Mokrus of 1./NSG 9 (second from left) was shot down near Ancona on 7 July 1944. At first posted missing, he was able to regain German lines and return to his unit.*

Air combats centred on Ancona on the east coast, *Komm. Gen.* signalling that two Ju 87s were missing from the night's work. From 2./NSG 9, *Obgfre.* Fritz von Bork and Ulrich Tröster were killed flying a Ju 87D-3 (WNr. 1266) at Mondolfo (PS) north west of Ancona and *Uffz.* Artur Ballok, gunner in Ju 87D-5 WNr. 141722 was slightly wounded near Castelfidardo (AN). A Ju 87D-5 (WNr. 141029, E8+HH) of 1./NSG 9, crewed by *Uffz.* Erwin Mokrus and *Gefr.* Hans Wagner went down at Osimo, roughly midway between Loreto and Ancona. Both men were initially listed as missing but it seems that Mokrus returned to his unit as he does not figure among the Allied reports of interrogated airmen and survived the war to gain a doctorate. It may have been news of this crew's experiences which later reached 3./NSG 9:

…we always had a certain amount of anxiety about being shot down and falling into the hands of the Polish Army. These people by no means adhered to the requirements of the Geneva Convention. One crew — I don't know now whether they were from 1. or 2. *Staffel* — managed to escape after various kinds of ill-treatment and get back to the German side. On their return they arrived in Villafranca.

A mechanic is in the rear cockpit of E8+HH and two more are at work beneath the centre section. Oversprayed camouflage paint has almost obliterated the fuselage Balkenkreuz and broad swathes of dark paint have been applied to the undersides. Uffz. Erwin Mokrus and Gefr. Hans Wagner went missing in a "Heinrch-Heinrich" on 7 July 1944.

Information to link individual casualties to the night's RAF claims is lacking. Flying Officer Tim Reynolds and P/O Mike Wingham in Beaufighter "R for Reynolds" of No. 255 Sqn. had already been headed for a bogey when ground control station "ADIEU" diverted them to another 10 miles ahead. Closing in, they "opened fire with three short bursts, and Hun, a Ju 87 dived steeply and hit the ground." Resuming their patrol offshore from Ancona they were given more trade, shooting a second Ju 87 into the sea, eight miles south east of the port. No. 600 Squadron's F/Os Jeffery and J.R. Brewer had lost their first potential victim and were stalking a second Ju 87 near Lake Trasimeno when it made a sharp turn to starboard and came at them head on. They began shooting at 1,000ft and started a small fire in its port wing root before engaging full boost, to climb and just clear their oncoming enemy. Turning tightly they saw an intense fire on the ground, "presumed to be E/A burning out", at 02.17. On landing, they found the Beaufighter had been hit by three rifle calibre bullets. The 2./NSG 2 aircraft that had deployed to Florence returned there after bombing but flew on to Rimini, only 40 minutes after landing in the case of D3+QK (Herbert Kehrer and Alfons Eck).

At twilight on the 8th, MAAF tried to pre-empt the *Luftwaffe's* efforts by sending Spitfires to Rimini, Ravenna and Forlì at last light in the hope of catching the "Stukas" between their disperals and their take-off point. No. 1 Sqn. (SAAF) saw nothing in two runs over Forlì, while 244 Wing claimed the destruction of one unidentified type on the ground at Rimini. Nevertheless, NSG 9 was able to dispatch 17 sorties against traffic between Monteriggioni and Siena (taken by Fifth US Army five days earlier). The early hours of the 9th saw the movement of a factory coded Ju 87 from Ravenna to Caselle and that night Kehrer and Eck deployed back to Florence, flew two sorties after midnight to an unnamed target then returned to Rimini.

At 15.30 on 10 July, *Komm. Gen.* announced that Ju 87s were to take off from Ravenna, Rimini and Forlì against targets around Castiglione del Lago (PG) and la Ripa (FI); alternates would be "Ferrero" (possibly Ferreto (PG)) and a road junction to the north west. The NSG 9 contingent at Florence was tasked with attacking the Rosignano area with Volterra as secondary. The weather was bad and in the event some eight sorties were sent off against Allied road traffic north west of Lake Trasimeno. At 01.20, Jim Bailey and "Shrimp" Wint were following a Ju 87 which peeled off to bomb a railway line and strafe a road 15 miles north west of the lake. They almost immediately engaged another, the ensuing action being described (undated) in Bailey's memoirs:

> ... the Shrimp and I were above the mountains when we were advised of trade coming south ... There was a sliver of a moon. We made contact with an aircraft, and a minute or two later I saw a Ju 87 ahead of me. As we closed in he caught sight of us, thrust his nose down and dived for the protection of the mountain-tops. I pushed my Beaufighter down and opened fire, letting him fly through the pattern. I saw one cannon shell explode amidships. We waited for a full minute and then the tell-tale fire broke out below.
>
> We were put after another Ju 87 soon afterwards. We attacked it twice and missed it twice ... With the second attack a shell pre-exploded at the muzzle, the flash blinded me for a second and when I could see again, the Stuka was gone.

It is not possible to confirm from the available *Luftwaffe* reords that any Ju 87 was lost or damaged in the area concerned.

Kehrer and Eck of 2./NSG 2 had again moved to the ALG at Florence but returned to Rimini next morning without logging a mission. Meanwhile, 1./NSG 9 had dispatched three Ju 87s from Ravenna at 22.00. They made an interim landing in Forlì to be refuelled and armed with an AB 500 and two AB 250 cluster bombs apiece. They were joined by a pair of aircraft from 2./NSG 9 and at midnight took off, tasked with attacking motor transport near Siena at one-minute intervals.

Oberfähnrich Klaus Wolff-Rothermel and *Gefr.* Hans Lankes (Ju 87 WNr. 141025, E8+GH) did not locate the primary target and so headed for the alternate, transport on the Ancona-Loreto coast road, at 2,200m and 250km/h. Their PATIN compass failed and they jettisoned their bombs in the sea off Loreto at 02.00, flew inland and took up a course for base, parallel to the coast. At 02.30 and 25 miles north of Ancona, they were attacked by the Beaufighter of S/L McLaren and F/O Tozer of No. 255 Sqn. whose first burst brought strikes on the fuselage and an apparent fire in the cockpit. After two more bursts, the fighter's crew was rewarded with the rare sight of two parachutes leaving the aircraft before it exploded and burned on the ground. Both crewmen, who reported hits in their engine, were taken prisoner. Klaus Wolff (as later he shortened his name) wrote in 1989:

> I was enlisted on 10 July 1942 in Quedlinburg... At 02.00 on the night of 10/11 July 1944, exactly two years later, we were shot down. My gunner, *Uffz.* [sic] Hans Lankes, bailed out first. He ended up in Africa ... At any rate, I did my duty and jumped last.
>
> Then a "delightful" journey from Naples and along the African coast, through Gibraltar to the USA where we arrived in Newport News on a splendidly sunny morning. By Pulman via Chicago to Colorado. The homesickness was oppressive.

Wolff had been questioned by CSDIC, apparently offering a jaundiced view of life in the *Luftwaffe*. Interrogator, W/C R.M.C. Day, noted under the heading of "Morale":

> ... a senior member of the *Staffel*, *Hptm*. REIMER is said to confine his operational activity to switching the airfield lighting on and off. A recent order, according to P/W, has forbidden officers to fly on operations, thus legalising a common practice. No troops are allowed beyond the confines of the camp after dark owing to the activities of the partisans.

Out in the open in broad daylight but bombed-up and apparently ready to go, E8+GH of 1./NSG 9. This may be WNr. 141025, shot down on 11 July 1944, with Ofhr. Klaus Wolff-Rothermel and Gefr. Hans Lankes taken prisoner.

This may refer to *Hptm*. Reither of 2./NSG 2 who, it seems, did not fly many missions in Italy but neither, as we shall see, had he endeared himself to Wolff. The late Eduard Reither courteously declined to discuss much about his *Luftwaffe* days with outsiders, so his perspective is unavailable. In reality, officers were flying missions then and would continue doing so until the last. Only the final count can be relied on as more than the synthesis of one airman's disaffection and his captors' wishful thinking and even this was not true of every place that NSG 9 was based. Wolff's recollections written down 45 years later are illuminating:

> I'd always been a lone warrior ... independent minded ... never had the requisite respect for superiors when I'd recognised them as prunes...

After completing his flying training:

> I was posted to night fighting but since I can never keep my mouth shut I kept getting moved on until I heard about NSG 9 wanting pilots with the blind flying licence, which I had in my pocket. So it came about that my path brought me to Italy which also held out more attraction for me than Russia. At first I was in the second *Staffel* under *Hptm*. Hegenbarth with whom I got on extremely well.

LEFT: *Hptm. Eduard Reither, Staffelkapitän successively of 2./NSG 2, 3./NSG 9 and 2./NSG 9, photographed by a Propaganda Company in the Summer of 1944. He did not get to see this portrait until more than 50 years later. Through the perspex can be seen (at left) the Revi gunsight and pilot's flare pistol and (right) one of the armour plates protecting the tail-gunner. Reither wears his flying helmet but neither parachute harness nor seat straps.*

Wolff came down with malaria and was hospitalised for a short time, after which:

> I was transferred to 1. *Staffel* since the *Major* wanted me under his wing. All the officers in this *Staffel* were married, including *Oblt.* Rolf Begemann. These "bourgeois husbands" stuck respectably to their quarters, which was supposed to reflect well on them.
>
> The *Major* noticed I was on first name terms with a lot of people and wanted to put a stop to it. There was simply nothing else for me at 20, as I then was, but to keep myself to myself. This explains why in my few months with 1. *Staffel* before I crashed, I had hardly any real contact.
>
> … in those days I was on special duties with the *Major* in 1. *Staffel* [and] I had to telephone [*Hptm.*] Reither for some reason and it took a long time before I got him on the line. It turned out to be an unpleasant discussion; he started shouting and I shouted back.
>
> A few days later I had to make a night landing on his field because my fuel was low. I got no fuel that night [and] next day he wouldn't see me. I only got my petrol toward evening, after I'd got the *Major* to intervene.
>
> … I never set eyes on Reither until last year in Schweinfurt [at the 1989 NSG 9 reunion].

Bad weather meant that NSG 9 could not operate on the night of 11/12 July and given the rapid decline in its sortie rate after the climax six nights earlier, the *Gruppe* appears to have been in dire need of rest and recuperation. Next day, 2./NSG 2 was formally redesignated as 3./NSG 9 and it was around this time that back in Berlin the *General der Schlachtflieger*, *Oberst* Hubertus Hitschhold, and the *Luftwaffe* Chief of Staff, *Gen.* Karl Koller, discussed NSG 9 late one night. The burden of their conversation was minuted as follows:

> The pilots from NSG 9 in *Lfl. 2* who have put themselves forward for *Reich* Defence should be setting off today. The *Geschwader* [sic] which was 14 crews short on 6 July, would, if further crews went to Home Defence, have a deficit of 25 pilots. This does not appear acceptable for the *Geschwader's* operational readiness, especially since the crews have special night attack training. *Lfl. 2* considers this withdrawal unacceptable.

Ancona, Arezzo and Livorno all fell between 15 and 19 July but waning moonlight meant a continued hiatus for NSG 9, with little activity other than some movements by groups of three and five CR.42s between Ghedi and Vicenza, picked up on radio and confirmed by

BELOW: *Oberst Hubertus Hitschhold, the General der Schlachtflieger (Inspector General of the Ground Attack Arm) intervened with the Luftwaffe's Chief of Staff, General Karl Koller, to prevent the transfer of NSG 9 volunteers to Reich defence duties in July 1944.*

ULTRA. Rather than return to Caselle, the new 3./NSG 9 moved to their next operational base, the small advanced landing ground at Cavriago (RE)[3], on or about 15 July. Herbert Kehrer who arrived there on the 17th remembers, "Landings in Cavriago were very difficult, only a narrow meadow. From overhead the flare path was hidden, only visible from the beacon due north when you were down to 300m." Personnel were quartered in a school in nearby Barco.

"That wasn't easy..." 17 July 1944: headset in hand, Harry Fischer after his 87th combat sortie, the dawn attack on Partisans holding the Castello di Bardi. The aircraft is D3+MK.

Allied radio monitoring detected Ju 87s E8+SH and E8+AB moving from Caselle to Piacenza on the evening of the 16th, in company with about four others. Among those involved were *Lt.* Volkmar von Grone and his *Bordfunker* Heinrich Lenz (E8+KK) and *Uffze.* Kurt Urban and Gottfried Lässig (E8+DK). Although an experienced combat airman, Harry Fischer of 3./NSG 9 had not flown a mission since the *Staffel's* arrival in Italy, logging only circuits, ferry and test flights. Now, with gunner Egon Zantow and ground crewman *Uffz.* Krämer crammed in the cockpit of D3+MK, he too flew to Piacenza. His 87th mission came the following morning:

> On 17 July 1944, we flew the mission to Bardi (PR). My take-off was at 05.10 to attack a castle. That wasn't easy. There was supposed to be an English Staff HQ in the castle. Aside from that, there was one particular house that was not to be hit since German prisoners were supposed to be quartered there. Round about were mountain peaks 1355, 1533 and 1284m high. Unfortunately I never heard any more about it. But actually there must be something to be found on it in your archives.

There is: Fischer's flight was part of the anti-partisan operation *Unternehmen Wallenstein* and his target, the Castello di Bardi, is an imposing fortress on a red rock commanding the valley below and with a small town huddled behind it. While Fischer took his two passengers on to "Reggio Emilia" (probably to Cavriago in fact) on the evening of the 17th, the *Gruppe* contributed a further 15 Ju 87s to *Wallenstein II,* another assault on Bardi and Varsi (PR). Ground forces probably took part because next day it was reported that 22 of the enemy had been killed and 81 German soldiers liberated during the action.

From the 17th onward, 2./NSG 9 was establishing itself at Vigatto (PR), 10km south of Parma. On 20 July, the *Staffel's* Italian SAIMAN 202 liaison aircraft (E8+ZK) took off from Gallarate at 03.45 for Pavullo nel Frignano (MO). Its business at these two airfields (both only tentatively identified by Allied code breakers) is a mystery. Another signal intercepted that day was from 2./NSG 2 – as it apparently still called itself – to NSG 9's battle HQ, reporting a strength of 16(14) aeroplanes and 17(11) crews.

In the rear area trouble had flared after "reproaches" from *Major* Frost over the service his *Gruppe* was getting from Caselle's *Platzkommandant, Oblt.* Heinert. The *Kommandant* of *Koflug 18/XI* went to the airfield to sort things out and, after talking to the warring officers, was able to settle the matter. The *Koflug* War Diary relates what happened next day:

> After 16.00... *Oblt.* Heinert's car... came to a halt a short distance beyond S. Maurizio on the journey from there to Caselle Airfield. *Oblt.* H. and the Italian interpreter accompanying him were trying to push the car... a Lancia car approached from S. Maurizio and stopped a short way off. Four guerillas got out and ordered *Oblt.* H., the interpreter and driver to put their hands up. When *Oblt.* H. went for his pistol, he was shot. The interpreter tried to get away and was shot, too. The Italian driver, who kept calm, was not attacked. The guerillas disappeared again with their car in the direction of S. Maurizio.

The partisans had not finished with Caselle however, for on the 24th:

> ...toward 13.30, an "Opel Blitz" medium lorry — WL Nr. 467423, chassis Nr. 5356, engine Nr. 588 — was stolen by guerillas from the Caselle aerodrome garage and driven away over the perimeter track and southern landing strip toward Leini (TO). A search by a Ju 87 of NSG 9 was without result. The lorry's Italian driver was arrested since, contrary to instructions, he had not removed its distributor cap. The theft can only have succeeded if it was aided and abetted by the Airfield Detachment's Italian civilian drivers.

On 23 July, the German 278. *Infanterie Division* signalled urgent requests for support by either bombers or *Nachtschlacht* aircraft but there were no bombers left in Italy and NSG 9 was not operating. On the 26th however, 16 sorties were dispatched to Ancona and *Uffz.* Richard Schwobe and *Gefr.* Günther Schlichting of 1./NSG 9 (Ju 87D-5 WNr. 141738, E8+EH) were posted missing as a result. Meanwhile 3./NSG 9 operated from Cavriago against the port of Livorno, a target where, Hans Nawroth remembers, "the defences were absolutely colossal [and] the ships' *Flak* wasn't bad either." Among the crews taking part were:

Fw. Hans Deutsch/*Obgfr.* Erwin Kaufmann	D3+CK	took off 21.32
Ofw. Herbert Kehrer/*Fw.* Alfons Eck	D3+QK	took off 21.45
Ofw. Toni Fink/*Obgfr.* Egon Zantow	D3+JK	took off 21.45
Obgfr. Harry Fischer/*Uffz.* Rudi Sablottny	D3+OK	took off 21.50

Deutsch (on his first combat mission[4]) reported direct hits on the harbour road following a sequential bomb release but he and Kaufmann bailed out, believing they had been hit by a night fighter although no corresponding claim has come to light. Deutsch did not fly again for six weeks and Kaufmann was hospitalised. The 3./NSG 9 had other casualties that night: the Ju 87D-3 (WNr. 212291) of *Fw.* Otto Brinkmann and *Obgfr.* Franz Till made an emergency landing at Barco. Till was hurt and the aircraft 45% damaged. There was fog when *Ofw.* Otto Gieger and *Obgfr.* Karl Gabauer were on landing approach and their Ju 87D-3 (WNr. 1369) hit a power line, killing both men.

Surviving logbooks suggest that 3./NSG 9 was briefly stood down but the other *Staffeln* were active on the 27th. Targets were vehicle columns round Senigallia (AN), Marina-Chiaravalle (AN) and Vallone (AN) on the Adriatic coast as well as south of the River Arno and in the Pisa–Pontedera area. Fires and explosions were seen and *Komm. Gen. Mittelitalien* reported the following day that at the same time as *1. Staffel* was operating, Allied aircraft had been about, possibly even bombing on German target marker flares. From 1./NSG 9, *Uffz.* Werner Waißnor, an original member of the *Gruppe,* was killed and his gunner, *Gefr.* Hermann Koch, was wounded at Cerasolo (FO), south west of Rimini. They were flying Ju 87D-5 WNr. 140755 and appear to have fallen victim to No. 255 Sqn. Despite being fired on by German ground forces, Reynolds and Wingham had closed in and near Rimini scored hits on the cockpit of a Ju 87 which dived into the sea and burned fiercely for five or six minutes.

From 2./NSG 9, *Bordschütze* Gottfried Lässig bailed out over enemy territory, "probably on account of severe hits on the aircraft" when Ju 87D-5 WNr. 110459 (E8+DK) was attacked by the Beaufighter of Flight Sergeants L.W. Waitman and J.G. Goss over Volterra (PI) at 23.25. The German aircraft evaded them once by a hard turn to port, passing under the night fighter, and when contact was regained it was slightly above, weaving and

E8+EH of 1./NSG 9 shows the extended wingtips of the Ju 87D-5 to advantage as well as a particularly dense underside meander camouflage. The MG 151/20 cannon lacks a flash suppressor and two parachute packs lie beneath the wing. This may be WNr. 141738 in which Uffz. Richard Schwobe and Gefr. Günther Schlichting were posted missing on 26 July 1944, during a mission to Ancona.

Seen here in Polozk USSR in April or May 1944, Ofw. Otto Gieger and Obgfr. Karl Gabauer were killed on 26 July of that year when their Ju 87 hit a power line on the approach to Cavriago airfield.

altering course and speed. Pulling up the Beaufighter's nose, Waitman registered hits on the port wing root before stalling, since the Ju 87 was doing no more than 110mph. It took him about ten minutes to regain control and reacquire the target which was still flying an evasive pattern. More bursts started a fire in the wing and deposited a stream of what turned out to be glycol over the fighter's nose. As he followed the Junkers down, an aircraft flew right across Waitman's front and he instinctively opened fire, his machine-guns scoring hits before he realised it was a friendly Baltimore. While ensuring that this unintended victim was in no difficulties (an aircraft of 13 Squadron, it belly landed at base with no one injured) the Ju 87 was reported to have struck the ground and burned fiercely southwest of Colle Val d'Elsa. In fact its pilot, Kurt Urban, nursed it back to Vigatto and crashlanded. The aircraft, hit in the starboard wing, incurred 70% damage (a write-off) and Urban was injured, not flying again for five weeks. *Obgfr.* Franz Spörr and *Flg.* Gustav Leumann (also of 2./NSG 9), flying Ju 87D-5 WNr. 2008, were slightly injured west of Modena (well within their own lines) but the cause is not recorded.

That evening too, the *Flivo* of 15. *Panzergrenadier Division* passed on a report from "very reliable civilians" that the Battle HQ of X British Corps at L'Olmo (PG) would be a worthwhile target for ground attack aircraft. A string of orders was issued next afternoon: Ju 87s were to take off from the Parma–Reggio Emilia area against targets around Pontedera (PI), Casciana Terme (PI), Certaldo (FI), Bucine (AR) and Arezzo. Accordingly, LXXV. *Korps*, I. *Fallschirmjäger Korps* and XIV. *Korps* were to mark their front lines from 19.45–22.30 by firing coloured lights or burning fires. At 17.30 however operations were scrubbed owing to the weather. Three hours later Montópoli in Val D'Arno (PI) and a nearby road intersection were put forward as targets for a *Nachtschlacht* operation. There was also a request for "further continuous operations" in front of 3. *Panzergrenadier Division* as constant Allied movements there pointed to imminent attacks against the division's left wing.

Flying resumed on the 29th, Toni Fink and Egon Zantow (D3+JK) taking off from Cavriago at 22.45 to bomb roads west of Perugia. In all, the *Gruppe* reported sending 13 or 15 *Straßenjagd*[5] sorties (signals differ) to the Bucine–Arezzo area, Harry Fischer and *Obgfr.* Rolf Möhrke (D3+AK) contributing three of them and recording opposition from both *Flak* and night fighters. Once again it was 600 Sqn. providing the defensive patrols and F/L Denis Thompson and F/O G. Beaumont were vectored on to a bogey south east of Florence which proved to be a Ju 87 flying an evasive pattern. A three second burst from dead astern set it on fire and they watched it spin down, followed by an explosion and fierce fire "in the exact spot for which the Ju 87 was heading" near Sársina (FO) but this is another claim yet to be matched to a known *Luftwaffe* loss.

Next morning, Ju 87 E8+CH left Caselle for Ravenna to be followed early in the evening by E8+CB, a Fw 58 liaison machine of the *Gruppenstab*. Fischer and Möhrke had made a 65 minute weather reconnaissance in D3+AK from 20.05 and, after an hour on the ground set off, this time in D3+KK, on an operation aborted by technical failure within 13 minutes.

A swift deciphering "break" on the 31st gave the Allies information on German intentions for the night's attacks just before they were due to get underway. There was to be no variation on the familiar theme: *Nachtschlacht* Ju 87s would start from the Parma–Reggio Emilia area against targets in the zone Pontadera–Casciana Terme–Certaldo–Bucine–Arezzo. Ground troops were to be ready to mark the front line any time between 19.45 and 22.30, should German aircraft fire white Verey lights. The *IV. Panzerkorps* had complained that day that, despite repeated requests for air support at Montópoli, friendly aircraft had been operating nightly over Pontedera (PI), just 10km to the west. By way of a response *Komm. Gen. Mittelitalien* explained just what NSG 9 had been going through of late (author's emphasis):

> The operations could not be carried out in the last few days owing [to the] weather. Area of operations decided according to possibilities of navigation and the defensive situation. *In operations from 26th one quarter of available aircraft and crews already lost.* At present no operations against single targets but only *Straßenjagd* on broad front being flown to disperse opposition.

The *Gruppe* ended the month with its strength markedly down on the 58 aircraft (27 serviceable) it had mustered on 30 June:

Einsatzstab	0	
1./9	13(7)	Ju 87D
2./9	11(8)	Ju 87D
3./9 (2./NSG 2)	10(8)	Ju 87D-3/D-5

Obergefreite Rolf Möhrke (left) and Harry Fischer of 2./NSG 2. The two flew missions together in late July 1944.

1. Probably a line marked on the Ju 87's ventral window

2. He died in 1990, aged 69.

3. There were two strips, Cavriago I and II, situated 7 and 10km west of Reggio Emilia respectively.

4. Albeit his 2171st flight, 18 of which had been attacks on Russian partisans.

5. Literally "road-hunting", this meant the bombing and strafing of motor transport.

Morale and Recreation

As seen by the Propaganda Ministry:

"The death of good comrades does not make them despondent... courageous hearts... great pride... great flying skill... aggressive spirit... fanatical desire for victory... unbending willpower."

As seen by Allied Intelligence:

"The morale in the unit seems to be very low largely owing to the understandable desire of one and all to avoid any unpleasantness so near to the end of the 5th Act."

As seen by themselves in hindsight:

"I liked flying but I'd rather it had been in peacetime."

"...our *Kommodore* in Italy greeted us: 'We're a forlorn hope, I admit, but we will have to do our duty.' A privileged bunch, we flyers, who could allow ourselves such talk and every one of whom — even the humblest *Flieger* — could listen to the BBC or other enemy broadcasts for soldiers without risking his life."

NSG 9 personnel enjoying the swimming pool at Torino-Caselle. The house at the rear centre was occupied by 2./NSG 2's Staffelkapitän, Hptm. Eduard Reither.

"I can't allow myself any verdict on NSG 9's morale."

"Morale was good although we were greatly outnumbered."

"Good until the end of the war in April 1945."

"Especially good, comradely atmosphere among the aircrew ... great enthusiasm for ops."

"I always found morale in 3. *Staffel* very good and have nothing bad to say in this respect."

"There was always harmony in the 3. *Staffel* "

"Morale was always good. This was because we were building a new unit. Besides it was an outfit that you could have an 'overview' of, where most people knew one another."

"...in Italy began the intermezzo with the night fighters that cost so many comrades their lives."

"On [my] arrival in Italy (16 September 1944) depressed mood on account of preceding losses. Fighting spirit of the aircrews was great."

"[On account of Allied air superiority] a feeling of oppression held sway, one had the feeling that the heat was on. On evenings out, usually drunk on wine."

"...the most important bit of our emergency gear was a mess kit and a pack of cards for *Skat* in case of being shot down (and surviving). Gallows humour? Quite definitely. That alone could still save us (at least as far as morale was concerned)."

"Oskar [Hug] and I had already been together in Russia and a real comradeship developed. We learned to value one another and formed a mutual trust. Then we came to Italy. Here began our hardest but also our happiest period. Difficult times alternated with happy evenings of drinking organised by the *Staffel*. So the time passed. The missions got harder, the odds worse and the number of losses mounted. We often sat around before taking off on dicey ops and talked about things that especially worried one of us. Mostly, it was always the same thing, our loved ones at home. He often told me about you and his little daughter he was so proud of."

As seen by captors and prisoners:

"Though not an intelligent type, P/W's morale is quite high…"

"P/W's… morale has remained high throughout."

"A more serious problem was the natural desire of the ground personnel to take cover when Allied aircraft were in the vicinity."

"But what a disgrace it all is! Do you know, they're actually using trained pilots as infantry? Of course I won't admit that to the interrogator, it would give him a chance to get me down. But it's true all the same."

Life among Italians:

"Contact with Italians? Only as much as came from staying in the Officers' Mess. I remember a really close contact between [an officer] and one Italian, name of Maria!"

"Across from the Officers' Mess lived three pretty Italian sisters whose mother had died. The eldest of them … was [an officer's] sweetheart…"

"We felt very good in Villafranca: we had contact with the locals, there were still things to buy, there was a cinema there, too."

"If the flying weather was poor, a couple of hours' sport. Otherwise, we had a lot of free time to kill during the day. Wherever my *Staffel* was, we had good contact with the Italian populace. At our last base, Villafranca, I even had the good fortune frequently to take my fill of relaxation with a sailboat on Lake Garda."

Life in quarters:

"One evening we were already lying in our beds in the dormitory, our machine-pistols hanging at the bed ends. [*Fhr.* Bernd] Jungfer comes into the room, grabs himself a machine pistol, aims at the lamp! "Stop! Quit messing around!" A salvo — lights out and darkness — lamp done for — holes in the ceiling. Next day, a visit from the *Staffelkapitän*, perhaps [it was] *Hptm.* Reither. Makes his way through the room, looks at the ceiling — Oh, Jesus! — sees the damage, walks on and says not a word. Well, well!"

ABOVE: *"Wherever my Staffel was, we had good contact with the Italian populace." Men of NSG 9 relax at a café in Caselle.*

BELOW: *NSG 9's adversaries needed relaxation too. A navigator takes aim during a darts match in the 600 Squadron officers' mess.*

"Without luck you're done for"

Twenty-one sorties were flown on the first night of August in the areas Pontedera – Bagni di Casciana – Certaldo – Bucine – Arezzo. Accurately placed bombs at the latter town produced big, sustained fires. To the south west, vehicle columns incautious enough to be showing lights were bombed and strafed. Flight Lieutenant Thompson and F/O Beaumont were patrolling between Florence and the target area when given a contact at 22.00. It was north of the former city when it turned east, attaining the unusually high speed of 240mph. As a result the Beaufighter gained only slowly until the bogey seemingly throttled back, allowing Thompson to close in astern until it did a port orbit before resuming a gentle weaving pattern. After 11 minutes' pursuit the contact was identified as a Ju 87 flying at 12,000ft. Two bursts of fire, the second from only 100ft away, blew the Junkers up, the Beaufighter being struck by debris and having its windscreen covered by glycol. Turning violently to starboard to avert a collision, the Beaufighter's crew watched the remains fall to the ground and an explosion ensue "as if a bomb had gone off."

It is possible that this aircraft was the Ju 87D-3 of 3./NSG 9's *Fw.* Werner Hensel and *Uffz.* Heinrich Laufenberg, WNr. 432614. As Hensel wrote 50 years after the event:

> …I was shot down in a Ju 87 by *Flak* on 3.8.44 and had to bale out from 3500m. The
> wireless operator crashed and burned with the plane.

The casualty report filed at the time put the incident on the 2nd but was later amended by hand to the 1st. Adding to the confusion about dates, an Allied Field Intelligence Team later looked over some Ju 87 wreckage near Cicogna (AR), "believed shot down on night of 31/1", finding that one crewman's parachute had failed, while his comrade could not be accounted for. Although Hensel thought AA fire had got him, Thompson's victim was apparently taken unawares and so the possibility for misapprehension is there. Furthermore, all other combat reports for this and the following night suggest that each Ju 87 spotted its assailant and carried out the standard evasive peel-off and steep

Pictured at Cavriago during July 1944, Fw. Werner Hensel and Uffz. Heinrich Laufenberg of 3./NSG 9 were shot down on the night of 1 August. Laufenberg was killed but Hensel evaded capture and made a three-day trek back to German lines. The armour-plating around the rear gunner's position of the Ju 87 is evident in this photograph.

dive. The upshot was that Hensel landed 25km behind Allied lines, evaded capture and walked back to German-held territory. The events of the three days it took him were, he says, "worth a book in themselves" but he is another who prefers not to dwell on his wartime experiences.

Herbert Kehrer wrote of the night 1/2nd August in the "remarks" column of his log book:

> Incendiary bombs on Arezzo. 8 big fires. Heavy *Flak*. Several night fighter attacks. *Fw.* Eck shot down NF.

Diary of NSG 9 Operations, August 1944
Aeronautica Nazionale Repubblicana
"Situazione Aeronautica — Aeri da Combattimento Notturno"

Night 1st/2nd Attacks against the roads Pontedera - Bagni di Casciana - Certaldo - Bucine - Arezzo. Good positioning of bomb hits at Arezzo. Large and long-lasting fires observed. Line of vehicles with their lights turned on attacked with bombs and machine-guns SW of Arezzo.

Night 2nd/3rd Attacks on roads in the area Marina di Pisa - Ardenza - Bagni di Casciana - Certaldo - Bucine - Arezzo. Harbour facilities hit at Marina di Pisa, fires and explosions observed. Small fires observed at the west and south ends of Arezzo.

Night 3rd/4th Attacks on roads around Marina di Pisa; attacks on Ardenza, Bagni di Casciana, Certaldo, Bucine, Arezzo, Gubbio, Fabriano, Cupamontana. Good results against vehicles north of Arezzo (about 50 vehicles), fires and explosions observed. Several houses burning at Fabriano.

Nights 4/5th – 7/8th No operations due to bad weather.

Night 8/9th Attacks on roads between Marina di Pisa and Arezzo. Good results against targets on roads west of Arezzo, roads South of Montevarchi, roads NW of Fergine and roads Arezzo - Chiassa. Fires and explosions observed.

Nights 9/10th and 11/12th No operations due to bad weather.

Night 11/12th Operations against vehicles on roads north of Fergine, NW of Figline, Certaldo, Marina di Pisa and Senigallia. Explosions and fires reported.

Night 12/13th No operations reported.

Nights 13/14th – 15/16th Units held in readiness to repel possible enemy landings.

Nights 16/17th – 21st/22nd No operations reported.

Night 22nd/23rd [Daily report missing from file]

Nights 23rd/24th – 25/26th No operations reported.

Night 26th/27th Operations west and SW of Florence, and South of River Metauro. In spite of poor visibility and fighter defence, enemy vehicle columns attacked effectively. Several fires observed.

Night 27/28th [Daily report missing from file]

Night 28/29th Attacks on vehicles west and east of Firenze, near Fano and south of River Metauro. Explosions observed. Bombs dropped on the exit of Fano and on Montemaggiore. Effective machine-gun attacks on the road Castelfranco - Loro. Large fire observed at Figline, vehicles burning SW of Firenze.

Night 29/30th No operations reported.

Night 30th/31st No operations due to bad weather.

Night 31/1st [Daily report missing from file]

Fifty-two years later he elaborated:

> On the homeward leg, my gunner, Alfons Eck, fired on a night fighter. He told me
> that flames were coming from one engine. On the strength of that I flew an orbit
> but we couldn't see any blaze from a crash.

From the night fighter's perspective, Thompson and Beaumont reported intercepting a Ju 87 that was taking "very violent evasive action" and losing height. When they got to within 200ft it greeted them with "one burst of twin red tracer. Inaccurate." As they closed in regardless, it turned hard to port, the Beaufighter following though on the point of stalling, and fired another burst which also went wide. The fighter had now come down from 11,000 to 7,500ft. Thompson recounted what followed:

> Pilot then obtained a visual on a Ju 87 slightly above, range 2000'. Started to close
> in when the E/A peeled off to starboard. Pilot throttled back and dipping starboard
> wing gave full right rudder and managed to follow in a practically vertical dive. The
> Ju 87 started to turn to starboard but pilot managed to get in a very short burst
> allowing for deflection. A few strikes were seen on the e/a's port wing. The Ju 87
> aileron turned underneath the Beaufighter while still diving. Pilot was unable to
> follow and pulled out at 3000 feet. This was below the tops of the surrounding
> mountains. No further contact could be obtained. The position of this contact cannot
> be established definitely but it was well north of the bomb line, roughly north east of
> Florence.
> ...When the e/a did its final peel off the aileron turn was too much for the
> Beaufighter which was out manoeuvred...

It seems that it was Herbert Kehrer's flying rather than Alfons Eck's gunnery which had saved D3+QK from becoming the Beaufighter's second kill of the night. Thompson and Beaumont had been shaken off but not shot down nor even hit.

Just five minutes after their victorious colleagues set down at Rosignano bearing a large piece of German fabric in one air intake, F/O N.J. Owens and F/S J.A. Walton had taken off in their turn. They duly obtained a contact of their own, only to lose it in a hard orbit. Their ground control, "SYRUP", could offer no help and they could only look on as their erstwhile target bombed Arezzo and strafed road transport.

On the 2nd, as three days before, a group of three CR.42s was on the move between the Torino area and other airfields in northern Italy, presumably passing on from NSG 9 and the FIAT factory to other *Luftwaffe* units and schools. Operations for that night would once more include the Arezzo area and friendly troops were asked, when aircraft requested it, to mark their positions with white Verey lights between 19.45 and 22.30. Twenty sorties were mounted, hitting not only the stated target but aircraft also went road-hunting round Marina di Pisa (where fires and explosions were caused among harbour installations), Ardenza (LI), Casciana Terme and Certaldo.

No. 600 Sqn. made two victory claims that night, the first by P/O's H.L. Jefferson and Spencer. At 22.30 and 8,000ft near Arezzo there was a nearly full moon and no cloud:

> Closed in to 1000 feet and pilot got a good visual on a Ju 87, even being able to see
> either flaps or dive brakes. Closed to 600 feet and 5° below. The Ju 87 peeled off
> steeply to port and dived. The E/A fired a long burst of twin yellow tracer ... levelled
> out at approximately 3000 feet and turned hard to port. The Beaufighter followed
> him down and opening fire at 200 yards range, kept on firing until he closed in to
> 100 feet. Numerous strikes were seen all along the fuselage and on the starboard
> wing near the fuselage. The return fire ceased after the first few strikes.
> [At 22.35 and 1,000ft] The A.I. contact went down to 6 o' clock and off the
> tube. The fire seen was taken to be the scattered remains of the [E/A] and was the
> only fire in the area.

The radars of the 1940s could require some ingenuity on the part of their operators, as Spencer reported:

> My set gave trouble and I had difficulty in keeping it working, having to hold a
> screwdriver on to the mag. slip phase screw to produce a picture on the set.

Pilot Officer Crooks and Sgt. Charles were orbiting near Livorno at 02.25 when GCI "RECRUIT" gave them a target which their AI could not pick up, then:

RECRUIT said, "You're right with him." Pilot saw tracer strikes on the road running west to east, to port and behind … did a hard starboard orbit and lost height to 4,000 feet. Still no A.I. contact. Searched the area for about 5 minutes but still no contact. RECRUIT called up and said, "we have another Bogey coming down from the north."

[At 02.45 and 6,000ft] Closed in to 4000 feet but so long as Bogey continued climbing unable to close in any nearer. Bogey was taking mild evasive action and finally levelled off at 12,500 feet and steered 030°, speed 140mph …

[At 02.58 and 12,500ft] Closed in to 800 feet and clearly identified the aircraft as a Ju 87 about 15° above. At the moment the pilot got his sights on to the E/A he attempted to peel off to port, having obviously seen the Beaufighter. Pilot opened fire immediately from 300 feet dead astern and on the same level, catching the Ju 87 before he could carry out his peel off.

The Ju 87 immediately exploded and the Beaufighter had to fly right through a great sheet of flame. Pilot did a port orbit and watched the remains of the E/A burning for two or three minutes on the ground. There was no return fire observed.

Jefferson and Spencer's kill came down in Allied territory and they received confirmation from Mobile Operations Room Unit "A" on the 4th. *Ofw.* Hans Wolfsen and *Gefr.* Hans Wilk of 3./NSG 9 were reported missing when their Ju 87D-3 (WNr. 331120, E8+PK) failed to return from a mission on the 2nd. The caption to a photograph of Wolfsen in Hans Nawroth's collection lends weight to this aircraft being the one shot down by Jefferson and Spencer:

Ofw. Wolfsen, Hans. KIA 03.08.44.[1] With Hans Wilk, failed to return from mission to Livorno, shipping targets. Only two aircraft assigned [the other was] Herbert Kehrer/Alfons Eck's.

After a 25-minute weather flight (in D3+QK), the latter crew had taken off again at 23.50 to attack Marina di Pisa with high explosive and incendiaries, claiming hits on harbour installations. Crooks and Charles' Junkers fell on the German side of the lines and was probably one of two *1. Staffel* aircraft lost on the 3rd:

Ju 87D-5 WNr. 131613, E8+DH: *Uffz.* Herbert Fietz, *Fw.* Karl Razinski missing (although both appear to have survived since post-war addresses exist for them. Author).

Ju 87D-5 WNr. 131150, E8+BB: *Uffz.* Helmut Krüger, *Obgfr.* Günter Tschirch missing (both later declared legally dead).

One of these however must have been surprised by F/O A. McDonald (RCAF) and Sgt Towell at 22.44 on the 3rd near Città di Castello (PG). Their victim was at 9,000ft, weaving gently and doing 140mph when Macdonald closed in to 50yds dead astern and opened fire with all guns:

A fairly large explosion was seen inside the cockpit and some pieces came away from it. The Ju 87 pulled up steeply and went over on its back and into a steep spiral dive. Black smoke was trailing out behind in a stream … Nav/Rad clearly saw the E/A strike the ground and explode with a terrific flash.

Another possible candidate was the aircraft in which Rudi Sablottny flew as gunner. Asked about any particularly memorable operations, he wrote:

Summer 1944, mission in Italy: destruction of dock installations, Pisa–Livorno. A Mosquito attacked us on the return flight, our rudder was destroyed right to the outer rim. But [we] landed OK.[2]

Herbert Kehrer also remembers that incident:

The "Rimini *Flak* Neck" was the area from about Ancona to Rimini. There was fierce fighting there, above all in the vicinity of Ancona, many artillery duels in which we intervened with our wing guns. Then we flew home as low as possible to escape the night fighters.

One night, it could have been in the region of Pesaro, they set up a *Flak* barrier between the Appenines and the Adriatic. When we found ourselves in this area on

ABOVE: *Ofw. Hans Wolfsen and Gefr. Hans Wilk with their aircraft "white 5"/D3+EK, which has an unusual quartering of its spinner tip. This crew was posted missing from an operation on 2/3 August 1944, shot down and killed by an RAF Beaufighter.*

LEFT: *Gefr. Hans Wilk of 3./NSG 9, missing from a mission to Livorno on 2/3 August 1944, was probably shot down by the Beaufighter of P/Os Jefferson and Spencer of No. 600 Squadron. His pilot, Ofw. Hans Wolfsen, shared his fate.*

RIGHT: *Ofw. Hans Wolfsen of 3./NSG 9 (seen here as an Unteroffizier) went missing during a raid on Livorno on 2/3 August 1944 along with his radio-operator, Gefr. Hans Wilk.*

the homeward flight, a curtain of fire suddenly rose up in front of us. I wrenched the machine around and made a detour over the Appenines.

Somebody who detoured over the sea had his rudder shot away by a night fighter. He made it home too, like all the others. It was a one-off. It may have been in August 1944.

Although some operations were apparently cancelled due to bad weather, Kehrer and Eck returned to Marina di Pisa on the 4th to drop fragmentation bombs on the approach road, starting two fires. A variety of other targets was hit that night with fires and explosions among a group of 50 vehicles north of Arezzo and several houses left burning at Fabriano (AN) on the Adriatic. Bad weather enforced a pause until the 8/9th when the *Gruppe* sent 17 sorties against road traffic between Marina di Pisa and Arezzo, with yet more fires and explosions ensuing. At noon on the 10th, *Nachtschlacht* missions were again scrubbed by the weather. There were 19 sorties on the 11/12th with targets on a broad front between Marina di Pisa on the Tyrrhenian and Senigallia on the Adriatic.

Florence was now in Allied hands, the moonlight was waning and the *Gruppe* took the opportunity to rest and refit but not, it seems, to withdraw to its rear area base. In fact, it was being held ready between the 13th and 16th against a possible landing by the Allies. This fear was to plague the Germans throughout the campaign because something of the kind had happened twice already — at Salerno and Anzio — but on this occasion it may have been based on reports of shipping assembled for Operation DRAGOON, the amphibious assault on the French Riviera.

On the 11th, Herbert Kehrer, with a ground crewman named Schlosser in the back seat, ferried E8+HL from Cavriago to Caselle. This entry in his log book constitutes the first documentary evidence that *3. Staffel* had begun to paint its aircraft with new codes, the process having begun on the 3rd according to a prisoner taken later in the month. Kehrer took +MK on a test flight at Caselle on the 12th and flew "D5+NH" back to Cavriago the next day (this entry follows a relatively common practice in that it probably refers to a Ju 87D-5 coded "+NH" rather than to one bearing the code of 1./NJG 3). Kehrer next flew on the 24th, when he brought the *Gruppenstab's* Fw 58, E8+ZB, down to Palata (BO); next day he was back at Cavriago for two short workshop flights in D3+QK. Toni Fink was similarly occupied, ferrying Ju 87 KQ+TS from Vicenza to Cavriago on the 20th and taking up D3+JK for practice flights on the 23rd and 24th.

On the 21st, Piacenza airfield belatedly received orders from *Luftflotte 2* that with immediate effect bases in *Koflug* 2/VI should only refuel aircraft of NAG 11, NSG 9 and FAG 122. On the 24th, *Luftflotte* 2 passed to its subordinate commands an RLM directive that for reasons of fuel economy workshop flights by single-seater aircraft were to cease immediately. On the 23rd, Polish troops crossed the River Metauro as a curtain raiser to the British Eighth Army's assault on the eastern end of the Gothic Line[3] beginning on the 25th. Next day, *Komm. Gen. Mittelitalien* signalled that operations by *Nachtschlacht* aircraft were to be expected near the front line from the night of the 27/28th onward with precise intentions to be notified each day.

In fact, the *Luftwaffe* reported that vehicle columns were attacked on the night of the 26/27th, west and south west of Florence and south of the Metauro despite poor visibility. On the morning of the 27th, *Komm. Gen.* announced that aircraft were to take off during the coming night from the Parma–Reggio–Ferrara area for road strafing in front of the whole main defence line with the principal effort on the German left wing. In what MAAF termed the "first Ju 87 activity this moonlight period" an estimated 20 sorties attacked traffic east and west of Florence, near Fano (PS) and south of the Metauro. Toni Fink and *Obgfr.* Egon Zantow bombed Fano and Pesaro in +GL; they were flying from Palata, having ferried the aircraft over from Cavriago earlier in the evening. Kehrer and Eck (E8+CL) meanwhile carried HE and fragmentation bombs from Cavriago to attack San Giovanni.

According to German records, two Ju 87s were missing from the night's operations. Although neither can now be identified with certainty, this is consistent with Allied claims: one by the anti-aircraft guns and the other by F/L Thompson and F/O Beaumont. At 22.23 they were near Arezzo at 10,000ft and had been vainly following vectors from "ZANEY" for 13 minutes when:

Ravenna, August 1944: Fw. Kaspar Stuber received the bronze mission clasp on the 8th and would get the silver award on 20 September. Here, comrades from 1./NSG 9 congratulate him after his 300th mission. He was to fly another eleven before being shot down and captured on 28 November.

> … contact picked up at 3 miles… E/A continued turning to port, dropping shower of incendiaries near Arezzo. E/A then made several half orbits to port and starboard, steadily climbing and continued north… Identified Ju 87 at 800ft. Opened fire at 400ft, 10° starboard and slightly below. Gave 1½ second burst, strikes seen on fuselage, clouds of smoke came from engine, bits seen to fly off. Swung in behind at same level and gave another 1½ second burst. Engine caught fire, glycol pouring back onto Beaufighter's windscreen. E/A went down in flames and was seen to explode and burn on the deck.

Desert Air Force recovered a list of navigational beacons and their identifying morse-code letters from the "pilot of Ju 87 shot down near Florence, night 27/28" but the report they signalled to MAAF gave no indication of his name nor whether he was alive or dead. One possible German loss (the date of the casualty report has been amended from the 28th to the 27th) was from 1./NSG 9: Ju 87D-5 WNr. 141039 whose pilot, *Uffz.* Günther Voss, was posted missing from an operation to Fano (PS). As this is a long way from Arezzo, Voss may have been the victim of AA rather than fighters.

At 21.20 the next night, six Ju 87s of 3./NSG 9 took off from Cavriago, each carrying 1 x AB 250 and 4 x AB 70 cluster bombs; others flew from Palata. Their targets were bridges and supply columns around Arezzo and Pesaro. Among the participating aircraft were:

Ju 87	E8+CL	*Ofw.* Herbert Kehrer/*Fw.* Alfons Eck
Ju 87	+GL	*Ofw.* Toni Fink/*Obgfr.* Egon Zantow
Ju 87D-3	E8+KL WNr. 100396	*Fw.* Otto Brinkmann/*Uffz.* Franz Scherzer

Kehrer reported attacking Figline Valdarno (FI) and road-hunting in the Arno Valley, causing four big fires, as well as encountering a night fighter on the return flight. In a second sortie from 23.00 this crew again went marauding in the Arno Valley, strafing, dropping fragmentation bombs and putting HE bombs on a lorry convoy. Fink bombed Pesaro and was shot up by a night fighter and wounded but brought his aircraft home to Palata. Brinkmann and Scherzer (callsign "ADLER" = eagle) had set a course of 120° from base, speed 270km/h and height 9,000ft. East of Florence they were suprised by a night fighter which set their starboard wing tanks on fire. Brinkmann jettisoned the bombs but the fire worsened and he gave the order to bail out. Scherzer, if he succeeded in this, was never found.

On reaching the ground, Brinkmann encountered Italian police who, after shooting him in the arm, directed him ostensibly to the German lines but actually to British troops. Shock and malaria laid him low for several days before he could be questioned by CSDIC who ascertained that he was a veteran of 59 missions who had begun his flying career as co-pilot and observer in a Ju 52 of KG z.b.V 102, transporting paratroops and mail to the Eastern Front. In November 1941 he had been shot down by a Beaufighter while en route between Crete and Derna in Cyrenaica (Libya), was badly burned and spent two weeks in hospital. In November 1942 he had been posted to *Nachtbehelfskampfstaffel 2* at Therespol on the Eastern Front, flying the Go 145. On 5 November 1943, with 2./NSG 2, he and his observer, *Ofw.* Hans Stein, had been injured when their Gotha crashed with engine trouble at Polozk airfield. Latterly, with *Lt.* Müller, he had volunteered for the Defence of the *Reich* (see page 61) and in July had received a posting to Berlin-Gatow but *Maj.* Frost had managed to get this cancelled, telling them they should be grateful given the life expectancy of fighter pilots up against Flying Fortresses.

Three claims of "destroyed" were made by 600 Sqn. that night, the first by P/O G.W. Judd and F/O Brewer (former Post Office workers from New South Wales and Sheffield respectively) at 21.10, altitude 6,000ft, south east of Pesaro. They had picked this one up as a freelance contact, got a visual and set it ablaze with a one-second burst; one more and it fell in flames and exploded. Twenty-five minutes later "BLACKBEER" sent them in pursuit of another bogey going due north at 290mph which sighted them and peeled off to starboard. They spiralled down after it to be rewarded with no more than a "momentary visual … on a single engined a/c with square wing tips" before losing it and returning to their patrol. At 21.45 they were given their next target which was heading west, weaving and gaining and losing height before levelling out at 10,000ft:

> Identified Ju 87 at 200yds. Fired one second burst at 100yds and saw strikes on fuselage and wings which caused E/A to catch fire. A further one second burst was fired into the flames. The Ju 87 stall[ed] up on its tail and collision was narrowly averted, pieces of the aircraft striking the Beaufighter. During a 180° turn observer watched aircraft falling in flames where it burnt - Position 60 miles west of Pesaro.

Debris had smashed the leading edge of the fighter's port wing and an oil cooler. The port engine

ABOVE: *A "black man" (mechanic) runs up the engine of Ju 87D-3, WNr. 3-1257 of 3./NSG 9. The final "L" of the unit code is visible on the rear fuselage and the Balkenkreuz has been toned down. Although the retreating airman hides the aircraft's individual letter, the rather cursory meander pattern appears identical to that of Ju 87D-3 "yellow D" on page 182 , suggesting they are one and the same.*

ABOVE: *Otto Brinkmann in the cockpit of his Ju 87D-3 in Polozk, USSR in the Spring of 1943. While serving with 3./NSG 9, Brinkmann was shot down and taken prisoner on 28 August 1944.*

LEFT: *Since joining the Luftwaffe in May 1939, Fw. Otto Brinkmann had been shot down over the Mediterranean in a Ju 52, crashed in a Go 145 in Russia and a Ju 87 in Italy. He was finally shot down and captured on 28 August 1944.*

RIGHT: *Uffz. Franz Scherzer of 3./NSG 9 was shot down and killed on 28 August 1944. His pilot, Fw. Otto Brinkmann bailed out and was taken prisoner.*

RIGHT: *Two Spitfire Mk. IXs of 241 Squadron, RZ•R (foreground) and RZ•U over the mountains of Italy in early 1944. It was in a later RZ•U (MT634, a Mk. VIII) that Capt. E.R. Dixon shot down Harry Fischer over the River Po on 31 August 1944.*

duly packed up but Judd was able to get home and land successfully on the other. Meanwhile south east of Florence, 600's CO, W/C L.H. Styles DFC and F/O H.J. Wilmer DFM had been put on to a bogey weaving slowly on a north westerly course. At 21.20 they saw incendiaries bursting on the ground but it was another 20 minutes before they obtained a contact. At 7,000ft near Florence they saw the Ju 87 which greeted them with a burst of fire passing below the Beaufighter's port wing and above its tail plane:

> Target, then to [Beaufighter's] starboard, peeled off to port. Pilot fired half deflection shot. Strikes seen all around Ju 87's cockpit. Target dived vertically and contact and visual were lost.

At 21.50, 7,000ft and 15-20 miles north east of Florence:

> Beaufighter did tight orbit and saw an explosion on the ground beneath and a petrol fire seen to start burning furiously.

Whilst all these reported positions are imprecise, it seems that Styles and Wilmer had attacked Fink and Zantow while Judd and Brewer's second claim was Brinkmann and Scherzer's Ju 87.

Although *Komm. Gen. Mittelitalien* announced at 13.00 on the 29th that NSG 9 would operate that night over whole front, concentrating on left wing, no more missions took place until the 31st. That morning brought one of the *Gruppe's* more unusual encounters with the Allies when Capt. E.R. Dixon (SAAF) and P/O D.F. White of No. 241 Sqn. were patrolling inland along the Po, looking for river traffic at first light. The two Spitfire Mk. VIIIs were down at about 30ft when White spotted an unidentified aircraft about three miles away, heading west at a similar altitude. They turned and closed in, identifying the bogey as a Ju 87 with "the usual dark mottled camouflage." White was in the best position, opening fire from dead astern but with no apparent result as the German tried to evade by making 40° turns but did not shoot back. Dixon then made a quarter attack, getting strikes on the port side of the Junkers' engine cowling, causing it immediately to give off smoke and crash in a field, bursting into flames on impact.

Dixon overflew the wreck but could spot no survivors amid the dust and smoke. No. 241 Squadron's diarist was moved to speculate that the Ju 87 might have been on a ferry flight and to hope that, "a high ranking officer of the Luftwaffe was flying it." In reality the Junkers was in the hands of the far from high-ranking *Obgfr.* Harry Fischer of 3./NSG 9:

RIGHT: *From mid July through early September 1944, 2./NSG 2's aircrew were billeted in a school at Barco. The casually dressed pilots on the school's steps are: Fw. Werner Hensel, Fw. Oskar Hug (+ 04.09.44), Fw. Hans Deutsch, Fw. Horst Rau, Ofw. Herbert Kehrer and Ofw. Wilhelm Böwing (+ 04.09.44).*

On 31 August 1944 they got me too. I was given the job of delivering a Ju from Vicenza to 2. *Staffel* in Ferrara but Flying Control wouldn't let me take off during the night [as] there were a lot of incoming hostiles reported. The stupid *Heinis* couldn't grasp that in such numbers they could only be bombers. So I was only allowed to take off at first light, at 06.15 when few incursions were reported — [but] of course these ones were … fighters.

I flew on the deck toward the Adriatic and then I wanted to steer a course due west to Ferrara with the sun at my back. It was certainly a beautiful experience finally to be flying in daylight for once, into the rising sun. When I'd been flying on the right course for a while (I'd been underway for about 40 minutes) all at once there were two Englishmen near me.

ABOVE: *This shot of Harry Fischer in the cockpit of a Ju 87D shows the injury hazard posed by the pilot's gunsight in a crash, as Fischer was to find out when shot down on 31 August 1944.*

Sat behind me was a little mechanic [*Obgfr.* Hüssmann] from 2. *Staffel* who hadn't the faintest idea how to operate the machine-gun. I immediately began turning tightly to bring my "comrades", flying so close to me, in front of my guns. One vanished very quickly but unfortunately I don't know to this day whether I got him or not. They'd have been easy meat for my [regular] gunner, since he was, as I'd seen so often, a first class shot.

After about 10 minutes I caught a packet in the port wing which started to burn as a result. There was only thing for it: land. But where? Close beneath was the Po, everywhere else fruit orchards. I preferred the latter, set down on a little patch, tore up a couple of small trees and thought I'd got away with it.

Then in slow motion the tail began to lift and slowly, gently the good old Ju laid itself flat on its back. Yet again I was in luck for I fell with the cabin right in a dried-up irrigation channel. Because I always flew with the cockpit open it was slid right back when we overturned and so I got out of the machine OK. Just my nose was slit open and hung down; after the shooting, I hadn't stowed the gunsight and so I'd demolished my nose on it. I also had a few splinters from my opponent's shells in my elbow. Again I'd been lucky; without luck you're done for.

Although Fischer was left with the end of his nose hanging by a thread, today he has only a faint scar line to show for this episode.

Evidently recovered from the events of three nights previously, Toni Fink and Egon Zantow were up again from Palata that night at 21.50 road-hunting south of the River Metauro, landing at Poggio Renatico at 03.00.

ABOVE: *"…I hadn't stowed the gunsight and so I'd demolished my nose on it." Obgfr. Harry Fischer of 3./NSG 9 (standing) shows the injuries he suffered when shot down in daylight by the Spitfire of Capt. E.R. Dixon (SAAF) of No. 241 Squadron. In the foreground are Fw. Alfons Eck and the Flugleiter's dog.*

1. The discrepancy in dates may arise from a reporting error or signify a mission begun before but concluded after midnight.

2. Dating this incident precisely is difficult. For the Livorno mission of 3 August, ostensibly only two 3. *Staffel* aircraft were assigned. On 26 July, Sablottny flew with Harry Fischer, whose logbook says nothing of a night fighter attack. In summer 1944 the night fighter concerned is unlikely to have been a Mosquito.

3. Its German name, *Gotenstellung* (Gothic Position or Emplacement) perhaps gives a better impression of the depth of what was in reality a system of successive "lines."

Harry Fischer

Born in Berlin in 1920, Harry Fischer started work as a "metal aircraft constructor" with *Deutsche Lufthansa* in 1934. During his time with the airline he gained experience on the Ar 77, Fw 56, Fw 58 V 13, He 70, He 116 and Ju 160 and by 1939 had qualified as a pilot to B II standard (at least 6,000km of flight experience and 50 night landings). On 11 August of that year, he joined the paratroops:

RIGHT: *Obergefreiter Harry Fischer, in aviation since he was 14: airframe fitter, paratrooper, cargo glider pilot, Nachtschlachtflieger, sports glider pilot.*

> That was an elite arm in those days, the training was long and arduous. We were trained as radio operators, combat engineers, drivers, locomotive drivers. Twelve parachute jumps at Wittstock… [champion boxer] Max Schmeling was there too.
> Because I was a sailplane pilot, I went for cargo glider training, something kept top secret at that time. There were three levels: DFS 230, Go 242, Me 321. My missions [with 2. (Gotha)/*Schleppgruppe* 3] in Russia followed, alternating between landing in pockets [of cut-off German troops] and transport flights from Smolensk to Warsaw.

His training on powered aircraft began on 18 April 1943:

> As a reward for my cargo-glider missions and because of my civil flying qualifications, I was transferred to Mogilev … where *Ritter* von Greim[1] had secretly established a school for powered flying. He wanted to give Hitler 100 trained pilots as a birthday present. I was on the first course and so was *Hptm.* Reither. After training we joined… *Störkampfgruppe* [*Luftflotte* 6] and flew operations on the Go 145 and Arado 66, practically the same thing the Russians were doing with their U-2. Here [on 27 November] was formed the *Nachtschwarm Oblt. Haimböck* [and] then came a further development, conversion to the Ju 87.

BELOW: *Harry Fischer in the cockpit of a Go 242 cargo glider.*

On 30 November 1943, came Fischer's first attempt at landing a Ju 87:

> The take off strip was completely iced-up and very steep from the mid-point on. I simply didn't make it from there to the dispersal area, I slid straight for the U-2 at the end of the airfield. All the same, with the engine switched off I managed to effect a small correction with the right brake and slid into the bomb dump. The only damage was to an airscrew blade.
> After that, further training at the Blind Flying School at Stubendorf in Upper Silesia… blind flying [stage] III, especially for the Ju 87 with *Roland* and *Egon* systems. Return to Lida [in] Russia[2] and Stuka training by *Oblt.* Lippach, the dive-bombing instructor. On 1 June 1944, ferry flight to Italy.

LEFT: *While serving with 2.(Gotha)/Schleppgruppe 3 in Russia, Harry Fischer recorded the recovery of two of the unit's Go 242s. Here, the tail booms of NL+GH are detached but the cargo door is still raised. The fabric of the wings has been badly damaged, perhaps through landing amongst trees.*

RIGHT: *The booms of NL+GH have been taken away, the door has been closed and a trailer lorry waits in the background.*

BELOW: *Another Gotha's fuselage (Nl+??), minus much of its fabric covering, is towed away by a half-track.*

THIS PAGE: *Borisov, USSR, 30 November 1943: Harry Fischer's first flight in a Ju 87 (WNr. 2325, "yellow K") comes to grief in icy conditions. The pale disc behind the cockpit is the antenna of the Peilgerät IV direction finder. In the background is a captured Soviet Polikarpov Po-2 "sewing machine."*

Fischer flew at every opportunity:

In the… *Staffel* there were 34 Ju 87s on the books, all of which I flew. For certain I was the only one who did… Why was that? Because there was no enlisted pilot in the whole [*Gruppe*] apart from me. I never wanted anything to do with the military, my heart belonged to flying and it's still the same today.

So no wonder I always had trouble with the *Hauptfeldwebel* (what we called the *Spieß* or "Mother of the Company"). In the mornings when the other ranks and groundcrew of the *Staffel* practised theory (as well as guard duty and exercises), I could enjoy my moment of freedom. This area of liberty remained for me even when we had no night operations on. Of course our *Spieß* was specially conscious of that. The *Unteroffiziere, Feld-* and

"I went for cargo glider training…" Harry Fischer at the controls of a Go 242.

Oberfeldwebel had their own Duty NCO roster [and] one day the good man had the idea of putting me down for an *Unteroffizier* course. Avoiding the proper channels, I wrote to the *Generalfeldmarschall*, Commander-in-Chief Italy, that I was more valuable on ops than on a useless *Unteroffizier* course. That was effective and it was really one in eye for the *Spieß*.

…The *Capitano* had an arrangement in which I'd already taken part in Russia. All those special jobs came in my direction: I made all the test flights on unserviceable machines and ferried the serious cases to a workshop. The same was true in Caselle. *Feldwebel* [Hans] Deutsch still had to finish his night flying training and "completed" a landing while still at about 10 metres altitude. A really beautiful crash; the port wing had a considerable upward bend but I flew the thing from Caselle to the workshop in Càmeri [NO] on 21 June 1944, a distance of about 80km. The D3+GK got a new wing there. A good thing it wasn't my fault[3].

It was the same in Russia, where I made a lot of courier flights. After concluding our Stuka training, I flew our instructor, *Oblt*. Lippach, in D3+PL to Biala Polska where new tasks awaited him. At the end of blind flying training I flew a dual-control Ju 87 [call sign DP+RX] from Stubendorf to Litzmannstadt[4]. That was like my courier flights up until [my posting to] Stubendorf. In Italy I often took off on weather recce before the *Staffel* set out on an operation. I got all those jobs.

I was particularly proud when, on 12 March 1944, I had to ferry an urgently needed Ju 87 from Wilna[5] to Lida for *Oberst* Rudel. For a few days I was grounded by severe weather; because of persistent fog, take-off was forbidden to all machines, large or small. A telephone call from Rudel secured my permission to take off. Fortunately, I knew the flight path. At the end of the take-off run was the Wilna-Lida railway. The trees had been cut back for a hundred metres either side of the line on account of partisan ambushes. So I chanced it and roared off… at the lowest possible level, almost along the rails, and came safely to Lida.

For Fischer, flying has lost none of its attractions:

To me, flying means being free. Gliding gave me this realisation from the outset and it's my hobby to this day. The battle with Nature is always a fresh challenge. In bad weather I squeeze myself into our powered glider but that's the exception.

---

1. *Generaloberst* Robert *Ritter* von Greim commanded *Luftwaffenkommando Ost*, its successor (from May 1943) *Luftflotte* 6 and, with Göring's dismissal in the dying days of the war, the entire *Luftwaffe*.

2. Now in Belarus.

3. It may not have been Hans Deutsch's fault either: his log mentions neither a crash nor a flight in D3+GK during June.

4. Now Lodz, Poland.

5. Now Vilnius, Latvia.

September

"Fly through the wreckage"

1944

"…Some night ground attack aircraft still at our disposal carried out several sorties to relieve troops at the front."

(*Luftflotte 2's* appreciation of the period 1-15 September 1944)

Thanks to the summer's intensive operations and the increasingly effective Allied defences, NSG 9 began September with 31(24) aircraft, half its paper establishment. The month would bring an influx of new personnel and several changes of base. During the 1st, the 3. *Staffel* moved aircraft to Palata, only to fly them back to Cavriago two days later and 1. *Staffel* was at Ferrara by the 5th.

Luftflotte 2 reported seven *Straßenjagd* sorties south east of Florence on 1/2 September and according to *Komm. Gen. Mittelitalien* there had been another six against roads in the eastern sector by 22.00. By the same time next evening, 20 Ju 87s had carried out 75 sorties against road traffic in the east and one *Staffel* had been active in the Florence area. Two aircraft were reported missing but there is no record of any personnel casualties.

The night of 3/4 September seems to have been a maximum effort, at least by 3. *Staffel*, against multiple targets on the eastern side of the peninsula. According to DAF, "Eight Ju 87s attacked 8th Army positions during the night on the 5th Div. sector" while the Air Ministry's Weekly Intelligence Summary spoke of 40-50 Ju 87s, perhaps 20 aircraft flying repeated sorties. While Toni Fink and Egon Zantow (in D3+GL)[1] made only a single trip from Cavriago to bomb Pesaro, Herbert Kehrer set out no fewer than four times. On the first occasion he had to put his Ju 87 (+CL) down again after 40 minutes due to engine trouble. Switching to aircraft +AL, he and Eck went first to Ancona, where their bombs started six fires despite *Flak* of all calibres, searchlights and night fighters. Returning to Palata, they were down only half an hour before heading off to attack Pesaro with fragmentation bombs and go road-hunting south of the town. After a 40-minute interval, their next mission was to Montecchio (PS), again with fragmentation bombs, followed by attacks on lorry columns toward Pesaro before landing at Cavriago. In all, this crew had clocked up 5 hours 25 minutes of combat flying between 20.00 and 04.45, to say nothing of a 20-minute transfer flight earlier in the evening. In Vigatto, Kurt Urban of 2. *Staffel* got only a 15-minute break between his two sorties in E8+DK while von Grone and Lenz flew three missions, logging three lorries shot to pieces on the first and an AA hit in the left wing of their +HK during the last.

This was another highly successful night for the RAF, No. 600 Squadron claiming 4-0-1. The first two successes went to P/O Judd and F/O Brewer. Having been in the air for only ten minutes and just 30 miles from base, they closed rapidly on a contact which peeled off to

3./NSG 9: Ofw. Herbert Kehrer (left) and Fw. Alfons Eck pose for the camera in the cockpit of Ju 87D-3, E8+AL as Uffz. Rafael ("Rolf") Szyglowski looks on. Kehrer and Eck made three sorties with this aircraft on the night of 3/4 September 1944.

starboard and was lost as the Beaufighter attempted to follow. "BLACKBEER" announced its reappearance 5 miles ahead and they were able, despite the enemy's violent jinking and loss of height, to get to within 150yds before opening fire. After four bursts the Ju 87 caught fire and went down apparently to attempt a landing near a road but hit some obstacle, exploded and burned fiercely for several minutes. This kill was timed at 00.08, some 10 miles north west of Rimini. Within two minutes, they were vectored after a pair of bogeys flying east at 7,000ft, got a visual on another Ju 87 and folllowed it through a tight port orbit after which it "straightened out, presenting an absolute sitting shot." One long burst from 100yds produced an immediate explosion and the Junkers dived flaming into the ground 20 miles south west of Rimini at 00.20.

Although the time was indelibly imprinted on the surviving crewman's memory as 23.55, it is probable that the second victim was the Ju 87 of *Fw.* Oskar Hug and *Obgfr.* Paul Sonnenberg. Hug had been wounded by ground fire on 4 November 1943 while serving with 2./NSG 2 in the East but was fated not to escape this time. In 1948, after four years as a PoW in Egypt, Sonnenberg described the night's events in a letter to Hug's widow:

> We readied ourselves for the second mission of the night. The first had already given us some difficult moments. We hardly spoke now, each of us attended to his own business and so we climbed, as so often before, into the aircraft. A few seconds later and we were already in the air. It was around 23.00. Then I heard a voice in my headphones; he asked why I was so quiet tonight. Myself, I had a strange feeling that evening, one I can't describe. We flew on for about an hour, it was now 23.55 and we had just recognised the target (near Fano on the Adriatic) and were heading for it when suddenly: crashes, splinters and flashes. Oskar cried out briefly and we went down in a vertical dive. I called to him several times without getting any reply. He must have been severely if not mortally wounded. There was only one thing that mattered now: every man for himself. I can only thank the great altitude that allowed me to get out of the machine a few moments before it hit the ground and let my parachute deploy. A burst of flame and ensuing fire told of the end of my pilot and aircraft. As for me, I was badly wounded and hospitalised.

Seen here in Turin in June 1944, Fw. Oskar Hug had been wounded in Russia the previous November and would be shot down and killed by the Beaufighter of No. 600 Squadron's P/O Judd and F/O Brewer on 4 September 1944. His widow only learned the full circumstances of his death in 1948 when his gunner, Obgfr. Paul Sonnenberg (who had been able to bail out), returned from a PoW camp in Egypt.

Four hours later and in much the same area, Flight Sergeants Cole and A.C. Odd (callsign "China 19") were rewarded with an interception after two hours in the air and having to cede contacts to their better placed colleagues "China 18" (of whom we shall hear more). When they at last got a contact of their own, it apparently spotted them and executed the customary peel-off to the right. The Beaufighter pursued from 7,000 to 2,000ft, opening fire from slightly above and somewhat to starboard. Hits were registered in the Ju 87's wing root and it turned to port, its gunner responding with a burst of white tracer which went wide. More fire from the night fighter produced whitish grey smoke from the Junkers before it disappeared under the Beaufighter's starboard wing. The RAF crew made a turn and witnessed "a terrific explosion and petrol fire" on the ground with "what appeared to be incendiaries burning in the centre of the blaze." They were then sent due north and, at 04.08, saw "a brilliant flash in the air about 10 miles to port." Their controller explained that "China 18" had just shot down a hostile and was returning to base damaged.

Squadron Leader P.L. Burke and F/L L.F.S. Whaley had been patrolling for over an hour and a half before being put on to a northbound bogey which they contacted 10 miles west of Rimini. They hit it with their first burst and followed it through a port turn before it peeled into a vertical dive. Despite lowering the Beaufighter's flaps and undercarriage, they lost sight of it and ground returns swamped the AI picture even after they descended to 50ft. It was almost 50 minutes before they found their next "trade", a freelance AI contact a mile off their 5 o' clock. Coming round to a southerly heading they closed on a Ju 87 flying straight and level, apparently oblivious to their presence. After a short burst at point blank range:

The Ju 87 exploded with a terrific blinding flash. The Beaufighter had to fly through the wreckage, sustaining considerable damage to the wings, fuselage and tailplane … some of the fabric was burned off the tail controls.

However, apart from rough running the engines performed satisfactorily and the pilot made a safe landing at base. The Ju 87 fell 15 miles south west of Rimini, both night fighter crews observing the crash.

There are three other known losses of NSG 9 crews from 4 September. None of them has a time attached and so they may have occurred in the early hours or during the following evening, meaning that they cannot be matched to particular RAF claims:

ABOVE: *Squadron Leader P.L. Burke and F/L L.F.S. Whaley and their Beaufighter callsign "China 18" (ND172, "B") which was badly damaged by the explosion of a Ju 87 they shot down west of Rimini at 04.05 hours.on 4 September 1944. NSG 9 lost four aircraft in that night's operations.*

2. *Staffel*:   *Uffz.* Kurt Urban (died of wounds 25.09.44)/*Gefr.* Erwin Schertel (killed, Borghi (FO))
3. *Staffel*:   *Obgfr.* Rolf Möhrke (*Bordfunker*, killed in crash)
              Ofw. Wilhelm Böwing/*Obgfr.* Josef Jantos (both missing, Cattólica (FO) area)

Böwing had been posted missing before[2] but this time he would not be coming back. Rudi Sablottny, *Bordfunker* in the aircraft following behind Böwing and Jantos's Ju 87, saw it blow up in mid-air from a "*Volltreffer*" (direct hit).

In three sorties on the night of 4/5 September, Herbert Kehrer and Alfons Eck (E8+HL) dropped HE and fragmentation bombs on Cattólica and strafed artillery positions; Fink and Zantow also made three trips, to bomb Pesaro, Montefiore Conca (FO) and Cattólica. At 00.15, *Komm. Gen. Mittelitalien* reported 50 Ju 87 sorties carried out. No. 600 Sqn. crews claimed more victories that night but, as stated above, it has not been possible to tie them up with specific German losses. At 20.45, F/O's Rees and Bartlett were guided on to a bogey coming south. When 20 miles south west of Rimini they saw bombs being dropped near the beach, just on the bomb line.

RIGHT: *The period of 3–5 September 1944 saw a run of successes by No. 600 Squadron against NSG 9. Here, F/O Rees logs his and F/O Bartlett's contribution.*

SEPTEMBER	4	BEAU	VI	1F	SEL1F	F/O BARTLETT	NIFT
SEPTEMBER	4	BEAU	VI	1F	SEL1F	F/O BARTLETT	(RIMINI) PATROL. Two JU-87's DESTROYED

An AI contact followed and they closed rapidly but must have been seen for the Ju 87 pulled up hard and peeled off into a dive, Rees's quick burst securing no strikes. At 22.50 they were given another bogey heading east and soon noticed tracer coming past the Beaufighter from behind. Two tight turns were not enough to shake off or get on the tail of what Bartlett identified as a single-engined pursuer and so Rees "opened up and climbed away." Ten minutes later, their next contact was seen to drop bombs in about the same area as the first before turning north:

> Target appeared to be concentrating on his bombing. No difficulty in bringing pilot to visual range … closing to visual, the Ju 87 fired a considerable amount of tracer.

A long burst from 250yds produced several strikes along the fuselage and a stream of smoke and oil before the Ju 87 glided down into the ground at 23.05 and burned for half an hour. Within five minutes they had a head-on contact coming south, turned to get behind it and fired a three-second burst from dead astern, down moon, with many strikes. This Ju 87 took "very violent evasive action" and fired greenish-white tracer which although coming close missed the Beaufighter. The German caught fire and went down in flames to explode and set the surrounding trees alight just south of San Marino, its fall witnessed by "China 24". At 02.30: F/L A.M. Davidson and P/O J.A. Telford went after a Ju 87 jinking and weaving its way home at 7,000ft and 10 miles south west of Rimini, pursuing it through climbs, a stall and violent turns and scoring a few hits before it flipped over, dived straight down and was lost.

On the evening of 5 September, Herbert Kehrer took Toni Fink and *Ofw.* Horst Rau in the back seat of E8+HL from Cavriago to Vigatto, returning after 10 minutes. Fink's next contribution to the Axis war effort was to ferry E8+A back to Cavriago. On the 6th, Spitfires of 239 Wing RAF claimed 1-0-3 Ju 87s on the ground. Even so, by 22.00 *Komm. Gen.* had reported 50 sorties by Ju 87s strafing roads along the eastern part of the front despite an earlier signal that no operations were intended owing to the weather.

In the early hours of the 9th, NSG 9 was back in action. The *3. Staffel* bombed Cattólica and San Giovanni (PS) while 2./NSG 9's Volkmar von Grone (+KK) reported starting a "widespread conflagration" in the city of Lucca. The RAF estimated that there had been a total of 30–35 sorties over the eastern and western sectors of the front and later in the day, 239 Wing reported strafing another Ju 87. Pesaro and Cattólica were again the targets on the nights of 10/11 and 11/12 September. *Leutnant* von Grone had transferred from Vigatto to Palata on the 9th and at 04.25 on the 12th attacked Riccione, landing at Vigatto at the dangerously late hour — for a unit that relied on darkness for its survival — of 06.00. According to a *Luftflotte 2* signal issued at 02.47 on the 13th, 14 Ju 87s dropped bombs "on Allied gun positions and in the area of the front" but thereafter *Nachtschlacht* operations were suspended for lack of moonlight.

On the ground, the eastern end of the Gothic Line had been breached by Canadian troops in the first days of the month, Pesaro being occupied on the 2nd. After this promising start, war's inevitable errors, German defensive tenacity and rain combined to dash Allied hopes. Firenzuola and Rimini were taken on the 21st and Eighth Army was into the Po Valley, only to be confronted by successive defended river lines. In the centre, Fifth Army had struck into the Il Giogo and Futa passes, aiming for Bologna. Despite notable successes they were still fighting in the mountains when September ended.

NSG 9 had meanwhile spent several days in repositioning, reinforcing and retraining its various elements. On the 13th, an advance party from 1. *Staffel* arrived in Bovolone and the Airfield Regional Command planned to transfer the other two *Staffeln* to Vicenza. The following day, the rest of 1./NSG 9 and the *Gruppenstab* were in Bovolone. Quarters were found for 1. *Staffel* in the town centre: a sizeable old villa set in its own park and belonging to *Cavaliere* Remo Gagliardi who continued to live with his family in the main part of the "almost chateau-like" building. On the 16th, 2./NSG 9 left Vigatto for Ghedi, a signal at 03.40 announcing that five Ju 87s were due to arrive there and six at Vicenza, while at 19.30 the first of seven 3. *Staffel* machines landed in Villafranca di Verona, beginning a long residence. Although this purpose-built aerodrome was in marked contrast to some of the rudimentary field strips NSG 9 had used during the summer, Villafranca had at least one drawback. Hans Nawroth again:

> The Catholic priest was a spy for the other side. As soon as the machines took off, he made it known by radio to the *Amis* or the English.

Quarters were requisitioned in the town for 3. *Staffel's* personnel. Harry Fischer:

> I was only an *Obergefreiter*. My billet was above our mess while [*Ofw.*] Horst Rau … and co. had their quarters with the Orderly Room near the railway station.

Hans Nawroth:

> It was some kilometres to the airfield… We were always brought there in a lorry. We felt very good in Villafranca: we had contact with the locals, there were still things to buy, there was a cinema there, too. On Saturdays, we aircrew marched to the shooting range and fired pistols and machine-guns there.

Another five Ju 87s reached Villafranca from Aviano and Vicenza on the 21st. On the 20th it was ordered that fuel and bombs were to be provided for a *Nachtschlachtstaffel* each at Bettola and Bovolone and that these preparations should be complete two days hence. On 1 October, the Regional Command's war diary duly noted "Bovolone and Bettola ready for past few days."

Many new crews were posted to the *Gruppe* during the late summer and early autumn. This became possible through changes in the *Luftwaffe* as a whole, with a drastically diminished role for multi-engined aircraft and progressive standardisation of the daylight ground attack arm on the single-seat Fw 190, freeing large numbers of aircrew for new employment. *Fähnrich* Dirk Bunsen:

It was believed that with the development of the V-1, the strategic bomber arm … could be done away with. So from summer 1944, experienced, highly decorated bomber pilots and their crews were parcelled out among *Störkampf* and *Nachtschlacht* units, lest they be retrained for ground fighting and lose rank in the process.

Unteroffizier Franz Fischer:

In August 1944, my unit… SG 3 in Estonia… was transferred into the then Protectorate for conversion to the Fw 190. Wireless Operators were put at the disposal of the *General der Schlachtflieger* and divided among the various sectors of the front.

Unteroffizier Heinrich Leinberger:

In summer 1944 I came from 7./SG 3 (formerly 7./St.G 3), which had been operating in southern Russia down as far as the the Crimean Peninsula … The pilots converted to the Fw 190 in Pardubice (Czechoslovakia). The wireless operators and gunners were divided among other units. I was posted to NSG 9, the converted pilots formed the new SG 151 under *Hauptmann* Pölz.[3]

Dirk Bunsen was called up in February 1941 and in November, after basic training, posted to the flying school in Plauen. The German reverses before Moscow in December of that year led to a fuel shortage precluding any flying training until April, leaving only theoretical instruction. Some gliding was done during the summer and then Bunsen was selected as an oficer candidate, becoming a *Fahnenjunker-Unteroffizier* on 20 December 1942. More glider flights followed and it was not until 27 February that he began to fly in powered aircraft. Eventually becoming an instructor, Bunsen – by now with *FFS A 43 II* in Crailsheim – was selected for a 3-month spell of evaluation at the front, joining *3./Einsatzgruppe der 2. Fliegerschuldivision* in Borisov on 13 June 1944. He spent two weeks standing guard against partisans, digging foxholes and fetching bombs in a lorry before the *Gruppe* was forced to retreat as the Soviet summer offensive gained ground, making its way back

to Bialystock by rail and harried all the while by Russian bombers. Not until 23 July could Bunsen begin conversion to the Ju 87 at Dubowo-North, flying his first three operations from Rostken, East Prussia during the night of 1/2 August. Four nights later, he flew five missions in one night before bending his left undercarriage leg in a rough landing. In the first days of September he found himself in Berlin-Rangsdorf, one of 23 instructors set to be divided among *Nachtschlachtgruppen* in Finland (NSG 8) and Italy.

A *Major* laid out the alternatives for us … In Finland we'd fly against ineffectual Russians, while in Italy we'd have to reckon with Allied night fighters who could latch on to their opponents with radar. Most of the younger pilots chose Italy, partly because of the attractiveness of this southern country, partly with a mind to the unpleasantness of Russian captivity.

After eight days home leave and a long rail journey from Berlin's Anhalter Station, Bunsen's party found themselves in Verona in the early hours of 13 September and after getting some sleep were divided among NSG 9's three *Staffeln*. Bunsen went to *Hptm.* Karl-Heinz Kuhle's 1./NSG 9 and was accommodated along with *Fhr.* Haas, a married 26-year old radio operator from Berlin, in a small turret room perched over the gateway of the Villa Gagliardi.

Leutnant Willy Ferling had joined the *Luftwaffe* in October 1940 and after training served as an instructor with *Blindflugschule 5*, latterly at Hagenow, until the school was disbanded. Since 26 March 1944 he too had been with *3./Einsatzgruppe der 2. Fliegerschuldivision* where he converted to the Ju 87. In action with this type, the Hs 126 and Fw 189 throughout the spring and summer as the unit was forced back from Ukraine to East Prussia, he won the Pilot's Clasp (*Frontflugspange*) in Silver. His gunner, *Uffz.* Stobbe, was killed on 29 July and on 9 August Ferling was awarded both the Gold Clasp and EK I. Then:

> On 29 August 1944, after over 100 combat missions, came the order from the *General der Schlachtflieger* in Berlin-Rangsdorf to transfer to 1./NSG 9 in Bovolone. I arrived there on 12 September after a stopover at the old school in Hagenow and home leave in Minden. I suppose I was meant to contribute my experiences as a former blind-flying instructor to NSG 9's testing of new radio guidance aids over the front.

Ferling's comment leads us to a number of measures being taken to prepare the unit for operations in the worsening weather of the autumn and winter as well as the necessity, from the new northern bases, of crossing the Appenine Mountains to reach its targets. Crews were to be taught the techniques of instrument flying, the use of Würzburg radar as a blind landing aid and the EGON technique. The version used in Italy, EGON-*Zweistand,* employed two Freya radars to interrogate the aircraft's FuG 25 IFF transponder, triangulating its position from the return signals as it flew along an arc centred on one of the ground stations and leading over the target. The controller could then use these plots to warn the pilot if he was straying from his allotted course and announce the moment to release his bombs. An evaluation in March 1945 found that with good crews, accuracies of plus or minus 200m in range and 0.25 degrees in bearing were attainable with this system.

As well as Bunsen (who was assigned *Uffz.* Heinz Eickhoff as his *Bordfunker),* Ferling and *Ofhr.* Bernhard Buckow also joined *1. Staffel. Oberfähnrich.* Helmut Schäfer — another veteran of the *Einsatzgruppe der 2. Fliegerschuldivision* — joined 3./NSG 9 at the same period, ferrying Ju 87 CC+FS from Vicenza to Villafranca on 21 September, with *Uffz.* Karl Hofmann in the rear cockpit. They had four brief flights in the same aircraft on the 22nd: three night landings plus homing on a radio beacon using the *Peilgerät IV* direction-finder. Two nights later, in E8+DL (as CC+FS had now become) they made a practice landing with the aid of Würzburg and on the 28th, two circuits with EGON control. This is Schäfer's assessment of these electronic aids:

> Control of flights via the EGON and Würzburg systems was still highly imperfect, although the in-flight night fighter warnings signified progress.

Dirk Bunsen's introduction to his new unit was a night in a Bovolone *trattoria* where, "the agreeable *vino bianco* ran in rivers." The next evening, Thursday 14 September, he, Buckow and *Fhr.* Hans Zander were sent south across the Po in a lorry to fetch aircraft from their *Staffel's* former airfield. At midday on the 16th, Bunsen and Eickhoff got the job of collecting another Junkers, this time from Càmeri, and flying it back at first light[4]. A bombed bridge cut their rail journey short and the rest of the trip entailed marching, hitch-hiking and a train from Milan, so that it was the 18th before they arrived at their destination. There had been a partisan ambush at Càmeri the day before with a guard shot through the lung and a lorry, 15 drums of fuel and an MG 81 with 2,000 rounds of ammunition stolen. So tense was the atmosphere that the dust-covered airmen were suspected by *Hptm.* Sonnenburg, the airfield commander, of being partisans in stolen uniforms and it took some time to establish their bona fides. Woken at 03.30 next morning, they went over to the hangar at the far end of the field where their machine awaited them:

> A cover on the left wing wasn't properly fastened and stood proud. A *cacciavita* or *giravite* [screwdrivers] must be fetched. Delay. We only got airborne when you could no longer talk of "morning twilight", let alone "first light." Marvellous flight east over the Po Plain. Thick morning mist still lay in the valleys of the rivers flowing down from the Alps. Interesting old cities from above: Milan, Cremona, Manerbio… Landed at 08.00 in Bovolone, had to report right away to *Maj* Frost by telephone. Got a fearful dressing down because in daylight American Lightnings could pick off the clumsy Ju 87 with ease.

On the 23rd, twilight training flights from Villafranca had to be broken off owing to enemy aircraft in the Mantua area but 3./NSG 9 managed four such sorties between Verona and Bovolone the next night. On the 25th, Willy Ferling had been visited by his father, a *Hauptmann* in a transport unit. He asked *Hptm.* Kuhle for leave to meet him but was told that first he must fly that night as operations resumed. Fifty-six years on, this officiousness — which Ferling says that it was not the norm in NSG 9 — still rankled.

The Ju 87s were to be at readiness from dusk to 20.00 for road-hunting on the German left wing. Despite "very bad weather" von Grone and Lenz flew from Bettola to Rimini, their E8+HK one of only six aircraft to attack searchlights and artillery in the Adriatic sector. It was probably this raid that made a vivid impression on Volkmar von Grone:

> I experienced a particularly critical situation from the airman's point of view, during a night attack by the entire *Gruppe* on a target south of the Appenines. As a target marker and pathfinder, my role was to take off ten minutes before the main force and mark the objective for the less experienced crews, with flares on the ground in the target area.
>
> Apart from an unpleasant twilight rendezvous with an English night fighter on the approach flight, I was able to put my markers exactly on target and head home satisfied. However, when I reached the Po Plain after flying north over the Appenines at about 2,000m, I realised to my horror that in the meantime a solid cloud and mist layer had formed, reaching up to 1,000m. Now I was in big trouble. On account of Allied superiority in radar technology and the associated constant night fighter threat, we were under strict orders to observe radio silence.
>
> When we got near to the Alps, our compasses used to exhibit deviations of up to 30 degrees, meaning that, without landmarks to navigate by, finding your own airfield again … was right out of the question. What should I do, bale out or make one last try to get a navigational fix by radio traffic in clear? I decided on the latter, expecting that in *Sauwetter* [filthy weather] like this our opponents would prefer to stay on the ground as well. So I finally got a course and distance for the field from our ground station and flew over the clouds to our "home port."
>
> But I was still far from being on the ground. The inventiveness of our dearly beloved station commander rescued me from this critical predicament... he'd alerted all our base's *Flak* searchlights who then built a cathedral of light from their intersecting beams that could be made out through the clouds. One searchlight oscillated all the while in a particular direction, indicating the direction of the runway. With this assistance I dropped down into the mist, lost altitude slowly and landed at last, safe and sound, guided on to the path by the wavering searchlight. Of course there was a great fuss that I'd got down in one piece but the most annoying surprise for me was learning that the whole operation had been scrubbed shortly after I took off because of the build-up of ground mist.

Others, including Ferling and Hans "Bruno" Grüning (E8+JH) and seven machines of 3./NSG 9 aborted due to the bad weather in the target area. Helmut Schäfer and Karl Hofmann attempted their first mission together in Italy, taking off at 19.14 in E8+DL:

RIGHT: *In the park at Bovolone in late September 1944 are radio-operator Uffz. Hans Eickhoff and his pilot, Fhr. Dirk Bunsen, both of 1./NSG 9. After Bunsen was posted to an Air Warfare School, Eickhoff crewed up with Ofhr. Karl Zander, with whom he died in a flying accident on 4 November 1944.*

RIGHT: *Obgfr. Egon Zantow was shot down and killed with his pilot, Ofw. Toni Fink on 28 September 1944 probably by W/C L.H. Styles DFC and F/O H.J. Wilmer DFM of No. 600 squadron RAF.*

ABOVE: *Ofw. Toni Fink, a pilot in 3./NSG 9, survived over 534 flights before dying in an accident on 28 September 1944.*

RIGHT: *The funeral on 30 September 1944 of Ofw. Toni Fink and Obgfr. Egon Zantow, killed in a flying accident north west of Verona on the 28th. Herbert Kehrer (front) and Flugleiter Dzykowski carry the first coffin with (obscured) Uffze. Franz Fischer and Rudi Sablottny. Karl Hofmann follows behind.*

On 25 September 1944, I had to break off a mission because there were low-lying clouds in the target area that rendered the approach flight to the target impossible. I flew back with the bombs and landed with them too. People weren't especially pleased with my "thrift" since both undercarriage legs were damaged during the landing (15% damage).

Although operations were cancelled again because of the weather, "Würzburg approach flights" were carried out from Villafranca on the 26th and 27th. At 16.50 on the 28th, the veteran crew of Toni Fink and Egon Zantow were killed in a crash north west of Verona on a non-operational flight. Although the Villafranca KTB entry for that day merely says "no special events", Schäfer's logbook records a two-hour mission on the evening of the 29th. In E8+HL, he and Hofmann attacked Riccione Marina (FO) with an AB 500 and four 50kg incendiaries, opposed by "Strong *Flak* defence, all calibres." Alfons Eck's memoirs recall one raid on this target:

> Our *Kapitän*… was giving the order for an attack on the neck of land [between the mountains and the sea] south east of Forlì where the Allies had broken through and which included [3./NSG 9's former quarters in] the little resort of Riccione: "Who doesn't have a friend or a sweetheart in Riccione? Then I hope that everyone knows what he has to do…"
>
> We knew! …the bombing of our little resort, so hospitable to us not long ago, was prevented.

Lfd. Nr. des Fluges	Führer	Begleiter	Muster	Zulassungs-Nr.	Zweck des Fluges		Abfl.				Flug						Bemerkungen
						Ort					Landung				Flugdauer	Kilometer	
							Tag	Tageszeit			Ort	Tag	Tageszeit			
129.	Templer, Lt.	Lotsch, Ofr.	Ju 87 g	L	80. Feindflug	Forpol	10.8.44	11 35			Forpol	10.8.44	12 50	75			
130.	"	"	"	"	81. "	"	11.8.44	19 00			"	11.1.	18 10	70			
131.	"	"	"	"	82. "	"	"	19 00			"	"	20 15	65			
132.	"	"	"	H	83. "	"	14.8.	18 00			"	14.8.	19 10	70			
											Die Richtigkeit der Feindflüge von Nr. 129 - 132 geprüft und beglaubigt.						
																	Paul Staffelkapitän
133.	Gerstenberger, Fhj.	Lotsch, Ofr.	Ju 87 D	F	84. Feindflug	Bettola	30.9.44	19 00			Notlandung 30 Km südl. Concordia	30.9.44	21 30	150	Flak	Nachteinsatz. Nachschubstrasse südl. Rimini.
134.	Müller, Lt.	"	"	K	85. "	Ghedi	20.1.45	17 10			Ghedi	20.1.45	19 00	140	Jagdflug	Artilleriestellung nördl. Bagnacavallo
135.	"	"	"	"	86. "	"	21.1.	17 35			"	21.1.	18 50	75		Dorf Grisanna südl. Bologna —

On 30 September 1944, flight 133 in the logbook of Obgfr. Werner Lotsch, his first mission with NSG 9, ended in a crash and a hospital. He would not fly again until 20 January 1945. The stamp certifying the accuracy of the log up to 17 August 1944 is that of his former unit, the Gruppenstab of I./SG 3.

Battle was rejoined on the last night of September, when 10 Ju 87s bombed their erstwhile home of Rimini airfield in bright moonlight and 19 attacked artillery batteries and vehicle convoys in same area and troops on the march near Riccione. Seven aircraft of 3./NSG 9 returned to Villafranca without loss at 21.15. The 2./NSG 9's von Grone and Lenz aborted with instrument failure while Ju 87D-5 WNr. 131440, E8+FK suffered 80% damage and *Fhj.Fw.* Edgar Gerstenberger and *Obgfr.* Werner Lotsch were both injured. They had crashed on the latter's first operation since transferring from the Eastern Front, where he had racked up 83 bombing and anti-tank missions with II./SG 2 and I./SG 3. Lotsch recalls that their Ju 87 broke into several large sections when it came down at 21.30 among farm buildings along the road between San Felice sul Panaro and Finale Emilia[5].

The E8+FK was an old aircraft (previously assigned, Lotsch believes, to *Ofw.* Artur Heiland) and had been taken up for two test flights earlier in the day on account of a defective fuel pump. Presumably the problem was thought to be fixed because they took off from Bettola at 19.00 for an attack on a supply route south of Rimini. They were underway when a light came on, indicating that the pump had failed again and that they would be unable to transfer fuel from the outer to the inner tanks. Werner Lotsch:

> Despite that, we decided to see the attack through to its conclusion — a fatal error in retrospect.
>
> On the return flight over the Adriatic, Appenines and Po Plain we almost rammed a high-tension line. Suddenly, Gerstenberger wrenched the machine steeply upward. Off to the side, the high-tension lines slid slowly by. We'd been lucky.

We flew further north. The engine ran regular and peaceful. For safety's sake, Gerstenberger jettisoned the landing gear [but] a bit later the motor stuttered, then silence. White house facades ahead of us in the moonlight, I sense us veering the left, then nothing more — out!

I'm still alive — lying on a bank apparently — see figures in the half light. "Would you like something to drink?" Yes. I drink: cocoa, perhaps? I fall back into deep unconsciousness right away. Wake up briefly: motor transport, violent pains in the chest, I hear someone groan. It's me. I wake for a short time lying on an operating table — field hospital [in] Concordia. My face is just being stitched — unconsciousness again.

Gerstenberger had had two or three teeth knocked out but Lotsch, despite his rear-facing seat, had severe injuries to his face and chest and various other bruises.

A week later [I'm taken] by casualty transport to the main hospital in Cortina d'Ampezzo (BL). After about three weeks, violent headaches and outbreaks of sweating — malaria infection, probably from lice in the wool blankets on the train. Atabrine sprays help me.

With all this to contend with, it was eight weeks before Lotsch, who had been awarded the black Wound Badge for his pains, rejoined his *Staffel* in Ghedi and was then sent on convalescent leave until 2 January 1945. Meanwhile Gerstenberger had been killed in action (see below) and Lotsch reflects:

That could have been my dying day, too, if the consequences of my crash on 30 September hadn't prevented it. That was what you call fortune in misfortune!

---

1. Whether aircraft ever were painted with this hybrid of the old *Gruppe* and new *Staffel* codes or whether it was a case of "old habits die hard" in filling out logbooks has not been possible to establish.

2. On 15 May 1943, with 2./*Störkampfstaffel Lfl.* 6, his Go 145 (WNr 2855, D3+OK) had been destroyed in an emergency landing after engine failure. The "missing" report was not corrected until 27 May.

3. Hubert Pölz had been *Staffelkapitän* of 7./SG 3 and was to command SG 151 until the end of the war, gaining the *Ritterkreuz* and flying 1,055 missions.

4. Hans Deutsch also fetched a Ju 87 (WNr. 100390) from Càmeri on the 16th.

5. According to the casualty report but logged by Lotsch as 30km south of Concordia sulla Secchia (MO)

In their
Operations
own words

Before the advent of electronic target finding systems, NSG 9's missions were constrained as much by meteorology and astronomy as by military necessity:

"If flying weather was poor, a couple of hours' sport. Otherwise, we had a lot of free time to kill during the day."

"Operations only at twilight or by night with clear skies and moonlight (orientation by landmarks)."

"Most operations took place on bright moonlit nights. The biggest problem with that was the mist that could set in so suddenly."

Ravenna, September 1944: aircrew of 1./NSG 9, their parachutes over their shoulders, set out for a mission.

If ops were on and the crews had not been flying the previous night, they followed a routine familiar to airmen the world over:

"Reveille about 06.00; breakfast about 07.00 (*Kasino*); assembly of whole *Staffel* at about 08.00 to give out orders; midday meal about 12.00 (*Kasino*)"

"In Italy: get up, breakfast, free time, midday meal, free time, mission preparations."

"Afternoon: aircrew to airfield for briefings and preparation of maps."

Meanwhile, the *Gruppenstab* would have been at work:

"Myself, I had about 40 ops, among them some with *Major* Frost… As Chief of Operations, I was mainly concerned with the preparation of night ops. The co-ordination of all the elements involved fell to me … meteorologists, *Flak* units along the route, contacts with the *General der Flieger* and getting the targets as well as summing up each mission and filling out the loss reports. The operational directives came from the *General der Flieger*, Ic *Abteilung* [Intelligence Section] and the briefings were conducted by *Major* Frost."

Because they were usually based on separate airfields, *Staffeln* were briefed individually.

In 1./NSG 9:

"Briefings mostly by *Major* Frost in the command post."

"Verbal briefing by *Maj.* Frost and the *Staffelkapitän*."

In 3. *Staffel*:

"*Hptm.* Reither always gave the briefings and after he went, *Hptm.* Buß, his successor."

As well as being assigned their targets, crews would be briefed on:

"…general weather conditions. Weather in target area. Possible *Flak* defence, possible night fighter activity to be expected en route."

When it was nearing time to go:

"…we were fetched by lorries and brought… to the landing ground… the aircraft stood way off along the perimeter – widely dispersed."

"The illumination of the real landing strips was less than that of the dummy and starts were often made without any runway lights."

"We always took off at one or two-minute intervals."

"Take-off in the Ju 87 was easy and needed only a short run but she was slow, clumsy and heavy with a restricted field of view."

"Mostly we flew singly [but] with EGON about three machines, one behind the other."

Although history shows that relatively few interceptions occurred away from the target area, no part of the flight felt truly safe:

"We were hellishly afraid of night fighters, especially as they were equipped with radar. Anyone sufficiently confident of his navigation took care to approach the target at low-level (about 50m above the ground) weaving continually (like hares)."

"As far as I remember, we didn't stick to a course but [flew] something of a zigzag to make things difficult for the defences."

"[to avoid] being picked up by English radar, we flew at low level from Villafranca to Bologna and then climbed to 3,000m. From there we flew on to the target area…"

When the aircraft went higher, the risks of interception multiplied:

"…dangerous climb to attack height of about 2,000m since with bombload, [the Ju 87 was] far too slow…"

"The Ju 87 was orbiting and climbing at the same time — climbing at about 100mph."

"When you got there you went 'to altitude', that is about 3,000m and that also while weaving."

"…rapid climb to attacking height (2,000m)."

It was during the approach to and departure from the target that most night fighter interceptions took place, commonly at heights between 2,000–3,000m. Although NSG 9 veterans give the impression that they spent little time at these altitudes, RAF sortie reports show that fighters often had ten or more minutes' warning of an approaching bogey and could then spend a similar period stalking the target with their own AI and/or in visual contact. The amount of evasive action the Ju 87s took could vary from:

"…target was weaving slightly."

or even:

"…Target was not taking any evasive action."

"…flying straight and level."

to:

"…weaving, jinking, altering height and speed."

"…weaving violently, altering speed and height."

Another tactic to throw off potential stalkers entailed the Ju 87 suddenly turning full-circle to either port or starboard before resuming its course, hoping to catch any pursuer off guard and cause him to overshoot or lose contact. This was not foolproof however:

"Pilot followed the Ju 87 through a tight port orbit after which the E/A straightened out presenting an absolute sitting shot."

An NSG 9 back-seater's main job was to watch and listen:

"On ops I always 'craned my neck' and kept a lookout for the night fighters."

"[According to prisoners] the approach of a night-fighter is generally indicated by a loud crackling in the inter-com."

"The old hands invariably evaded by a corkscrew falling turn, the young boys often tried straight dives, with little success."

As seen by the night fighter crews:

"Ju 87 turned sharply to starboard and then whipped over to port in a steep dive."

"Target pulled hard up and peeled off going straight down."

This manoeuvre often sufficed to break both visual and radar contact:

"The Ju 87 peeled off to starboard and vanished into the valley mist."

"Ju 87 peeled off and was lost in the ground returns."

Ground crewmen hitch a ride on the wings of Ju 87D-5 "C", probably to act as the pilot's eyes while he taxies.

Sometimes however, something bolder was tried:

"Ju 87 turned into Beaufighter, jettisoned its bomb. Contact and visual were lost."

"The Ju 87 turned port and fired a burst at the Beaufighter."

Those who made it past the fighters on the way in still had to find the target:

"In the dark it was difficult to recognise the designated target exactly (rather you suspected or surmised it). Other than from visual beacons, you oriented yourself by the reflections of the meandering rivers — that is the Adige, the Po and their tributaries — glittering in the moonlight.

The window in the floor between your feet was mostly filthy with oil and opaque. To recognise the target — which you were supposed to bomb in a dive from 3,000m — correctly during the approach flight, you had to sideslip alternately to left and right…

Diving on the target, you fell from 3,000m to 800m before the contact-altimeter sounded a warning on the Bosch klaxon."

"Dive, salvo the bombs [followed by] harassing attacks on ground targets."

"Approach target in a dive. Recover machine after bomb release at about 1,000–1,500m. After bomb release, gun attacks on vehicle columns."

Afterward, evasive patterns were resumed in all their variety:

"E/A then made several half orbits to port and starboard, steadily climbing, and continued north."

"…target was jinking violently and losing height and going north."

"E/A gently losing height and weaving. Northwesterly course."

Once across the mountains and back over the Po Plain:

"Back to base at low level."

"…Myself, I always had my first radio contact at a maximum of 30km from the airfield. I reported my approach to the ground station each time so that they would illuminate the flare path for landing."

"We found our base (1) by compass; (2) by the German *Flak's* "cathedral of searchlights" [cone of lights over the base]"

"To make things as difficult as possible for the enemy night fighters… we altered our landing procedure frequently. The normal flare path… comprised two green lamps marking the touch-down point, a line of six or seven white lamps down the right hand side of the runway, and two red lamps marking the runway's end. Sometimes, by prior arrangement, the lamps were repositioned so that the reds in fact marked the touch-down instead of the stopping point; or the white lamps might mark the left hand side of the runway instead of the right."

"…dummy landing strips were illuminated when… intruders circled the field [but] it was possible to land … when the intruder was relatively far away, by quickly illuminating the [real] strip and then dowsing."

Finally:

"After missions that ended at dawn, the first thing was to get a few hours sleep right away."

"…until one o' clock in the afternoon."

he campaign in France successfully concluded, Allied strategic bombers — the Americans with enthusiasm, the British with grudging mutterings about "panacea targets" — returned to the bombing of Axis oil production facilities they had embarked on earlier in the year. It worked: output plummeted and the *Luftwaffe* in Italy was compelled to surrender almost 60% of the 3,600 cu.m. of fuel in stock at the beginning of October in favour of other fronts. In future (and in theory) NSG 9 and the resurrected Italian fighter units would share a mere 200 cu.m. per month (which would fill the internal tanks of about 250 Ju 87Ds if the fighters got none). In practice, all piston-engined flying in Italy would soon be drastically curtailed. What was more, Italy's climate and geography were combining to place obstacles in NSG 9's path that autumn. Missions from the bases on the Po Plain were now likely to entail night flying over or among the mountains, the airfields themselves were alarmingly prone to becoming fogbound and bad weather would recur more frequently.

*Werner Hensel,
Herbert Kehrer and
Alfons Eck of 3./NSG 9.*

Soon after midday on 1 October, the 26. *Panzer*, 278. *Infanterie* and 114. *Jäger* Divisions were told to expect night operations by Ju 87s from Verona with strafing in front of the German left wing but these were cancelled at 20.00 owing to the weather. Nevertheless, Desert Air Force's diarist noted on the 2nd that:

> The Hun was active in a small way during the night, dropping flares and butterfly bombs in the RIMINI area. No damage or casualties have been reported.

Intentions were signalled at 11.30 on the 3rd for Ju 87s to fly from Verona if the weather permitted, road-hunting on the central and eastern sectors from dusk to 04.00. The Allies estimated that 80 or 90 sorties were flown, the Germans recording some 60 tons of bombs dropped by NSG 9's three *Staffeln* in the Rimini area, although the targets on which there is more detail were all in the western-central part of the front. Seven Ju 87s operated out of Villafranca between 19.30 and 04.45, Hans Deutsch and Hans Nawroth (D3+CL) flying four sorties:

> 19.41–20.54 Heavy *Flak*. Junction of pass road on Monte Oggioli destroyed by direct hit. Resultant traffic columns strafed with guns. 1 x SD 500, 4 x SD 70
> 22.07-23.16 Nightfighters, heavy *Flak*. Florence-Firenzuola road attacked. Incendiaries and AB among vehicle columns. 1 x AB [500?], 4 x Br. C 50
> 00.26-01.34 Attack on part of Firenzuola town. 1 "furnace" [conflagration]. 1 x AB 500, 4 x Br. C 50
> 02.19-03.25 Sequential bomb release on pass road, Monte Oggioli. 1 x AB 500, 4 x Br. C 50

Herbert Kehrer and Alfons Eck (flying E8+CL) aborted five minutes after take off for reasons not recorded. Helmut Schäfer and Karl Hofmann (E8+HL) made four sorties, first bombing Firenzuola itself and then bombing and strafing traffic north of the town. After midnight they attacked vehicle traffic in the Raticosa Pass and on their last flight bombed a village north of Firenzuola and strafed marching columns. In their four sorties to Firenzuola, Peter Stollwerck and Franz Fischer (E8+AL) claimed several hits on lorries which, they noted, travelled with their headlights on full. From Bovolone, Willy Ferling and Bruno Grüning (E8+NH) flew three operations "road-hunting in the Firenzuola area."

LEFT: *In an earth revetment at Villafranca, Herbert Kehrer and Alfons Eck pose in front of a Ju 87D-5. This photograph shows to advantage the aircraft's MG 151/20 wing cannon and its flash suppressor as well as the engine exhaust flame damper.*

Wing Commander Styles and F/O Wilmer were airborne from Falconara on a defensive patrol near Ravenna when vectored toward a contact coming south at 6,000ft. They got a visual near Cesena:

> Beaufighter lowered 30° of flaps and closed in to 400 feet range. Target turned to port and was clearly visible against the moon. Identified as a Ju 87. Beaufighter opened fire immediately and followed the Ju 87 down in a diving turn to port, firing all the time. There was no return fire.
>
> Numerous strikes were seen all along the fuselage and at the wing roots ... a fire started in the cockpit accompanied by smoke and at the same time pieces were seen to fly off the E/A.
>
> The Beaufighter followed the Ju 87 down ... and clearly saw the E/A go straight down, crash against a hillside and explode.

BELOW: *Commanding Officer of No. 600 Squadron from March to December 1944 was W/C Lawrence Styles DFC. With his navigator, F/O H.J. Wilmer DFM, he shot down Ju 87s of NSG 9 on 28/28 August and 3/4 October 1944.*

This victory was timed at 20.20hrs, six miles south east of Cesena. Despite this precision and the expenditure of no fewer than 600 cannon shells and 1,800 machine-gun rounds, the *Kommandierender General der Deutschen Luftwaffe in Italien*[1] Staff Intelligence Officer's report says that the month's sorties passed off without loss.

On the night of 4/5 October, 23 aircraft made 86 sorties against targets in the centre and east. Their main effort was again at Firenzuola, Ferling and Grüning going there twice. Planned operations from Villafranca between dusk and 05.00 had to be cancelled at 20.30 in the face of bad weather which put paid to any operations over the next week. Even before that Dirk Bunsen seems to have found it a frustrating month:

> Not assigned to any missions. On the few operational nights during October only the two *Oberfähnriche*, Buckow and Zander were "on." As for me, I served nights of "apprenticeship" in the concrete bunker of the Ops Room, getting to know how missions were supervised and how they unfolded.

On the 8th, 1./NSG 9 lost *Obgfr.* Heinz Schönauer and *Uffz.* Siegfried Hellman, both killed when their Ju 87 crashed at Roverbella (MN) during a non-operational flight. The next day, the Italian *Littorio* Division urgently requested the bombing of five locations in ostensibly friendly territory south west of Piacenza and south of Alessandria and Asti but no anti-partisan missions are known to have been flown by NSG 9 during this period.

Fifth US Army continued battling its way through the mountains toward Bologna and *Komm. Gen.* now announced that from the 11th nightly attacks would be flown against roads in the central sector, this in spite of the unfavourable phase the moon was entering. Moonlight however was something on which NSG 9 would come to rely less and less and attacks were reported on columns south of Bologna on the night of the 11/12th. Next day, orders were given for the "immediate evacuation" of Bettola with 2./NSG 9 transferring to Ghedi. More operations were now scrubbed because of the weather but the lull did permit further training. From 16–19 October, Willy Ferling undertook ten "instrument flights" in Junkers W. 34 E8+WB, the longest lasting 48 minutes. Dirk Bunsen was one of his pupils:

> In mid-October pilots were checked out on blind flying. These tests were always done by a *Leutnant* of the 1. *Staffel*. He was small in stature and had a pleasant, quiet and settled manner. We took off from Bovolone in a W. 34, early one sunny and very warm October afternoon. The test lasted barely an hour, following various instructions like flying 2°/sec. curves blind at a constant height as well as at specified rates of climb and descent. Additionally, running through a qgh landing procedure[2]. The instructor was satisfied.

On the 14th, Peter Stollwerck bombed an island in the River Adige, west of Verona and futher sorties with concrete practice bombs were flown from Villafranca on the 17th and 20th (against a dummy aerodrome south west of Bovolone). The 2. *Staffel* also carried out bombing training from Ghedi on the 17th. On the 19th, NSG 9 acquired some back-up when *Sonderstaffel Einhorn* arrived in Villafranca with 12–14 "special aircraft" under the command of *Hptm.* Schuntermann. Planned as Germany's answer

BELOW: *Pin-up "Georgia" adorns a German propaganda leaflet dropped in the Fifth Army zone.*

RIGHT: *Overleaf, American soldiers are invited to ponder what lies ahead of them. This leaflet dates from October 1944, when an American breakthrough to Bologna and beyond seemed imminent. In fact it would be another six months before they reached the River Po.*

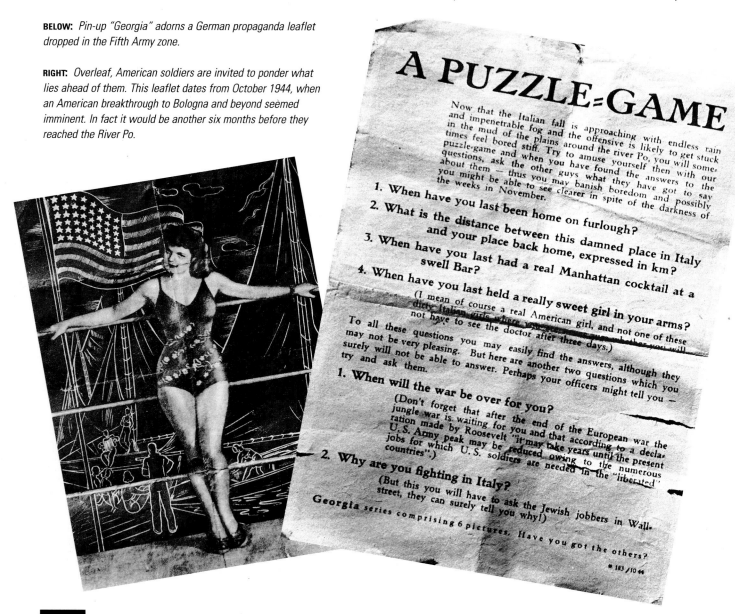

A PUZZLE=GAME

Now that the Italian fall is approaching with endless rain and impenetrable fog and the offensive is likely to get stuck in the mud of the plains around the river Po, you will sometimes feel bored stiff. Try to amuse yourself then with our puzzle-game and when you have found the answers to the questions, ask the other guys what they have got to say about them — thus you may banish boredom and possibly you might be able to see clearer in spite of the darkness of the weeks in November.

1. When have you last been home on furlough?

2. What is the distance between this damned place in Italy and your place back home, expressed in km?

3. When have you last had a real Manhattan cocktail at a swell Bar?

4. When have you last held a really sweet girl in your arms? (I mean of course a real American girl, and not one of these dirty Italian girls where you .... rather you will not have to see the doctor after three days.)

To all these questions you may easily find the answers, although they may not be very pleasing. But here are another two questions which you surely will not be able to answer. Perhaps your officers might tell you —

1. When will the war be over for you? (Don't forget that after the end of the European war the jungle war is waiting for you and that according to a declaration made by Roosevelt "it may take years until the present U.S. Army peak may be reduced owing to the numerous jobs for which U.S. soldiers are needed in the "liberated" countries".)

2. Why are you fighting in Italy? (But this you will have to ask the Jewish jobbers in Wall-street, they can surely tell you why!)

Georgia series comprising 6 pictures. Have you got the others?

* 183/10 44

S c h l e c h t w e t t e r l a n d e v e r f a h r e n

I. Das QGH-Verfahren.

1.) Grundsätzliches.

Das qgh-Verfahren soll es ermöglichen, bei qbi qgw, in Notfällen auch bei qbi qgz-Wetterlage in Platznähe Höhe aufzugeben und zur Aufnahme der Erdsicht durchzustoßen.

Es kommt darauf an, sobald man den Platz erreicht hat (qgf), sofort auf den nächsten Senkrechtkurs zu qms zu kurven und mit dem Fallen auf af zu beginnen. Bei Anliegen des Senkrechtkurses müssen mindestens 30 sec vergangen sein seit qfg (andernfalls noch bis Ablauf von 30 sec geradeaus fliegen), worauf man auf den Gegenkurs von qms kurvt. Dann beginnt der A b f l u g, der normalerweise 1 1/2 Minuten dauert. Nach dem Abflug in einer der letzten gleichsinnigen Kurve auf qms kurven (rd. 180° - Kurve). Im A n f l u g zum Platz wird weiterhin die restliche Höhe von af bis zur Landung aufgegeben. - Siehe Skizze.

qms = Landerichtung, d.h. Anflugrichtung für die Landung

qmp = ha = Höhe, in der man am vorliegenden Platz ankommen soll (meist 1.500 m)

Abflug — 1½" — Kurve

Senkrechtkurs liegt an — 30 sec

qms 270° — qfg"

qmp ha — Anflug — af

KK = 24°, nächster Senkrechtkurs=360°, 12 sec kurven

af = Höhe, die man bis zum Beginn des Anfluges erreicht haben soll (meist 800 m)

2.) Die Berücksichtigung des Windes (Bestimmung des Luvwinkels).

Würde man beim Anflug mit qms als KK anfliegen, wäre eine Windversetzung nicht zu vermeiden. Es muß also an qms ein Luvwinkel

to the *Kamikaze*, *Einhorn* ("Unicorn") finally evolved into a ground attack *Staffel* with Fw 190F-8s adapted to carry bombs of up to 1,800kg, although in practice only 1,000kg weapons were ever used in action. The unit's pilots were promptly detached to Ghedi for ten days and Willy Ferling ferried E8+WB there from Bovolone on the 20th. This may have been for the benefit of both *Einhorn's* pilots and 2./NSG 9. In November, *Major i.G.* Erich Seebode, Intelligence Officer to *Komm. Gen. Italien*, reported that *Einhorn* "has been converted to night operations in quick time." However, although the *Sonderstaffel* would later add its weight to some of their missions, none of the dozen or so NSG 9 veterans with whom the author has raised the question remembers or has even heard of *Einhorn*.

On the 20th, target information was requested from the ground troops with a view to operations resuming the next night. At 13.30 next day, orders were duly issued for Villafranca's Ju 87s to go road-hunting in the central Alpine sector from twilight to 19.00 but yet again the weather supervened and it was not until the 22nd that an estimated 6-10 aircraft operated between Ferrara and Rimini, dropping bombs to the west of the latter town. Early on the morning of 26 October, Ju W. 34 E8+WB was flown from Vicenza to Innsbruck and seems never again to have figured in NSG 9's history. Training continued, with no fewer than 61 practice flights logged from Villafranca over the next two days although some or all of these may have been by the Italian fighters based there.

The onset of winter was steadily bringing the ground campaign to stagnation. His infantry's casualties outstripping the flow of replacements, General Clark was now compelled to call off the bloody struggle to reach Bologna, just nine frustrating and intractable miles short of the city. Eighth Army was still making progress up the Adriatic Coast, crossing the River Ronco on the last day of October. Moving or static, enemy troops would have supply lines and NSG 9 would have targets.

Barely six weeks after arriving in Italy, Dirk Bunsen was already moving on:

Fri. 27.10: letter to Father and Mother. News that on Mon. 30.10 I am to leave here for Bug-auf-Rügen for a course at the Air Warfare School.
Mon. 30.10, 14.00: Departure in persistent rain by Wehrmacht vehicle to Verona along with [Fhr. Haas] …
The train leaves about 23.00. Bloody cold in the Alps. Fortunately I'm able to organise two woollen blankets for myself.

ABOVE: *Extract from Ofhr. Dirk Bunsen's course notes on the qgh bad-weather landing procedure. This method, codenamed "Fischer" was part of the blind-flying training that Lt. Willy Ferling gave to NSG 9 crews in a Junkers W. 34 during October 1944.*

BELOW: *The 2./NSG 9 was based in Ghedi from late October 1944 until the last days of the war. Reputedly built there as a hunting lodge for Mussolini, this building served as the Staffel's Officers' Mess.*

Herbert Kehrer and Alfons Eck of 3./NSG 9. The E8 code of NSG 9 can be seen on the Ju 87's fuselage just by Eck's left shoulder. Note also how the fuselage Balkenkreuz has been toned down and the scuffed paint around the wing walkway.

To date, Bunsen's flying with NSG 9 had consisted of fetching a Ju 87 from Càmeri's workshops and practice in the vicinity of Bovolone, including a twilight flight in company with a second aircraft and testing new R/T gear in solid cloud cover. Helmut Schäfer was sent on the same course but had at least been allowed six operational flights before he left.

The final 15 of the month's 108 sorties were flown on the 31st, mainly against Allied troop positions south of Bologna and a radar station near Florence, strafed at 20.15. In E8+EL, Peter Stollwerck and Franz Fischer were turned back from a mission south of Bologna by the weather but Hans Deutsch and Hans Nawroth ("D3+GL") braved searchlights and light *Flak* to deliver an AB 500 and 4 x SD 50, claiming a direct hit on their target "in area JI", among the Appenine passes. As the British Air Ministry summed up:

> The only offensive operation reported during the [late October] period was a strafing attack by Ju 87s, late on 31 October, north of Florence, which caused no casualties or damage. The enemy still appears to be worried most over the central sector of the Italian Front.

---

1. By the autumn of 1944, *Luftwaffe* forces in Italy were so reduced that maintaining a full *Luftflotte* structure was no longer justifiable. *Luftflotte* 2 was withdrawn and a "Commanding General" installed. The post went to *Gen.* von Pohl.

2. Codenamed *"Fischer"*, this was a method of losing height safely in bad weather when near base.

Us and Them

The Junkers 87:

"She was too slow due to the fixed undercarriage."

"Not unsuitable for night ops but nevertheless not fast or manoeuvrable enough."

"I can't come to a conclusion. The Ju 87 was relatively slow [at] 280–320kmh. I think on account of that many night fighters were deceived and we got away."

"The Ju 87 was acceptable for night operations but much too slow, though this was towards the end of the war and we had nothing better."

"Ju 87: Advantages — very good manoeuvrability; good diving capability; very robust airframe; enormous ability to withstand bullet damage. Drawbacks — too slow with bombload and sluggish in level flight and in the climb; too restricted in defensive armament. Poorly suited for instrument flying."

The Focke-Wulf 190:

"…very good."

"The Fw 190 was a day fighter!! Only used on night ops out of necessity."

"We were hellishly afraid of night fighters." Here, a USAAF officer poses before NSG 9's worst enemy, a Beaufighter Mk VIF. This particular machine, V8700/"F" was flown by successive CO's of No. 600 Squadron RAF, Wing Commanders Paddy Green DSO, DFC and Lawrence Styles DFC.

Allied Defences:

"Of course, the night fighters were a first class misfortune for us."

"We were hellishly afraid of night fighters."

"In my opinion the defences were very effective as we were pursued from take-off to landing and had no fighter escort. We didn't hear propaganda broadcasts."

"[Enemy] night fighters very effective and successful. Radar technology good."

"Anglo-American defences with night fighters and *Flak* were very strong."

"*Flak* defence was also effective during the climb prior to [crossing] the lines."

"The American *Flak* was very heavy and the American night fighters very active."

"I never encountered *Flak* or searchlights."

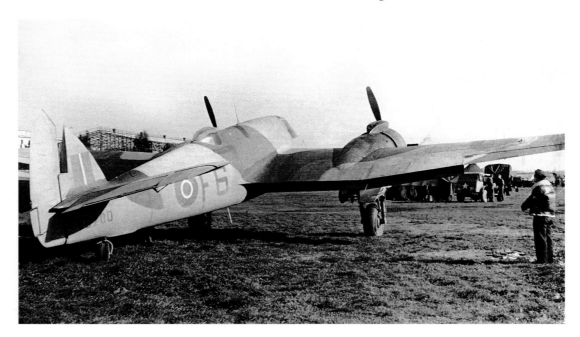

LEFT: *A rear view of Beaufighter V8700 showing the distinctive marking style of No. 600 Squadron which substituted a "6" for the official identification code "BQ." These photographs are thought to have been taken at Naples-Capodichino in February or March 1944.*

RIGHT: *Beaufighter V8700 shows off the nose and starboard wing aerials of its AI Mk. IV radar. Although this aircraft shot down Ju 88s on 25 January and 17 March 1944, German jamming was by now becoming a problem and the Squadron went over to AI Mk. VIII centimetric radar during the spring. V8700's last mission with No. 600 Sqn. was on 22 April 1944 with W/C Styles and F/L Kownacki (Polish) aboard.*

Results:

"Troop movements, supplies and nights' rest were disrupted. Losses in men and material [caused] were limited. I can hardly remember [receiving] information about the results of attacks."

"Now and again thanks came from the front lines but I never encountered a direct briefing. They must certainly have got more of that in the *Stab*. One time I heard from the Bologna area that, thanks to our efforts, the ground troops finally got to eat in peace that night."

"The operations were very well rated by the ground units. All the same, NSG 9 was one of the few units that was on hand until the end. In early 1945 we suffered a lot from the operations of British night fighters (Mosquito) fitted with very good radar. There were losses while our machines were landing and the *Flak* couldn't improve the situation. The Anglo-American defences were highly effective, especially toward the end of the war. Their principal advantage was [their] radar and [radio] interception technology. *Flak* hardly played any role, rather it was the night fighters."

"We got no reports back from the front because our ops were confined to the supply [lines]… Our missions couldn't have a decisive influence on the situation at the front. It was rather a disruption of supply traffic and that only on moonlit nights."

"Operations must have been very successful in part because the Americans frequently bombed our base, Villafranca di Verona… NSG 9's successes were mentioned in the *Wehrmacht* communiqué."

"Russia: nuisance attacks good [effect]. Italy: no influence on the enemy's strategy — perhaps delayed his advance."

"The night operations had hardly any effect: "nuisance raids" was the best you could call them, disturbing the enemy soldiers' sleep…"

"In retrospect, I have the impression … that our superiors knew how ineffective our missions were, that is they were aware of their ineffectiveness but had the feeling that "it's an order from above and something must be done." I never heard information about the outcome [of attacks]. Perhaps the infantryman up forward in his trench was more content whenever he heard something from German aircraft."

"…initiation and deployment of the NS units must be regarded in the light of an emergency measure dictated by circumstances. They did, however, achieve local successes, and caused the Allies considerable expenditure of men, planes and ammunition in combatting their activities, besides helping to maintain the morale of the German troops on the ground."

In October 1944, a new ground attack unit, Sonderstaffel Einhorn, was posted to Italy. After converting to night operations at Ghedi, its Focke-Wulf 190s flew three operations from Villafranca alongside NSG 9 during late November and early December before returning to Germany. While in Italy it had lost two aircraft in accidents as well as one destroyed and five damaged in the Allied raids of 18 November. Here, the scraped fuselage and torn wings of an Einhorn Fw 190F-8/R1, WNr. 581447, A3+LX, lie in Villafranca's scrapyard. Darker paint has been added to the fuselage top and sides since the national and unit markings were applied, possibly to improve the camouflage effect for night flying.

PREVAILING BAD WEATHER DURING NOVEMBER–DECEMBER IN UPPER ITALIAN AREA AND THE STRAINED FUEL SITUATION WILL ALLOW NIGHT G/A OPS ONLY IN ISOLATED CASES. OPS TO BE ORDERED ACCORDING TO INDIVIDUAL CIRCUMSTANCES. FLAK TO BE WARNED IN GOOD TIME. OTHERWISE UNRESTRICTED PERMISSION TO FIRE.

Decrypted signal from General Commanding *Luftwaffe* in Upper Italy,
2 November 1944

Villafranca di Verona, early November 1944: Hptm. Heinz Buß presents the Iron Cross First Class to Fw. Werner Hensel, Alfons Eck and Horst Rau, all of 3./NSG 9. When taken prisoner, Eck was relieved of his medal by a GI who, he wrote, "was prouder to wear it than I had ever been."

At the beginning of November, Stab and 1./NSG 9 were based in Bovolone, 2. *Staffel* in Ghedi and 3. *Staffel* was in Villafranca, as was *Sonderstaffel Einhorn*. On the 3rd however, orders were issued for 1./NSG 9 to transfer from Bovolone to Villafranca as soon as the airfield situation permitted.

On the 4th, the *Gruppe* returned to action with 11 machines leaving Villafranca from 20.00. Twenty minutes later, the Ju 87D-5 (WNr. 130699, E8+FH) of *Ofhr.* Karl Zander and *Uffz.* Heinz Eickhoff crashed 14km south of the aerodrome. The men's deaths were initially blamed on a night fighter but subsequently classed as an accident, as was the destruction during the same mission of another aircraft about which no details have emerged. A further Ju 87 was apparently lost during the day although not on ops. Deutsch and Nawroth's "D3+GL" bombed "roads in area FH", probably those leading into Loiano (BO) and at 20.45, there was strafing on the US II Corps front south of Bologna, where Volkmar von Grone shot up searchlights. On the 5th, targets were the same as for the night before and the *Gruppe* put up 20 sorties, including seven that 3./NSG 9 flew from Villafranca, starting at 17.05 with *Ofw.* Carl "Sepp" Wintermayr and *Uffz.* Karl Hofmann (E8+HL) claiming a direct hit on Loiano village. German archives record a total of 32 tonnes of bombs dropped over these two nights, so if each aircraft carried 1 x 500kg and 4 x 50kg munitions (as Hans Deutsch's did) there were around 45 sorties in aggregate. Three nights later, three training flights were made from Villafranca, Deutsch and Nawroth going up for 20 minutes to practise homing on a transmitter.

The MATAF daily summary provides a more than usually vivid picture of the raids of 10/11 November. NSG 9's effort included 27 sorties from Villafranca and targets were along Highway 65 around Pianoro (BO) and Loiano, with the apparent main objective north of Traversa (FI) at 22.30. The arrival of the Ju 87s was "preceded by the firing of red and purple smoke shells which may have been used to designate targets to the enemy aircraft" and the Americans watched as the Germans were engaged by their own *Flak* from Pianoro until white recognition flares were dropped. Peter Stollwerck's E8+HL was hit in the starboard wing by a 2cm shell and after dive-bombing he returned the favour by shooting up an AA position north of Loiano. At 20.45 in the Camugnano (BO) area, five or six enemy machines approached low over the River Savena from the north and climbed to attack their objectives, splitting into flights of two or three. The recipients reckoned that the bombs dropped that night included at least one of 500kg along with phosphorus and fragmentation weapons; Deutsch and Nawroth achieved a direct hit on a road in the face of light AA fire; in his two sorties, von Grone again fired on searchlights and attacked lorry convoys along the Florence–Castiglione road.

The next night's attacks spread from dusk to dawn and were remarked by MAAF as a departure from the usual moonlight ones. Seven sorties took off from Villafranca in the late afternoon: Willy Ferling and Bruno Grüning in E8+NH to Castel del Rio (BO); Stollwerck and Fischer dive-bombed

Loiano, the incendiaries from their AB 500 starting a major conflagration; Wintermayr and Hofmann attacked an AA position to the north. A second wave of seven went out around 05.35 next morning. Volkmar von Grone went road-hunting round Loiano and ten of Villafranca's aircraft returned there from 16.45 that afternoon.

While the ground forces were being notified that air support against guerrillas at Mondovi (CN) was not possible owing to fuel restrictions, Villafranca was able to send up 35 practice sorties over the next two days (although it is not clear how many were by NSG 9). Operations resumed from the base on the 16th, with eight Ju 87s up in the late afternoon. Peter Stollwerck dropped E8+AL's SD 500 and SD 70s in the centre of Forlì but Volkmar von Grone quickly returned to Ghedi when E8+HK's radio failed.

Allied reconnaissance on the 16th had detected 13 Ju 87s in Villafranca's northern dispersal area and another five at Vicenza, knowledge that was to be put to use in a major series of raids on Axis airfields two days later, when Liberators smothered Villafranca in fragmentation bombs from 09.55, killing four civilians and injuring seven service personnel and 12 civilians. Willy Ferling wrote:

> 18.11: Carpet bombing of the Ju 87 dispersals (3. *Staffel*) in Villafranca (experienced at first hand, up close, lying in a trench), only a few machines undamaged.

The airfield's war diary recorded three Ju 87s burnt out and five damaged[1], while strafing Thunderbolts set fire to another Junkers that afternoon. It was reported from Ghedi that only two out of 15 aircraft remained undamaged. Another source indicates that two Ju 87s were destroyed and six damaged on the 18th and three more damaged next day. Whatever the precise figure, losses of this order cut deep into the *Gruppe's* already low inventory and it was three days before NSG 9 was back in the air, four or five Ju 87s attacking Forlì from 17.10-17.30 on the 21st, the Germans having evacuated the town on the 9th.

On 22 November, NSG 9's needs were being discussed by no less than the *Luftwaffe's* Director General of Signals, *Gen.* Wolfgang Martini. Just as the unit was making increasing use of electronic guidance systems, so thoughts had turned to the protection of its aircraft against enemy radar. The conference concluded that Italy's mountainous terrain would rule out line-of-sight jamming from ground stations and noted that:

ABOVE: *The 3./NSG 9's Orderly Room was on the ground floor of this building in Villafranca (seen here in 1988) with personnel quarters in the rest of the building. The town's railway station lies about 100m along the road to the left.*

At present only the *Kettenhund* [Watchdog] jammer is available for active airborne jamming. This incurs the danger of enemy night fighters homing on to the jammer, whether it is carried in the *Nachtschlacht* aircraft or in a special jamming aircraft. So long as no more suitable jammer is available, airborne jamming is not recommended.

Passive jamming with *Düppel* (German "Window") would require spoofing aircraft which would consume scarce fuel and might give premature warning of an attack and so the only other possibility seemed to be that the artillery might fire barrages of *Düppel*-filled shells. The negative tone of these deliberations stands in stark contrast to the scale and enthusiasm of the Allies' embrace of radio countermeasures and it seems that nothing further was done even though German bomber units had begun using *Düppel* over a year earlier and it continued to be used in Italy by FAG 122's night reconnaissance aircraft.

A pilot's map showing the front line in northern Italy (top left) between the evacuation of Forlì on 9 November and the Allied capture of Faenza on 10 December 1944.

Around seven aircraft bombed and strafed Forlì that evening, Wintermayr and Hofmann (E8+KH) hitting the Via Emilia (Highway 9) east of the town. The target was the same on the 23rd with four aircraft up from Villafranca, including the Ju 87D-5 of *Ofhr.* Bernhard Buckow and *Uffz.* Arthur Berkemeyer (WNr. 141018, E8+JH) and E8+MH, flown by Ferling and Grüning who had also been on the previous day's raid. They took off at 16.18 toward a target area with 10/10 stratocumulus from 3,000-6,000ft and 7/10 stratus at 10,000ft but they would not be bombing visually. Willy Ferling describes:

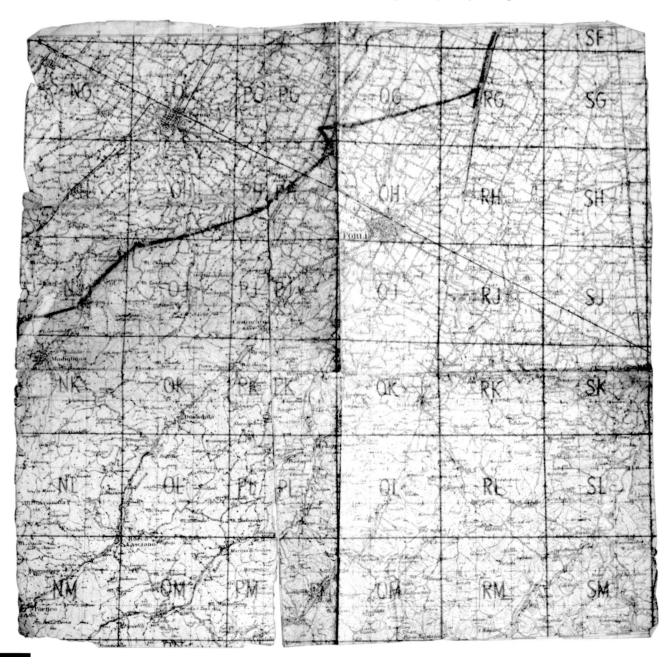

… NSG 9's tests of a new radio-guidance system using the R/T… On 23 November a special mission to test the guidance system: fire bomb raid on Forlì with two(!) Ju 87s. Bombing height 4,000m, keeping on course with instructions over the R/T from the control station: "*Autobahn*" [= "magnetic course to me is …"] and so on. You can imagine the result! The *Flak* fired on us at their leisure: Buckow and I had to dance the "*Flak* waltz."

Our control station had probably lost us at this point, not far short of Forlì, and the night fighters too could be vectored on to us at leisure. And the Lightnings were already there.

The "Lightning" in question was a Beaufighter crewed by W/O D.B. Smith and F/S J.B. Dunford. At 17.05, over Ravenna, they were alerted to a bogey 20 miles away and coming south; ten minutes later, they were ordered to maximum speed and advised that there were two bogeys. Darkness was fast setting in when, at 8,400ft and five miles east of Lake Comàcchio:

> …got an A.I. contact at 2¼ miles range. Closed in to 1 mile and then had two contacts, nearest dead ahead and second 10° to starboard … at 1000 feet range obtained a visual on two aircraft flying loose line abreast formation and weaving gently. Closed in to 800 feet and identified the aircraft as being two JU.87's, the undercarriages being distinctly seen in both instances. Estimated speed of enemy aircraft as being 160 m.p.h.

At 17.18, 25 miles east of Lake Comàcchio:

> Closed in from dead astern to 600 feet. Opened fire with cannon and machine-guns at the aircraft on the left. Immediately saw strikes all over the JU.87. The port wing came off near the fuselage and the E/A immediately blew up with a terrific explosion. The light from the burning aircraft lit up the other hostile clearly. Without stopping firing attacked the right hand aircraft as it started to peel off to port. Saw some strikes on the starboard wing. This aircraft returned fire inaccurately as it was diving away. Last seen the E/A was diving straight down into 10/10th cloud at 6000ft.

From Willy Ferling's viewpoint:

> Our own defence was somewhat ineffective, so Buckow's machine was hit, burning like a torch as it fell and vanished from sight. I myself could no longer reach Forlì with my couple of incendiaries and extricated myself from the night fighter's attack by diving. The bombs later went for a bath in the Po.

However, the enemy had not finished with him yet and he continues:

> My flight back to Villafranca turned out really bad: the traffic from a ground station suddenly became audible again with strange directions about which course to take, considering the Alps were getting dangerously close. Later it transpired that an English transmitter was trying to mislead me. The red warning lamp for low fuel level came on. Just as we were on the point of bailing out, the Villafranca beacon came like a gift from the Gods. Perfunctory circuit, landing and the engine cut out as I was taxying to dispersal – after 2hr 18min flying time.
>
> Buckow and his crewman had to pay for this test flight with their lives and it was only by a whisker that a second crew avoided their fate.

There was another consideration, as Dirk Bunsen recalls:

> Of the four new crews, those of the two *Oberfähnriche* were always "on"… so these two officer candidates could attain the prescribed total of 22 missions as soon as possible and be promoted to *Leutnant*. On 4 November I arrived in Bug-auf-Rügen for the Air Warfare School course. After a few weeks a letter from a *Staffel* member reached me there [and] I learned that both these *Ofhr.* crews had crashed on operations.

Buckow, a Berliner, was 24 and Berkemeyer, from Kellen near Kleve, was 25. In 1996, the wreck of a Ju 87 was found in the sea at a position consistent with their crash. At the time of writing, attempts to recover it had been frustrated by fishermen's nets snagging the aircraft and moving it from its original location.

Leutnant Willy Ferling joined 1./NSG 9 at Bovolone on 12 September 1944 and in October gave blind flying instruction to his comrades in a Junkers W.34. On 23 November, he witnessed the shooting down of Ofhr. Bernhard Buckow and Uffz. Arthur Berkemeyer during a test mission for EGON ground-controlled bombing.

The airfield of Vicenza, seen here with the city beyond, served as the "gateway" for Luftwaffe aircraft entering and leaving Italy from the Reich.

Following this disastrous experiment, operations were not resumed until the 27th when 16 aircraft dropped HE and incendiary bombs over the front. At 06.20 next morning, Volkmar von Grone and Heinrich Lenz (in E8+HK) left Ghedi on an anti-partisan mission against a bridge at Bobbio (PC). New aircraft were being brought in: Herbert Kehrer delivered E8+XL to Villafranca from Vicenza but that afternoon Harry Fischer and *Gefr.* Heinz Staudt had barely taken off from Villaverla (Thiene) when they realised that E8+FL's coolant temperature was 150°C and were forced to turn back. The problem was only resolved in time for them to bring the aircraft to Villafranca 24 hours later.

Plans announced for the night of 28/29 November included *Nachtschlacht* operations in the central and eastern sectors, NSG 9 contributing 24 Ju 87s and *Sonderverband Einhorn* five Fw 190s. Fourteen of these aircraft (including all the Focke-Wulfs) operated from Villafranca, Willy Ferling's E8+KH among them. Other members of 1. *Staffel* set out from Bovolone, including *Hptm.* Kuhle, their *Kapitän*, (possibly in E8+CH), closely followed by *Fw.* Kaspar Stuber and *Uffz.* Alois Adami (Ju 87D-5 WNr. 131086, E8+DH). They took off around 16.10, carrying an SD 500 fragmentation bomb and four Br. C 50 phosphorus incendiaries. Their assigned targets were troop and transport concentrations, artillery positions and bridges in the "English/Polish sector" around Forlì. Stuber, accustomed to flying independently by moonlight, had this time been ordered to keep his leader in sight and do exactly as he did.

Kaspar Stuber, just back from three weeks' leave, was a highly experienced pilot with 236 war flights in Russia, where he had flown the He 46 with *Störkampfstaffel 1* from December 1942 before transferring to SG 111 the following October. After six weeks' training on Capronis, he had come to Italy in December, joining NSG 9 and flying 74 more missions without mishap. He held the *Deutsches Kreuz*, EK 1 and gold *Frontflugspange*. Adami had the EK I and silver FFS (awarded on 19 July and 20 September 1944 respectively) and his postings from October 1943 onward had mirrored Stuber's although apparently they had not crewed up together until June.

At 16.30, S/L Archer and F/L Barrington (who had been evaded by two Ju 87s over Cassino back in April) were scrambled "for enemy activity in the Forlì-Faenza area." It was 17.05 when GCI "SYRUP" gave the night fighter a vector for "possible bandit at angels 12", advising a minute later that, "there were two bogeys near, possibly friendly." Barrington got a radar contact and they climbed to 12,000ft, getting a visual from 2 miles away on two aircraft, one 500ft higher than the other and 300yds to starboard. Archer closed on the latter and was able to confirm it as a Ju 87.

> At this moment both aircraft seemed to sight us. The port aircraft dived away to port, the other one that we were following dived steeply for cloud cover below.
> Followed down after it at 290 IAS and closed fairly quickly to 600ft range. Opened fire at 600ft with cannon and machine-guns. Closing in to 600ft saw numerous strikes on fuselage and port wing. The JU.87 still turned to starboard, pouring out smoke as pieces were seen to break off wings and fuselage. A large centrally placed bomb was seen to come away at this moment. The JU.87 now spiralled steeply to the ground and blew up.

Stuber had been unable to control the aircraft and ordered his gunner to bail out before following suit, landing near where E8+DH exploded. Adami, who was not seen to leave the aeroplane, was killed: he had turned 23 not three weeks before. Willy Ferling remembers him as a fluent speaker of Italian, acting as 1. *Staffel's* interpreter. Once in Bovolone, the two were on their way to arrange with the town's Mayor for the supply of a stove when American fighter-bombers attacked a train standing in the station. When the raid was over and Ferling and Adami emerged from cover, the Mayor's office had been destroyed and so the *Staffel* never got its stove. Dirk Bunsen recollects another link between Adami and the Mayor:

> I remember Adami well. He was of medium height with black curly hair, came from
> the South Tyrol and of course spoke fluent Italian. He was in love with the pretty
> daughter of the Mayor of Bovolone (a good, cultivated man). She was called Lisa or
> Luisa. In October 1944, when the aircrew quarters were in the villa of *Cavaliere*
> Remo Gagliardi, the two of them used to make small talk and so forth in a little
> summer house in one corner of the park.

Events came thick and fast during the night of 28 November. At 17.16, between four and six single-engined fighters (*Einhorn's* Fw 190s) and Ju 87s attacked in the Forlì area. At 17.17, a Ju 87 bombed a Fifth Army command post, dropping – it was estimated – "2 x GP, 4 x AP and 7 or 8 incendiary bombs … from 6,000ft" and wounding two enlisted men and two Italian civilians while a third Italian was killed. Three minutes later, in the mountains south of Bologna, a lone German aircraft was seen to bomb its own side's positions near Vergato (BO). Allied ground troops reported that two Fw 190s had attacked Forlì at 17.25, a "believed Ju 88" dropped fragmentation bombs east of Vergato five minutes later and a single aircraft strafed Highway 65 at 19.00 but no damage was reported. Although a Ju 87 was reported shot down by AA in the Forlì area, this may have been a competing claim for Stuber and

*Leutnant Volkmar von
Grone's map showing the
front line in the mountains
south of Bologna in the
late Novenber-early
December 1944 period.*

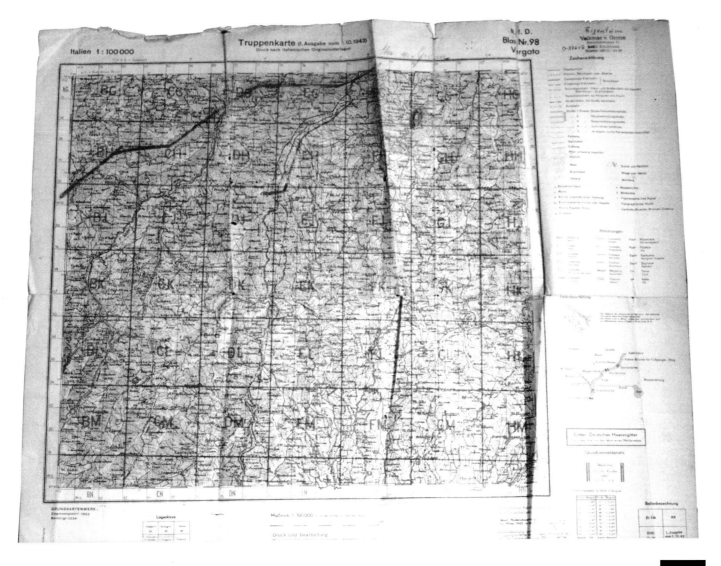

By November the crisis before Bologna had passed and and the fifth in the "Georgia" propaganda series was dwelling on the miseries of winter warfare in the mountains.

WINTER WEATHER AHEAD!

The days are shortening and you are still here. "Beautiful Italy" has changed. That bit of sun during the day cannot warm you any more after you have been lying for days and days in your foxholes perhaps knee deep in water.

True enough Jerry is giving up a bit of ground here and there. Perhaps he will give up a few miles again some day, but only after he has exacted the highest possible toll of blood from your infantrymen.

WHAT WOULD YOU BE FACING THEN?

The mighty swift-flowing Po river with its deep ice-cold water and a merciless fire sweeping across from the other side.

WHAT WOULD YOU SEE after you had perhaps managed to build a bridge over the river on the bodies of your comrades? Just new fortifications, a maze of barbed wire entanglements, thousands of pillboxes, earthworks, concrete and steel for miles! All the long weary way to the Alps, the highest and most difficult mountain barrier in Europe, with ridges of tenthousand feet and an eternal winter.

EACH LINE MUST BE STORMED AND THOUSANDS OF AMERI-CANS WILL HAVE TO GIVE THEIR LIVES!

AND AT HOME?

They know very little about your sufferings out here in Italy. The ignorance on the subject has never been greater than now. The home-front warriors, especially the Hebrews, are rolling in cash and praying that this war may go on for ever. They are launching "reconnaissance parties" too, but into the bedrooms of lonely women. Their ammunition is a fat roll of bills and their war-cry is: MORE DOLLARS AND GIRLS. They get them!

HAS IT NEVER OCCURED TO YOU HOW SENSELESS all this is, and that nobody will give you any thanks afterwards?

You can do nothing about it? Oh yes, you can!

You can think of your own nearest and dearest at home. You know in your hearts that, whatever their sentiments about dead heroes may be, the very best news any of them can receive is that you are waiting for the end of the war safe and sound in a decent camp.

Give them a Happy Christmas!

Georgia series comprising 6 pictures. Have you got the others?

330 - 11.44

Adami's plane. NSG 9 did however lose *Uffz*. Franz Spörr of 2. *Staffel* in a fatal crash at Fornaci (BS), well away from the front and attributed to accidental causes.

The evening's raids gave the Allies something new to think about. Signals Intelligence had listened in as one aircraft radioed to ground control that it had released its bomb and "…there were indications from other sources that an attack … on Fifth Army CP was under ground control of bombers and bomb release." There had been a break in transmissions but they had reopened at 17.45 until, 16 minutes later, the aircraft being guided was reported lost and the ground station went off the air soon afterward. Stuber, rated by his interrogators as "not an intelligent type", was pressed repeatedly about the radio equipment in his aircraft. He claimed it had carried nothing special, admitting only to the presence of FuG 25A in his usual (and currently unserviceable) E8+BH, saying this had been unique in the *Staffel*, at least up until he had gone on leave. He had made two EGON practice flights some weeks previously but with only partial success and he denied ever receiving instructions from the ground while on an actual mission. He said there had been no briefing about EGON for his final flight but suspicions were aroused by his admitting to the orders to follow and imitate his leader, suggesting that Kuhle's aircraft had been receiving guidance from the ground.

NSG 9 had flown 166 sorties throughout November and, thanks to MAAF's airfield attacks, suffered probably its highest losses for a single month. However the operational introduction of EGON to Italy and night bombing by Fw 190s had pointed the way forward. Another milestone was the award of the *Ritterkreuz* to Rupert Frost on the 25th, the *Gruppenkommandeur* being the first *Nachtschlachtflieger* to receive this decoration. However one veteran has remarked to the author:

> It seemed to me that the higher my *Staffel*'s losses became, the greater was the *Kommandeur's* prestige.

---

1. *Einhorn* lost an Fw 190 plus 5 damaged.

Commanding Officers

*I*t would have been gratifying to be able to set this out in a simple table but while many things became clearer while researching this book, the precise sequence of appointments and tenures of NSG 9's *Staffelkapitäne* did not, in part because of the limited information from 2./NSG 9 which seems to have undergone the most changes of leadership.

1./NSG 9 was established with *Hptm.* Rupert Frost as its *Kapitän.* When 2./NSG 9 was formed, *Hptm.* Robert Hegenbarth became its *Kapitän* and Frost took on the additional role of *Gruppenkommandeur.* At some point after 27 March 1944 (when he signed a casualty report as *Staffelkapitän*), Hegenbarth was transferred to a unit in Romania and went missing in action on 24 August, reportedly on his first mission there. (Although a postwar document in the German archives places Hegenbarth at the head of 1./NSG 9, no other source suggests that he ever held this position).

Between 28 April and 2 May Frost became a *Major,* probably on the 1st of May if considerations of tidy administration played any part.

The report of *Oblt.* Rolf Martini's death on 22 May 1944 describes him as 2./NSG 9's *Staffelführer,* a post that could exist either alongside or instead of a *Staffelkapitän.* His initial successor was *Oblt.* Bernd Schewen, followed on 1 June by *Maj.* Robert Rohn, who signed his last casualty return as *Staffelführer* in the first week of July.

The 2./NSG 2 arrived from Russia at the beginning of June under the command of *Hptm.* Eduard Reither, who continued to lead the *Staffel* through its redesignation as 3./NSG 9.

By 5 July 1944, a PoW claimed Frost was leading the *Gruppe* as well as commanding 1./NSG 9 in place of its *Kapitän, Oblt.* August Müller, who had been grounded with fatigue and sent home to Germany. This information is not necessarily reliable for according to veterans Müller was in fact NSG 9's Technical Officer. Another prisoner taken on the 11th said *Oblt.* Schewen was now the *Kapitän* of 2./NSG 9 and a third, interrogated on 28 August backed this up (Schewen had been signing or counter-signing 2./NSG 9's casualty reports throughout July but with no post indicated, just his rank). Nevertheless, the report of four casualties on 27 July bears the signature of *Oblt.* Hermann Kuchenbuch as *Staffelführer.*

ABOVE: *Gruppenkommandeur of NSG 9, Maj. Rupert Frost was a veteran who had won the Narvik Shield (sleeve patch) with KG 27 in Norway before becoming a pioneer Störfkampflieger on the Eastern Front. He led NSG 9 from first to last and was awarded the Ritterkreuz in November 1944.*

ABOVE: *Hptm. Robert Hegenbarth, the first Staffelkapitän of 2./NSG 9, was later posted to Romania and killed in action on 24 August 1944.*

RIGHT: *Maj. Robert Rohn (left) and Hptm. Eduard Reither both served as Kapitän of 2./NSG 9, Rohn until July 1944, Reither from the end of September that year. From February 1945 Rohn commanded NSG 2 in western Germany. After the Allies crossed the Rhine, NSG 2 was constantly changing bases and Rohn was shot and killed by a Hitler Youth sentry while surveying a potential new airfield, apparently in the period 27 March–5 April.*

Commanding Officers

ABOVE: *Hauptmann Eduard Reither, Staffelkapitän of 2./NSG 2, 3./NSG 9 and, later, 2./NSG 9.*

From his signature on a casualty report it seems likely that *Hptm.* Karl-Heinz Kuhle took over 1./NSG 9 from Frost on 1 September 1944 and he was definitely in post by the 13th of that month. On 28 September, at Frost's insistence, Reither was transferred to command 2./NSG 9 and he signed Werner Lotsch's pay book as *Kapitän* of this *Staffel* on 16 October. When conversing with the author, Reither could not recall from whom he took over, only his disappointment at being separated from the men he had led for so long.

A surviving *Luftwaffe* document, annotated with the date 13 November 1944 but apparently referring to the situation somewhat earlier, names NSG 9's commanding officers as follows:

Einsatzstab NSG 9	Bovolone	*Kdr. Maj.* Frost
1./NSG 9	Villafranca	*St.Kpt. Htpm.* Kuhle
2./NSG 9	Ghedi II	*St.Kpt. Maj.* Rohn
3./NSG 9	Villafranca	*St.Kpt. Hptm.* Reither

Oberleutnant Bernd Schewen had been *Adjutant* since at least the beginning of November when he signed a pilot's travel warrant. Rohn may also have served as NSG 9's Operations Officer before going on to take command of NSG 2 in western Germany early in February 1945. He was to be shot and killed by a jumpy Hitler Youth sentry while surveying prospective airfields as his unit fell back before the American advance in late March.

Leutnant Volkmar von Grone was appointed *Staffelführer* of 2./NSG 9 late in 1944, before contracting hepatitis and being posted back to Germany after a period of convalescence[1]. In the second half of March 1945, Reither was posted away from the *Gruppe*, becoming a "*Nachtschlacht* Advisor" to the *General der Schlachtflieger*. His successor in 3./NSG 9 was *Hptm.* Heinz Buß – known to his men as the *Capitano* – who would command the *Staffel* to the last.

On 5 January 1945, an *Oberstleutnant* signed a casualty report, styling himself Deputy *Gruppenkommandeur*. This individual's signature has not yet been deciphered but since he outranked Frost it seems likely that he was on a temporary assignment.

In mid-January, *Hptm.* Willi Wilzopolski came to Italy to take over 1./NSG 9. Where Kuhle had been posted meanwhile is not known but he survived the war. Wilzopolski however did not, being killed in action on 3 March but again the author has been unable to determine whether he was officially replaced.

Accounts of the leaving of Thiene on 27 April 1945 (see page 174) suggest that *Oblt.* Schewen was then in charge of 2./NSG 9 once more, while Rupert Frost commanded NSG 9 in Italy to the end.

RIGHT: *Early April 1945: Hptm. Heinz Buß, Staffelkapitän of 3./NSG 9, inspects his unit's improvised Flak emplacement alongside of Highway 62, some 500m south of Mozzecane (VR). The other personnel are: (from left) Ofw. Dzykowski of NSG 9's Ops Room; Ofhr. Dirk Bunsen; Fw. Soukopp, from a Propaganda Kompanie ("among other things, they threw pamphlets and leaflets out of a plane"). To the right is the ammunition belt and box of one of the guns, while two gun pit parapets are also in evidence. The gun crews slept in requisitioned rooms in the single-storey farmhouse on the far left of the picture. The position existed between 1 and 22 April 1945.*

---

1. His last mission in Italy was on the night of 22/23 January 1945, his first on the Oder front on 3 March.

Arado Ar 66C of 2./*Störkampfgruppe Luftflotte 6*, Eastern Front, Autumn 1943

Flown by *Obgfr.* Harry Fischer in the autumn of 1943 during his time with the *Nachtschwarm Oberlt. Haimböck*, part of 2./*Störkampfgruppe Luftflotte 6* which became 2./NSG 2 in October 1943 and 3./NSG 9 in July 1944.

Standard two-tone green splinter camouflage on the upper surfaces; undersides painted black for night operations; Eastern Front yellow tail band and wing tips. Photographs suggest that all code letters were black, outlined in white. The white *Werk Nummer* on this aircraft's rudder is not legible in the reference photograph.

Caproni Ca.314 of 1./NSG 9, Campoformido-Udine, January 1944

This profile marries the appearance of 1./NSG 9 Capronis known from photographs with documented individual markings: E8+EH (MM. 12740) crashed at Campoformido-Udine on 10 January 1944 in an accident killing all four crew.

Italian olive green and light grey camouflage with an overpainted *Regia Aeronautica* white cross discernible on the rudder; the white fuselage band is a German Mediterranean Theatre marking. While at least one NSG 9 Caproni had yellow spinners, apparently none had the yellow nacelle undersides and wingtips specified for captured aircraft in *Luftwaffe* service at that time.

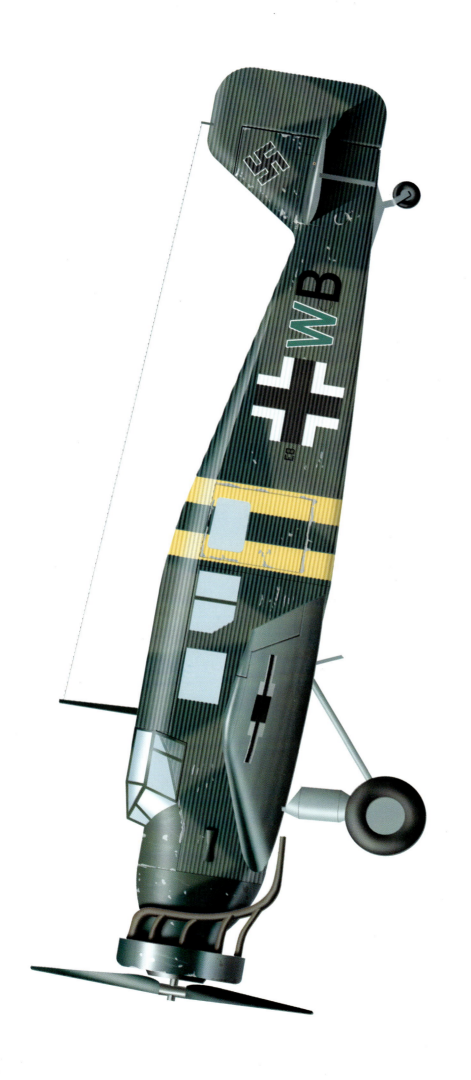

Junkers W.34 of _Stab_/NSG 9, Villafranca di Verona, October 1944
There are no known photographs of the Ju W.34 which served briefly with _Stab_/NSG 9 in October 1944. This speculative profile combines the standard paint scheme for the type (two-tone green splinter camouflage and pale blue undersides) with the E8+WB code recorded in the logbook of its pilot, _Lt._ Willy Ferling. Twin yellow stripes were commonly applied to _Luftwaffe_ blind-flying trainers.

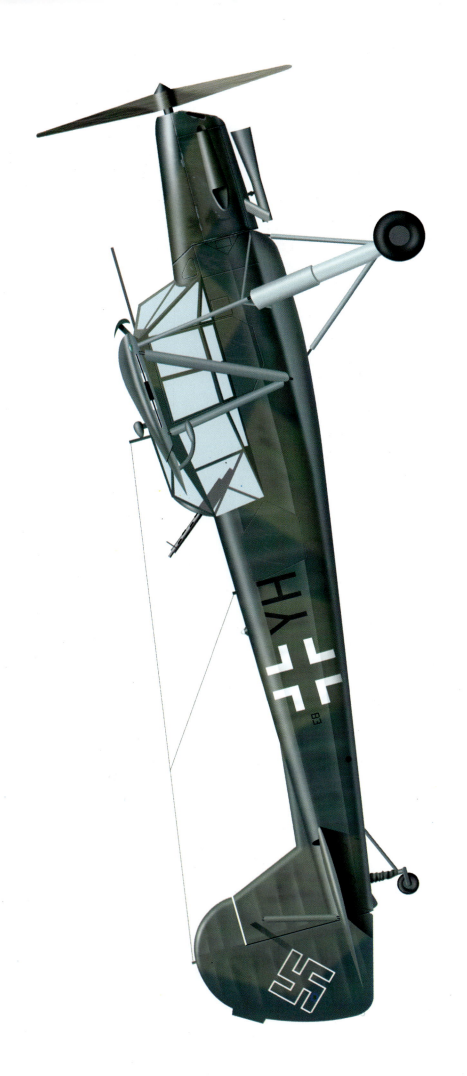

Fiesler Fi 156 *Storch* of 1./NSG 9, Caselle-Torino, early 1944
This aircraft was camouflaged in standard two-tone green splinter camouflage and pale blue undersides while its code letters were all black. It had an enlarged air filter. *Hptm.* Robert Hegenbarth, is reputed to have used this liaison aircraft for weekend trips to his home in Klagenfurt, Austria.

Fiat CR.42 *Falco* **of 1./NSG 9, Fabrica di Roma, March 1944**
For nocturnal operations with NSG 9, the CR.42's basic Italian camouflage was oversprayed with cloudy patches of brown and grey (or pale blue) on the olive green upper surfaces and dark grey (or green) on the light grey undersides. 1./NSG 9's aircraft had white spinners. Modifications included cutaway wheel fairings, an enlarged air filter and exhaust flame suppressors. None of the known photographs shows a 1. *Staffel* code but an E8+AH is documented among the first NSG 9 Fiats to go into action.

Fiat CR.42 *Falco* **of 2./NSG 9, Caselle-Torino, Spring 1944**
The aircraft is similarly modified and camouflaged to that in the previous profile but with the red spinner and code letter (outlined in white) of 2. *Staffel*. Like its sister, it has yellow tips to its propeller blades, following Italian practice. This aircraft was flown by *Fw.* Horst Greßler.

Ju 87D-5 of 1./NSG 9, Tuscania, April 1944

Feldwebel Günther Gräßer's "new aircraft" photographed on 20 April 1944, a week before it deployed to Tuscania, one of the first NSG 9 *Stukas* into action. It had the signature camouflage of the *Gruppe*, a brown meander pattern over the basic two-tone green splinter while the pale blue undersides were darkened by grey "tiger stripes." The tip of the spinner was white and there was a small white "S" on the front of the port wheel spat.

Ju 87D-5 of 2./NSG 9, Ghedi, December 1944

Based on a photograph of a "red J" of 2./NSG 9, possibly E8+JK, WNr. 140750, in which *Fhj.Ofw.* Artur Heiland und *Uffz.* Artur Ballok were shot down by a USAAF night fighter on 22 December 1944. The brown meander pattern was less convoluted than on most NSG 9 machines. As the war progressed the *Gruppe* tended to remove the dive brakes from its aircraft; *Werk Nummern* were usually hidden by oversprayed camouflage.

Ju 87D-3 of 2./NSG 2, Byelorussia, May 1944

Flown by *Ofw.* Toni Fink and *Fw.* Hans Nawroth on one of their last missions before transferring to Italy. The two-tone green splinter camouflage, pale blue undersides and yellow band are typical of Ju 87s on the Eastern Front but the photograph of "White 8" suggests the tailpane's upper surfaces may have been unpainted. *Staffel* aircraft had white tail numbers, repeated on the port wheel spat. The white unit code and the white-tipped spinner are derived from another, contemporary Ju 87 of the *Gruppe*; the red individual letter outlined in white is provisional.

Ju 87D-3 of 3./NSG 9, Villafranca di Verona, April 1945
This aircraft's fuselage was found at Villafranca when the airfield was captured. 3-1193, E8+KL is last known to have flown on 16 February 1945, *Flg.* Wolfgang Holtz and *Uffz.* Kurt Wagner carrying out night landing practice and a searchlight co-operation sortie. This profile's green/white segmented spinner and the grey meander on the aircraft's undersides derive from another late-war 3. *Staffel* aircraft. The hyphenated *Werk Nummer* was unusual but not unique in NSG 9.

Fw 190F-8/R1 of 1./NSG 9, Villafranca di Verona, April 1945

E8+DH, WNr 581632, was found in a hangar at Villafranca by advancing American troops. Its standard camouflage of three greys had been toned down by the application of dark green, possibly to make it less conspicuous on the ground or in the night skies. Not all Fw 190s of the *Gruppe* were repainted in this way, however.

North American F-6C of 15th TRS, USAAF, Fürth, April 1945
This F-6C, in which Lt. Haylon R. Wood shot down two Ju 87s of NSG 9 over Austria on 27 April 1945, lacked the clear vision Malcolm hood. Aside from the blue/white 15th TRS checkers and the nickname "Millie, My Baby, And Me", its appearance was standard for the USAAF in Europe in 1945.

Beaufighter VIf of No. 600 Sqn. RAF, Marcianise, June 1944

Flown by F/O Stewart Rees when he shot down the CR.42 of 2./NSG 9's Horst Greßler. No. 600 Squadron used just a "6" to denote the unit, along with the individual aircraft's letter. The placement of the codes here derives from photographs of two other squadron aircraft in 1944 (different permutations appeared on earlier Beaufighters and a later Mosquito). A small letter "M" was painted in red on the front of the radome. Camouflage and national markings were standard for an RAF night fighter in 1944.

Spitfire Mk VIII, No. 241 Sqn. RAF, Piagliolino, August 1944
Flown by Capt. E.R. Dixon (SAAF) when he shot down the Ju 87 of *Obgfr.* Harry Fischer on 31 August 1944. This profile is an impression based on photographs of a Mk IX which was MT634's predecessor as RZ•U. Camouflage and markings were standard for an RAF day fighter in 1944.

NSG 9's TACTICS

Evasive Action

A Sighting a Beaufighter on its tail, the Ju 87 peels off left or right into a "falling corkscrew", extremely difficult for the fighter follow.

B Visual contact is broken. If the Ju 87 has bombs aboard, they are jettisoned during the dive and the Beaufighter crew sees fires and explosions on the ground, sometimes mistaken for the impact of a stricken aircraft.

C The Ju 87 can pull out of the corkscrew on any heading its pilot chooses and escape at low level, its radar return lost in the ground "clutter."

"...target: roads south of Bologna"

1 The Ju 87 sets out from base at low level across the Po Plain to escape detection by Allied radar. To complicate any attempt at interception, it weaves and changes height frequently.

2 Approaching the Apennine Mountains, it climbs in a spiral to its attacking height of 3,000m. Most night fighter attacks take place when the Ju 87s are at medium altitude, approaching or leaving the target area.

3 Locating its target, the Ju 87 makes a shallow dive attack, in this case through one of the mountain passes. After bombing, it may follow up by strafing.

4 Its attack completed, the Ju 87 regains sufficient height to cross the mountains before setting course for base, again weaving and changing height.

5 The Ju 87 may suddenly pull a hard left or right orbit, in the hope that any pursuer will overshoot and lose radar and visual contact.

6 Nearing base, the Ju 87's *Bordfunker* may briefly break radio silence to announce its imminent arrival so that the flarepath can be lit or — if the recurring valley fog has descended — the airfield searchlights can make a "cathedral of light" to guide it home.

7 The aircraft lands, the flarepath is swiftly extinguished to avoid attracting the attention of Allied intruders and it taxies to dispersal.

December 1944

"Signs of aggressiveness"

After a two-night hiatus, Forlì was again the target on 1 December. The nine aircraft from Villafranca apparently took off just after 16.00, too early as it transpired to gain the full cover of darkness. Warrant Officer H.G. Baits and F/S Lothian had taken off from Falconara at the same time and were near Forlì just over 40min later when advised of four bogeys coming from the north west at 13,000ft. On reaching 10,000ft they were told to hold altitude as the contacts were now at that height, 15 miles off. Since it was still fairly light, they were able to get a visual from no less than 8 miles on four aircraft in line astern with another a few hundred feet below and slightly to port. On closing in, the gull wings and fixed landing gear of Ju 87s were identified; the Germans had by now descended to 8,000ft and were making an estimated 200mph. Baits opened fire at the last in line:

> Observed strikes along the fuselage and black smoke start to come from the engine. There was considerable return fire which came fairly close. Then the Ju 87 peeled off to starboard, emitting larger quantities of black smoke from its engine. The return fire ceased abruptly and the E/A went into 10/10 cloud at 6,000ft. Last seen it … gave the impression of being out of control.

Baits claimed this one as probably destroyed but events were now to take an unaccustomed turn.

> At that moment the other JU. 87s began to show signs of aggressiveness. They turned in towards the Beaufighter and as the aircraft that had originally been to port of the formation turned to starboard he flew right through the burst from the Beaufighter. Strikes were seen along the fuselage but the return fire … did not stop.

This Ju 87 was claimed as damaged. Baits' early sighting of the enemy had meant that Lothian's radar was not needed and so:

> I concentrated on watching the tail. As events proved, this was necessary…

One of the Germans now attacked from 600yds dead astern:

> Tracer was seen to be coming unpleasantly close … The Beaufighter opened up to full speed and took evasive action by skidding … This did not however shake the JU.87 off and he continued to press his attack, without gaining much distance … The Beaufighter was obliged to put [its] nose down and make for the cloud below. At this moment a JU.87 carried out an attack from the starboard quarter [and] the tracer was seen to be coming fairly close. Beaufighter entered cloud and shortly after climbed up to even the attack. He saw that the JU.87 [which] had been attacking from astern was still in position to carry on … so entered cloud again. When he broke cloud the JU. 87s were nowhere to be seen.

Which aircraft the Beaufighter hit is unknown. Despite night fighters and AA fire, Kehrer and Koch (E8+CL) at least were able to bomb Forlì by EGON whereas Ferling and Grüning (E8+KH) were twice compelled to abort by a defective radio and Wintermayr and Hofmann's E8+ML was turned back by a coolant temperature of 120°C. Both target and timing were the same on the 2nd. At

The Piazza Castello, Villafranca di Verona at 9.17 on a winter's morning. The woman passing by on the right is huddled against the cold. The temporary building at the left, with German service personnel in front of it, carries the prominent sign "Villafranca Anhalter Bahnhof, Flieger Horst Kommandantur." This alludes to what was then Berlin's largest rail terminus and the one serving Italy. Although at the opposite end of Villafranca town from the field itself, the name suggests a reporting centre for arriving and departing personnel of the Aerodrome Command.

11.00 *Komm. Gen.* had issued his orders for the coming night which, as decrypted by the British three days later, were:

> Night ground attack ops also, should opportunity arise, by *Sonderstaffel Einhorn*, using bombs and aircraft armament against road targets in area north west of Forlì with part forces in order to split Allied night fighters. Attacks on road targets and localities in Futa area and (strong indications Porretta) Pass. Bombing targets Forlì, Loiano, Grizzana, Castiglione, as well as the area covered in the "special order".

Some 14 Junkers and Focke-Wulfs flew from Villafranca and this time it was Kehrer and Koch's turn to abort soon after take-off. EGON radio traffic was detected from stations PAUL 1 and SIEGFRIED 1 and since *Einhorn* went for Desert Air Force's Advanced HQ near Forlì, it seems probable that NSG 9 had been assigned the remaining targets, all in the mountains to the south of Bologna. Airfield Regional Command 10/VII recorded that NSG 9 had dropped AB 500 containers, SD 70 bombs, and AB 36 canisters filled with incendiaries in the course of the night's operations. At least one aircraft was out after midnight for there was strafing along Highway 65 near Monghidoro (BO) at 01.08 and again ten minutes later.

No flights were scheduled for the night of 3/4 December beyond ferrying a single Ju 87 to Thiene. Willy Ferling (E8+EH) and Herbert Kehrer (+CL) made test flights from Villafranca on the 5th. The 1./NSG 9's former base of Ravenna fell on the 8th and a Beaufighter chased and lost a Ju 87 near Faenza that night but it was not until the next day that orders for another operation were issued (and decrypted): road-hunting and EGON-guided harassment of Grizzana (BO), Castiglione (BO) und Forlì. Although Villafranca logged three combat sorties, these plans appear to have fallen through but it would be a different story on the 10th when, according to MAAF:

> Approximately 12 sorties of mixed Fw 190s and Ju 87s carrying bombs were flown in the Fifth Army area and about the same number of Fw 190s operated in the Eighth Army area. Attacks were made at dusk and up to 18.00 hrs. Military and civilian casualties were caused in both areas. Demolition, anti-personnel and incendiary clusters were dropped…
>
> The Ju 87s are believed to be from two squadrons at Villafranca and Vicenza and the Fw 190s from a squadron at Villafranca.

At twilight, around six Ju 87s overflew the Forlì-Cesena area and from 16.15–17.00 four of *Einhorn's* Fw 190s bombed and strafed Forlì Aerodrome, then at 16.52 the Focke-Wulfs bombed Forlì town, hitting the Main HQ of Eighth Army. In the mountains at 17.15, four aircraft dropped anti-personnel bombs west of Loiano (BO) and near Cásola Valsénio (RA) and at 17.22 another released two bombs east of Montérenzio (BO) but no damage was done. At 18.00 however, a lone aeroplane bombed Gággio Montano (BO), destroying one building and causing civilian casualties. Once again, EGON traffic was picked up by Signals Intelligence. From the German perspective, von Grone and Lenz (E8+HK) met "very heavy *Flak* defence" when attacking Loiano; Deutsch and Nawroth ("D5+FL") reported dropping an AB 500 and 4 x SD 70s on traffic "in area GH" — the Idice Valley — while Kehrer and Koch (E8+HL) logged "bomb release by EGON in the Ligano area, south of Bologna, *Flak* and night fighters." Both Germans and Allies were fallible when it came to Italian place names and the non-existent "Ligano" was probably Loiano or Liano.

An Allied report that anti-personnel bombs were dropped in the II Corps area south of Bologna on the moonless night of the 15/16th lacks corroboration from German sources so far. *Einhorn* left Villafranca for Holzkirchen, Bavaria on the 17th, assigned a role in the Ardennes offensive launched the previous day. Meanwhile on the 11th, ten or eleven of NSG 9's pilots had been posted to Schroda in Silesia (now Sroda, Poland) to convert to the Focke-Wulf 190. Willy Ferling was among this group, spending three days leave in Dobbiaco (BZ) with his father before arriving at his destination on the 18th. Ferling's flights in the Fw 190F-8 began on the 23rd, none of the five he made that day exceeding nine minutes, which suggests a succession of "circuits and bumps." Other NSG 9 pilots converting to the Fw 190 included *Ofhr.* Günther Gräßer, *Fw.* Horst Greßler, *Fw.* Werner Hensel and *Lt.* Fritz Resch. One immediate consequence was the creation of a pool of spare Ju 87s in Villafranca and log books show that aircraft in the markings of 1./NSG 9 were being flown by pilots of the other *Staffeln*.

After their mission on the 10th, Deutsch and Nawroth had landed in Bovolone, only to be grounded for the next ten days by the fog which hung around the airfield all through the hours of twilight and darkness. Daylight flying was reckoned as suicidal and so they stayed put. They could only bring "D5+FL" home on the 21st, in time to take part in NSG 9's next combat, on the night of 22 December when eight Junkers were up from Villafranca and (almost certainly) the same number from Ghedi. Wintermayr and Hofmann (E8+EL) aborted with engine trouble; Harry Fischer and Heinz Staudt (E8+HL) took off at 16.43 with Forlì as their objective but ended by dropping their bombs through 9/10 cloud cover south west of Ravennna, as did Deutsch and Nawroth. With the advantage of EGON, Kehrer and Koch (E8+CL) and Stollwerck and Fischer (E8+KL) did report bombing the target and causing a large fire, despite "*Flak* of all calibres." NSG 9's normally strict radio silence seems to have slipped that night, allowing MAAF to overhear Ju 87 E8+KH "active between two airfields."

Again *Fl.H.Ber.* 10/VII meticulously listed the bombs expended:

Ju 87s from Villafranca
[1. and 3. *Staffeln*]: 16 x SD 70; 6 x AB 36 Brand; 2 x Brand C 50; 6 x AB 500; 2 x SD 500.

By Ju 87s from Ghedi
[2. *Staffel*]: 28 x SD 70; 2 x SD 500; 6 x AB 500.

Since 2. *Staffel* carried eight centreline loads but only seven complements of underwing bombs, it may be that one aircraft was "armed" with either flares or leaflets.

The evening's flying was not long underway before the first casualty occurred: *Ofw.* Herbert Schink, a 3. *Staffel* pilot, suffered minor injuries when the engine of his Ju 87D-5 (WNr. 131434, E8+BL) failed and he was forced to make an emergency landing 4km south of Villafranca at 16.53. The aircraft itself incurred 50% damage. At 20.05, the Beaufighter of F/L Rees and F/O Beaumont was 30 miles north east of Bologna orbiting a beacon (which flashed the letters "AD" in white light) at 9,000ft when directed toward a southbound bogey a little below. Radar contact came north of Forlì at 4 miles' range and visual, by the light of a three-quarter moon, at 700yds:

Rapidly overtook target and, overshooting, passed underneath it at the same time identifying it as a JU. 87 ... did a tight turn and came in behind ... closing to 200 yards dead astern and on the same level. The JU. 87 apparently sighted the Beaufighter and immediately peeled off to starboard. Beaufighter followed down, firing a period of short bursts. Strikes were seen ... but it still appeared to be under control when last seen at 6,000 feet. No return fire was experienced ...

All contact lost, Rees and Beaumont resumed patrol, waiting a quarter of an hour for their next "trade." Alerted to another bogey, they flew back to the beacon which it appeared to have orbited before heading south. Radar contact again gave way to visual, this time on an enemy weaving gently and climbing at an estimated 130mph:

Opened fire with cannon and machineguns. Saw a heavy concentration of strikes all over the JU. 87 which immediately burst into flames. Beaufighter followed it down through a thin layer of cloud and clearly saw it strike the ground ... 16 miles North west of FORLI. There was no return fire from this E/A.

At 21.20, over Bologna, GCI "ZANEY" called in yet another contact. Beaumont's radar was now performing badly and only gave a trace at one mile. When seen, the target appeared to be orbiting and, owing to the Beaufighter's approach angle, could not be held – in fact "ZANEY" advised that it was now behind them but nonetheless managed to steer them round to a stern chase. They rapidly closed on what they now saw was a Ju 87 making about 120mph. When they opened fire from just 150yds, they:

Saw a good concentration of strikes and numerous pieces were seen to break off the JU.87. The target stalled and went into a spin. There was no return fire ... The Nav/Radio saw the aircraft strike the ground and burst into flames. Both pilot and Observer saw the aircraft burning on the ground.

Dec	22	Beau VI	Q	Self	F/o Beaumont		N.F.T.
Dec	22	Beau VI	Q	Self	F/o Beaumont	卐卐 Patrol.	Forli Area. Both left burning on ground Two Ju 87's Destroyed. One Ju 87 Damaged

Two crews, thought be from 2./NSG 9, with their ground staff and aircraft "J". The man in the rear cockpit appears to be dismounting the MG 81Z machine-guns. The Unteroffizier (third from right) wears a Frontflugspange mission clasp, EK I and pilot's badge on his Fliegerkombi flying suit.

Beaufighter "Q" landed at Cesenatico at 22.15, after three highly successful hours in the air. While the aircraft it damaged cannot be identified as yet, its second and third victims, both from 2./NSG 9 were, respectively:

Ju 87D-5	WNr. 140747, E8+KK:	*Fw.* Edgar Gerstenberger/*Gefr.* Hans Mechlinski, both killed: Lugo (RA).
Ju 87D-5	WNr. 130532, E8+FK:	*Ofhr.* Hans Kolster/*Gefr.* Gustav Leumann both killed: Calderara di Reno (BO).

Confirmation that Gerstenberger had crashed and burned reached Werner Lotsch on his return to Ghedi from convalescent leave. An armourer showed him his former pilot's pistol, recovered from the wreckage: its grips were charred and the ammunition inside had exploded.

The night also brought the only air-to-air victory against NSG 9 by an American night fighter. The Beaufighter of 1/Lt. Albert L. Jones and Flight Officer John Rudovsky of the 414th Night Fighter Squadron had taken off at 20.05 on an intruder mission to Verona. At 21.30:

> While flying W of Mantua at 800ft, seen unidentified aircraft flying N at 900ft. Given chase, was then picked up by radar and identified as Ju 87. Attack was made from dead astern and the e/a went into a dive to starboard and crashed near ASOLA [MN] where it was seen to be burning.

The time and northerly heading suggest that Ju 87D-5 WNr. 140750, E8+JK was returning from its sortie. At such a low level, *Fhj.Ofw.* Artur Heiland und *Uffz.* Artur Ballok may have felt comparatively secure from interception, especially one from below, and were nearing their home airfield. The attack seems to have caught them unawares and both were wounded. NSG 9 had lost a quarter of the small force dispatched; 2. *Staffel*, losing three out of its eight aircraft taking part, had suffered a truly dreadful 37.5% casualty rate.

Although an operation appears to have been planned for Christmas Eve, none took place but on Christmas Night the *Gruppe* put up around 30 sorties. Despite its losses, 2. *Staffel* fought on: *Lt.* von Grone (E8+HK) dropped flares over Loiano on his first trip and claimed a direct hit on the Futa Pass road on his second; *Ofhr.* Ernst Messerschmidt (E8+LK) twice bombed Loiano and then the Faenza–Forlì area. From 3./NSG 9, Kehrer and Koch's E8+CL was guided to Faenza (captured nine days earlier) by EGON and the pilot duly logged, "Widespread conflagration. Vicious *Flak.*" Deutsch and Nawroth (E8+DL) may also have been directed from the ground for, despite solid cloud in the target area, they dropped an AB 500 and four SD 70s from 1,500m on a road junction south of the town. Harry Fischer and Heinz Staudt (E8+LH) dropped their bombs south and south west of the built up area, also remarking on "*Flak* defence of all calibres." Allied sources say only that at 17.32 bombs fell on Faenza and its outskirts.

Bombs

NSG 9 had begun operations with Fiat CR.42s carrying a pair of 50kg general purpose HE bombs. Soon, however, the emphasis shifted to munitions designed to cause damage over the widest possible area rather than destruction at a single point. These included canisters which split to scatter small anti-personnel bomblets; fragmentation bombs of (nominal) 50, 250 and 500kg calibres; 50kg phosphorus bombs and canisters of 1 and 2kg magnesium incendiaries. Flares and propaganda leaflets were also sometimes carried.

ABOVE AND BELOW: *The AB 70 container carried 50 x SD 1 anti-personnel bombs. Total weight loaded 56 kg (111 lbs). Container body diameter 203 mm (8 inches), overall length 1,103 mm (43.5 inches)*

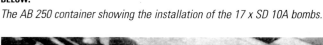
BELOW:
The AB 250 container showing the installation of the 17 x SD 10A bombs.

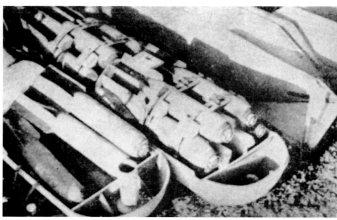

BELOW LEFT: *A Fw 190 being loaded with an AB 250 container which could carry either 224 x SD 1 anti-personnel or 17 x SD 10A fragmentation bombs. Total weight loaded 215 kg (474 lbs).* **BELOW RIGHT:** *Container body diameter 375 mm (14.7 inches), overall length 1,620 mm (63.7 inches).*

ABOVE: *The AB 500 container could carry either 37 x SD 10A fragmentation bombs or 184 x B 1 3 EZ or 116 x B 2 EZ incendiary bombs. Total weight loaded 470 kg (1,034 lbs). Container body diameter 482 mm (19 inches), overall length 2,286 mm (80 inches).*

ABOVE AND ABOVE RIGHT: *The SD 2 known as the 'Butterfly Bomb' was a very effective anti-personnel bomb and could be loaded in varying numbers in different containers. Total weight 2.2 kg (4.8 lbs). Bomb diameter 76 mm (3 inches), overall length and tail 89 mm (3.5 inches).*

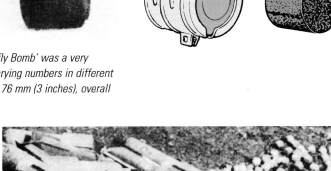

RIGHT: *The AB 23 container was similar to the AB 70 and differed only with the internal fixings for 23 x SD 2 anti-personnel bombs. Total weight loaded 61.6 kg (135.3 lbs). Container body diameter 203 mm (8 inches), overall length 1,103 mm (43.5 inches)*

ABOVE: *The Brand SC 50 incendiary bomb. Total weight 45 kg (99 lbs). Body diameter 203 mm (8 inches), overall length 1,096 mm (43.2 inches).*

BELOW: *The SD 50 fragmentation bomb. Total weight 51 kg (112 lbs). Bomb diameter 203 mm (8 inches), overall length and tail 1,092 mm (43 inches).*

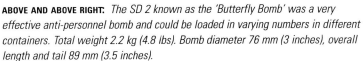

BELOW: *The SD 70 fragmentation bomb. Total weight 66 kg (145 lbs). Bomb diameter 203 mm (8 inches), overall length and tail 1,096 mm (43.2 inches).*

BELOW: *The SD 500 fragmentation or semi-armour piercing bomb. Total weight 535 kg (1,177 lbs). Bomb diameter 445 mm (17.5 inches), overall length and tail 2,286 mm (80 inches).*

Fw. Hans Deutsch (left) and Johannes Nawroth in Villafranca, late December 1944. On the Ju 87's fuselage, behind Nawroth's left shoulder is the E8 unit code of NSG 9. Note also the toned down Balkenkeuz.

Setting off again at 19.25, Deutsch and Nawroth got only as far as Ostiglia (MN) before engine trouble compelled them to turn back, while Harry Fischer attacked a "target south of Bologna." At 22.22, Kehrer and Eck took off in E8+EH to bomb and strafe Faenza and, after an hour back on the ground, went out again to bomb and shoot up artillery positions to the west of the town. Deutsch and Nawroth meanwhile had switched to E8+KL and again bombed a road south of Faenza with an SD 500 and four SD 70s from 2,000m; this time they were able to report direct hits. According to a MATAF Intelligence Summary, bombs also fell on Ancona.

NSG 9's aircraft dropped the following bombs during the night's raids:

From Ghedi: 12 x AB 500, 2 x SD 500, 2 x AB 250, 52 x SD 70

From Villafranca: 6 x AB 500, 9 x SD 500, 54 x SD 70, 8 x AB 70

While Ghedi's figures suggest 14 sorties (one aircraft burdened with a 500kg weapon on the centreline and an AB 250 under each wing), the second set is less clear. Villafranca put up 17 sorties, one of them abortive, while the bombs used equate to 15 main loads and 15.5 wing loads. On the first of three trips, Wintermayr and Hofmann (E8+EL) carried leaflets to Forlì and Faenza. The *Gruppe* dropped 174,000 leaflets during December, as Herbert Kehrer recalls:

> From Villafranca we dropped propaganda material. The Americans had black books of matches with a white "V" on them. We dropped these books with information inside about illnesses that you could fake: 8-10 illnesses, stomach complaints for instance. There were exact descriptions of how you should act, what you should say. A short time after, these books came back in droves with a note — in German — to say our soldiers needed them more than the Allies did.

Warrant Officer Baits and F/S Lothian were about to get shot at by NSG 9 once again. Their Beaufighter ("H") had been patrolling in the Ravenna area for almost two hours before they were given their first bogey at 22.30. When contact proved elusive they were moved across to Bologna and at 22.50 were steered toward a new target, getting to within a mile before an AA barrage came up across their path and they lost the contact while taking avoiding action. At 23.00, word came from "ZANEY" of another bogey coming from the north at 5,000ft; this one was picked up on AI while weaving hard and doing about 120mph. With 30° of flap and lowered undercarriage, they came within 500yds to identify it as a Ju 87 and were past 300yds before it saw them and peeled off before they had it properly in their sights. The Ju 87 dived straight past the Beaufighter, firing tracer from its rear guns. As Baits moved to follow, his starboard engine failed, he immediately feathered the airscrew and set course for base, making a successful landing even though his brakes had gone u/s as well. Later, a single rifle-calibre bullet was found in the defunct engine.

At 00.30, another Beaufighter chased an enemy aircraft from initial contact 10 miles south east of Ghedi to the aerodrome itself, where the bandit landed without lights. The blackout necessitated by the presence of intruders probably helped bring about NSG 9's only "casualty" of the night, a Ju 87 which taxied into a trench on landing at Villafranca and was damaged, this incident passing off without anyone being hurt. Marauding Allied aircraft had long been disrupting NSG 9's take-offs and landings and the American night fighters in particular flew a great many such missions as the war entered its final months. As a passive countermeasure, the *Gruppe* would illuminate a dummy airstrip brightly while starts were effected from the real one without benefit of a flare path. An intruder would often circle a German base for a lengthy period but it was still possible to bring returning friendlies in safely by waiting for the hostile to reach the furthest point of its orbit, rapidly turning on the runway lights and dowsing them before it again drew close. Generally the *Flak* would only open up if it was thought that the Allied machine had spotted a target and was about to bomb or strafe. Rupert Frost told his interrogators after the war that:

> Particularly hectic moments occurred when flares were dropped whilst mechanics were tuning up a motor. Not having heard the approaching plane the resultant overwhelming and not unnatural desire to take cover had to be discouraged by the severest punishments.

Fw. Hans Deutsch (left) and Johannes Nawroth with Ju 87D-5 (yellow "C" on wheel cover) in Villafranca, late December 1944. This aircraft has the shorter exhaust flame damper. Note also the cannon shell ejection chute and the two lugs for the discarded dive brakes.

Early in the evening of the 26th, for their first sortie Fischer and Staudt (E8+LH) dropped bombs south of Faenza and leaflets on artillery positions to the south west. From 2./NSG 9, Ernst Messerschmidt went twice to Brisighella (RA) while Volkmar von Grone registered two direct hits on the Futa Pass road. RAF aircrew noted that two flares fell north of Forlì and that bombing started large fires there. Deutsch and Nawroth were unable to see what they had hit because:

> We were chased by a twin-engined night fighter which either had jammed guns or had run out of ammunition. We started twisting and turning wildly and my plane flew east. Then we were over the Adriatic and [he] tried to drive us into the water. We managed to escape over Comàcchio.

A composite image of a map marked up by Leutnant Volkmar von Grone while Staffelführer of 2./NSG 9 to show code letters of navigational beacons and courses from Ghedi to targets north of Barga (LU), near Monzuno (BO) and south of Forlì. The first of these locations indicates that the map dates from around 27/28 December 1944, when his Staffel supported the German Wintergewitter (Winter Storm) offensive in the Serchio Valley north of Lucca.

For us it was a completely crazy business. He was hard on our heels. We always wondered why he didn't fire. My feelings at the time weren't the best. You saw the enemy and nothing happened apart from him wanting to drive us into the ground or the Adriatic.

The author has been unable to find any Allied report of this pursuit. No. 600 Squadron put up six sorties in the Forlì area that night and noted that two unidentified aircraft had orbited north west of Bologna but these were not contacted; P/O M. Seepish (RCAF) and F/S Paterson were vectored toward a bogey but subsequently advised that it was friendly; the same happened to W/O Smith and F/S Dunford but after midnight. No. 255's two Beaufighters at readiness were not called on to fly; 256 Squadron sent intruders to Sarajevo in Bosnia. As for the USAAF, the 414th NFS had seven Beaufighters on patrol and intruder missions between Bergamo and Ghedi but they attacked only ground targets. The 416th NFS dispatched six Mosquitoes to the Po Valley, one of which encountered an unidentified twin-engine aircraft near Modena but was given the slip. Therefore, whichever Allied aircraft "chased" E8+RH probably never knew how badly it had rattled its crew.

Another wave took off from Villafranca around 19.00 for targets south of Bologna. Fischer and Staudt met bad visibility and, unable to identify the German lines, turned back and landed with their bombs still aboard. Wintermayr and Hofmann carried leaflets and an AB 500 to Loiano; Kehrer and Eck (E8+EH) were able to bomb road traffic while Deutsch and Nawroth (in E8+DL this time) dropped an SD 500 and four SD 70s through solid cloud. Villafranca's total of 10 sorties suggests the night's effort was smaller overall than on the 25th.

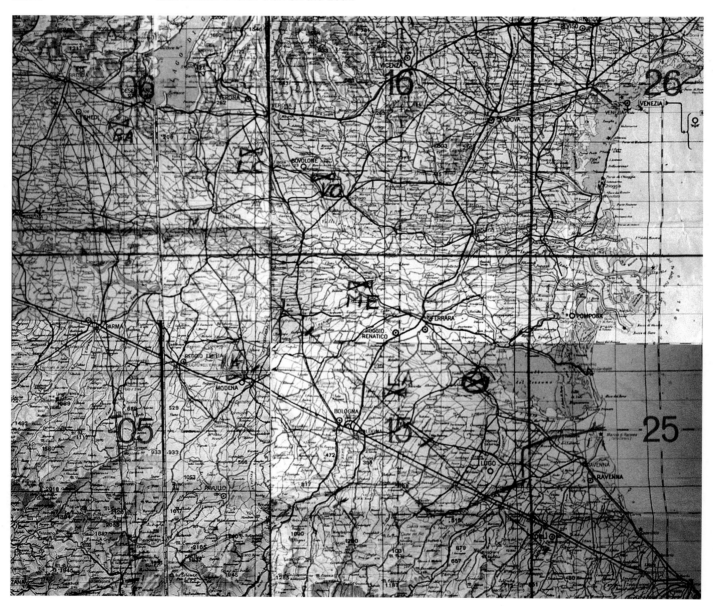

For the night of 27/28 December, targets were assigned in both the eastern and western sectors. Five Ju 87s left Villafranca around 17.00, Kehrer and Eck (E8+CL) bombing artillery positions south of Faenza while Deutsch and Nawroth dropped an AB 500 and four SD 70s on roads south of the town, their E8+DL sustaining hits in its propeller and starboard wing tank from light AA. Fischer and Staudt (E8+LH) found fog up to 1,000m over their target and, unable once again to distinguish friendly positions, jettisoned their bombs before landing in Ghedi. A German counterattack along the valley of the River Serchio was supported by 2./NSG 9 raiding the city of Lucca and the Lucca–Viareggio (LU) road. Warrant Officer Jack L. Ingate (RAAF) and F/O Brewer got into visual contact with a Ju 87 south of Fano at 18.45 but its gunner spotted them, opening fire as his pilot peeled off for a successful evasion, despite the Beaufighter following down to 500ft. This may have been been Ju 87D-5 E8+AL whose *Bordfunker*, Franz Fischer, reported engaging a twin-engined nightfighter. His pilot, Peter Stollwerck had that night used a weapon or technique he had first practised on the 21st: codenamed *Flattermann* ("bat") it entailed dropping four AB 70 containers in level flight.

Although plans were announced next day at 13.00 for a *Nachtschlacht* operation over the eastern sector, this failed to take place. Reinforcements for NSG 9 were in prospect however: a Ju 87 was due to be ferried to Thiene that night and three more to Vicenza on the 30th. Even so, on 31 December the *Gruppe* could muster just seven Ju 87D-3s and 14 D-5s with a total of 12 aircraft serviceable.

Leutnant Volkmar von Grone of 2./NSG 9:

> 1944 was drawing to a close. In the meantime I had been appointed *Staffelführer*...
> Of the ten comrades with whom I'd come to Italy a year before, only two-had survived. That really got to me.

"...That really got to me"

By the end of 1944 the fates of the men who made up the original nucleus of NSG 9 had been:

Maj. Rupert Frost	surviving	
Hptm. August Müller	surviving	
Oblt. Rolf Begemann	shot down by AA, prisoner of war	05.07.44
Lt. Volkmar von Grone	surviving	
Ofw. Horst Greßler	shot down by NF, wounded	02.06.44
Fw. Johann Deffner	killed in crash	06.05.44
Fw. Artur Heiland	shot down by NF, wounded	22.12.44
Uffz. Benno Müller	killed in crash	24.03.44
Uffz. Heinz Müller	shot down by AA, killed	28.04.44
Uffz. Kaspar Stuber	shot down by NF, prisoner of war	28.11.44
Uffz. Werner Waißnor	shot down by NF, killed	27.07.44
Gefr. Ewald Kapahnke	killed in take-off collision	03.07.44
Gefr. Johann Horn	killed in training accident	10.01.44
Gefr. Richard Schwobe	missing in action	26.07.44
Gefr. Franz Spörr	injured	27.07.44
	killed in flying accident	28.11.44

A life in
Wolfgang Leo Hugo Holtz
aviation

During the evening, a mighty drinking session (not to say "piss-up") with the *Staffelstab* from *Ofhr.* downwards. An older *Obgfr.* … took part. At a late hour, he made some humorous-ironic remarks. The *Capitano* bellowed with feigned exaggeration, "Holtz, lie down!", which Holtz immediately did, sharp and brisk, just like a new recruit.
(Dirk Bunsen)

Born in 1905, Wolfgang Holtz began learning to fly aged 18, on an Albatros B. II at Danzig. After his father died in 1927, he crossed the Atlantic, working variously as a carpenter, farmhand, dishwasher, translator, gold miner and porcelain importer. He also found time to gain further civil flying qualifications in Canada and the USA from 1928–29, working as a pilot and instructor and a correspondent for two aviation journals.

At the invitation of the Society of British Aircraft Constructors, he took part in the 1935 flypast for the King at Hendon. Returning to Germany from England on holiday, he reported for duty with the newly formed *Luftwaffe* that August, resigning from his Canadian job. After a spell as personal pilot of

In the snows of the Alps, on their way out of Italy, men of 3./NSG 9 pose for a group portrait with their producer gas powered lorry.
From left: unknown, Uffz. Karl Hofmann, Uffz. Wolfgang Holtz and Uffz. Kurt Wagner. Holtz wears the Gold Pilot's Mission Clasp, EK I and Deutsches Kreuz.

the commander of *Luftzeuggruppe 5*, Holtz joined the *Luftwaffe* Reserve in March 1937, serving with 2./KG 155. He was made a *Flugkapitän* and became a *Leutnant* in October of that year, embarking on a 12-month probationary period prior to acceptance as a regular officer.

He served in the Spanish Civil War between August 1936 and February 1937, amassing 52 troop transport flights across the Straits of Gibraltar and 147 combat sorties. In the Polish campaign he held a staff appointment but made four operational flights over France in October 1939. In 1940, as III./KG 26's Technical Officer, he flew 17 missions over Norway, hitting the Port Admiral's HQ at Narvik and bringing his Heinkel home, despite 23 AA hits and with every other member of his crew wounded. In the days that followed, he was credited with direct hits on four merchant ships, winning the EK II and Narvik Shield. During the Battle of Britain he nursed an He 111 back from Scotland over the North Sea on one engine to a belly landing in Stavanger and racked up another 16 missions during the night *Blitz* on Britain's cities.

With III./KG 76 in Russia, he flew 38 more ops on Ju 88s and Heinkels before being posted as *Staffelkapitän* to 3./*Störkampfgruppe Luftwaffenkommando Don* from 1 November 1942. Over the next four months he undertook 52 day and night sorties, being awarded the Gold Pilot's Clasp on 31 January. His unit fought in the retreat from the Oskol River to Kursk and over Poltava, attacked partisans in the woods around Bryansk and supported the recapture of Kharkov. It was near that city, on 17 March 1943, that he was wounded in one knee and sent home on convalescent leave. Returning to the front on 3 June, he flew another 85 missions over the Kuban River bridgehead in the Caucasus. Leading the *Einsatzstab* of 3. and 6. *Störkampfstaffeln Luftflotte 4* from 20 July, *Hauptmann* Holtz covered the withdrawal from the bridgehead without a single loss and was duly mentioned in dispatches; on 16 August, he was awarded the *Deutsches Kreuz*.

During October, Holtz was again convalescing — this time from nervous exhaustion — in a sanatorium in Zakopane, Poland. Returning to duty in November, he was arrested, charged with contravening Article 92 of the Military Code[1] and court-martialled. His wife, *Dr.* Mathilde Holtz, did not learn of these proceedings until the following March, being told that an *Oberleutnant* had denounced him[2]. The precise allegations remain obscure but seem to have involved both sabotage and failure to carry out orders.

By this time, Holtz was incarcerated at Spandau outside Berlin and although his wife was permitted to visit, the whole affair was classified top secret and the State Prosecutor would not let her see any papers. She was however tipped off by a prison guard that one "*Rittmeister X*" had handed correspondence between her and her husband to the *Gestapo* and that she should expect her home to be searched.

The capriciousness of the Nazi system which had imprisoned Wolfgang Holtz now came to his aid. Returning downcast to her Berlin hotel, his wife encountered an old college friend and poured out her woes. He, it transpired, was a high-ranking officer in the SD. Next morning he drove *Dr.* Holtz to the State Prosecutor's office, leaving her outside in the car until eventually he emerged and pressed the secret dossier into her hands. He went on to say that there had been a denunciation against her on file and that he had torn it up. Her benefactor then took her straight to the station and the next train home.

On the journey, Mathilde Holtz was at last able to read the charges laid against her husband. In Berlin she hired a lawyer who charged her RM3,000 (almost her yearly income as a physician) and took custody of the files. She amassed evidence of her husband's innocence, even stowing away on a troop train to the Eastern Front to track down witnesses there. People in high places she "bombarded with letters", *Frau Göring's* reply offering tips on how to get through to the *Reichsmarschall* himself. For a week *Dr.* Holtz stood outside the Interior Ministry on Berlin's Unter den Linden. She made daily visits to Göring's chancellery, only to be politely shown the door until one day his car passed the gate she was waiting by. Seizing her chance, Mathilde Holtz dashed over and pushed her petition through the car's window. Next, she "fought my way through the War Ministry", finally reaching the office of one *Freiherr* von Hammerstein where she found a school friend of her lawyer and demanded that her husband "be set free immediately and his rank restored — no more and no less."

To the astonished von Hammerstein she made — "in a kind of trance" — an "inflammatory speech" about the huge patriotic commitment of the *Luftwaffe's* young men, telling him he should look elsewhere for saboteurs, in the Army for instance. She suggested he ask himself why thousands of officers and umpteen thousand other ranks should be sitting in prison for trifling offences, deliberately pulled out of the front lines. In the same way, "the sparrows were already singing from the rooftops" about the wrong supplies delivered to the Front: there was his sabotage!

Wolfgang Leo Hugo Holtz

When she had calmed down somewhat, von Hammerstein gently explained that convicted men could not simply be released, even when there was evidence that they were innocent, and that the proper retrial procedures had to be followed. However, two weeks later came the 20 July bomb plot against Hitler; three days after that, Wolfgang Holtz was back home, one of the first in a wave of prisoners let out at this time (presumably to make way for conspirators, real and imagined). His health had suffered during confinement and he was admitted to a *Luftwaffe* sanatorium. As for "that nice *Rittmeister*" who had denounced Mathilde Holtz, "he became a hero of the 20th of July."[2]

Meanwhile, *Dr.* Holtz passed word via her lawyer that she would agree to her husband going back to the Front provided his rank was restored and during December 1944 she got a letter from the authorities saying that, given the strained military situation, he could either return to operations or be posted to the *Volkssturm*. She was promised that after flying five missions he would get his *Hauptmann's* rank back and his retrial would go ahead even if he were killed in action. So it was that in January 1945 *Flieger* Holtz was sent to Italy and 3./NSG 9. It turned out however that *Major* Frost knew nothing of the promised restoration of rank, leaving Holtz to work his way up again — as far as *Unteroffizier* before the war ended. At 39, he was older than most of his fellow airmen and seems to have been a popular and respected figure, not least in the eyes of his *Staffelkapitän*, Heinz Buß. He would do sterling service to his new comrades as the *Reich* that had condemned him fell apart. He would survive the war but never return home.

BELOW: *A resumé of Wolfgang Holtz's flying career in the Spanish Civil war, the Norwegian Campaign, the night Blitz on Britain and in the East, copied from his pass book.*

ABOVE: *The achievements that won Wolfgang Holtz his many decorations, summed up in March 1943 by his Gruppenkommandeur as "tact, courage, excellent flying skill [and] exemplary aggressive spirit..." Seven months later he would face a court martial for sabotage and failing to carry out orders.*

---

1. Dr. Holtz understood that her husband's unit was simultaneously broken up and its personnel dispersed. In fact the two *Staffeln* became 1. and 2./NSG 6 respectively as part of the general reorganisation of the *Nachtschlacht* arm then underway.

2. Subsequently she heard that this officer had been a spy and had defected to Sweden.

"The Ju below struck us"

NSG 9's first operation of 1945 was probably a 2. *Staffel* attack with bombs and gunfire on partisans south of Monte Rosa, close by the Swiss border, on the afternoon of New Year's Day. On the 3rd, another early evening start from Villafranca began inauspiciously when E8+LH's oil feed failed on take-off. Its crew, Harry Fischer and Heinz Staudt, were forced to jettison their fuselage bomb (not yet armed) into Lake Garda before attempting a landing from this, their third abortive mission in a row. At 18.00, after 40 minutes in the air, E8+AL (Deutsch and Nawroth) too landed back at base, with electrical failure. Kehrer and Eck's E8+EH attacked Monghidoro (BO) under the instructions of EGON controller "KASPAR", meeting searchlights and all calibres of AA. The 2./NSG 9's Ernst Messerschmidt flew a mission to Bagnocavallo (RA) in Ju 87D-5 E8+KH. MATAF logged three unidentified aircraft over Highway 65 around 15-20 miles south of Bologna at 17.30 and there was a report from ground forces of one aircraft brought down near Pianoro (BO) at that time but no record of a corresponding German loss has come to light. Allied troops also counted 30 incendiaries and six anti-personnel bombs dropped near Sassoleone (BO) during the night.

The parlous state of fuel supplies and the dormancy of 1. *Staffel* had their part to play in depressing the sortie rate, as did the miserable winter weather which scrubbed missions planned for the night of 6/7 January. Six bombs reportedly fell near Lucca on the 15th and four nights later "a small formation

Aircrew of 3./NSG 9, Winter 1944/45. Off-camera, someone has just shaken the snow from a tree on to (from left) Uffz. Franz Fischer, Uffz. Kurt Wagner, Obgfr. Harry Fischer, Gefr. Kurt Schölzel and Obgfr. Heinz Staudt (MIA, 22.04.45).

of Ju 87s" operated over Eighth Army's front but none of these missions features in the available pilots' log books. As for the ground fighting, Allied offensive activity had closed down after Christmas and the lines were to remain virtually fixed for the next three months apart from local efforts by the Allies to improve their positions in the expectation of a spring offensive.

The *Gruppe* had ended 1944 with a mere 21 aircraft and on 10 January this had not changed. ULTRA gives us a breakdown between the *Staffeln* for the 15th:

Stab	1(0)	Ju 87D
1.	–	–
2.	13(11)	Ju 87D
3.	10(8)	Ju 87D

On the 20th, orders were given for road strafing on the eastern part of the front by Ju 87s flying from Verona from 15.00 onward but only a small force, possibly as few as six, took part. Kehrer and Eck – again in E8+EH and again with EGON – dropped their main bomb on Russi (RA) and went on to place their incendiaries near Ravenna. Deutsch and Nawroth (E8+DL) also bombed Russi with an AB 500 and four SD 70s. From 2. *Staffel*, *Lt.* Friedrich Müller and *Gefr.* Werner Lotsch (Ju 87D-5 E8+KK) took off from Ghedi at 17.10 and bombed an artillery position north of Bagnocavallo, returning to base at 19.30; Ernst Messerschmidt and *Gefr.* Hettling (E8+NH) followed a few minutes behind them.

Lotsch subsequently entered "defence: night fighters" in his logbook and among them was "China 28", flown by S/L Coleman and F/O Frumar who had last intercepted a Ju 87 the previous May (see page 36). After only a quarter hour in the air, they had seen incendiaries burning on the ground 3 miles north east of Forlì and two minutes later, at 17.47, had a contact 3 miles away at their own 10,000ft altitude. The target was making 200mph but executing no more than a gentle weave by way of evasive action. Apparently unseen, they closed in to 400yds and opened fire from dead astern:

> Saw a good concentration of strikes and the target burst into flames and went straight down, being seen to explode on hitting the ground. There was no return fire at any time during the combat.

Claim one Ju. 87 destroyed

Within a minute they were alerted to the next bogey, 1½ miles away and coming head on. This passed them 200yds to starboard and they could do no more than identify it as a Ju 87 before losing contact. There was a wait of six minutes for their third target which was apparently being engaged from the ground by Bofors guns. Again they were able to come in from behind without themselves being fired on by the Ju 87 and opened fire as it began to dive:

> The aircraft was last seen diving for the ground. Army and RAF Regiment report a JU. 87 crashing 2 miles N.E. of FUSIGNANO [RA] between 17.58 and 17.59 hrs. The pilot was seen to bale out and landed in enemy territory. The rear guns were recovered from this aircraft.

This aircraft is claimed as destroyed

The first of these claims is not confirmable from German records but there is ample evidence to pinpoint the second. An RAF Field Intelligence Team visited the crash site and reported:

> Ju 87D shot down by fighter into No Man's Land c. 18.00hrs 21 [sic] January 1945. One crew member bailed out on Allied side of SENIO but evaded. Name on harness: FISCHER. Dropped 4 x 50kg bombs. Crash at MR M.4443 (approx.)

This was Ju 87D-5 WNr. 140717 (E8+AL) of 3./NSG 9 which had been flown, under EGON guidance, by *Ofhr.* Peter Stollwerck. His *Bordfunker*, *Uffz.* Franz Fischer, recalls the incident:

RIGHT: *Ofhr. Peter Stollwerck of 3./NSG 9 was shot down on 20 January 1944. He and his Bordfunker, Franz Fischer, bailed out into No Man's Land but regained their own lines.*

> Fired on by night fighter … at about 4,000m altitude. Dropped the bombs [1 x AB 500 incendiary and 4 x LC 50 flares] and dived to 600m. Fired on by light *Flak*. Coolant loss, engine fire. Baled out from about 300m, landed in No Man's Land with a heavy blow to the right foot and shrapnel in right hand. Fired on by machine-guns in forward outposts. After recognition, guided through minefield and taken by motorcycle to the command post of a *Waffen-SS* battalion. There I met Peter Stollwerck. At dawn taken by lorry to the Po. Taken across the Po by night and then on to Villafranca. There I put myself in the hands of the doctors.

Stollwerck too had jumped into No Man's Land. As his parachute opened, the name card in its pack had fluttered down on the east wind to be picked up by German soldiers. Unaware of thus having introduced himself and trying to get his bearings, he was taken aback to hear shouts of "Stollwerck, over here!" After regaining friendly lines, Stollwerck was back with 3. *Staffel* on the 22nd, becoming "quasi-adjutant" to its *Kapitän, Hptm.* Heinz Buß.

Coleman and Frumar had meanwhile gained a freelance contact; coming head on and closing rapidly, it passed right over them with only 50ft clearance, readily recognisable as a Ju 87. They orbited but could not find it again and within a minute were sent north by "ZANEY" as the bandits were now heading for home. At 18.02, ten miles north of Ravenna, they got an AI contact at four miles and, descending to 4,000ft, closed in until they could identify it against the lighter part of the sky as yet another Ju 87. They fired three bursts at the comparatively long range of 600yds and registered hits but the Junkers did not catch fire. Their target in this case may well have been E8+FL since Harry Fischer and Heinz Staudt attacked roads between Russi (RA) and Bagnocavallo and returned to report being fired on by a night fighter. After one final, fruitless chase, Coleman and Frumar returned to Cesenatico, completing a singularly busy 70 minutes in the air. Fischer and Staudt set out twice more, the first time bombing traffic columns on the move near Castel del Rio (BO), on the second trip turning back with a failed generator.

The second night fighter crew on patrol, W/O C.M. Ward and F/S J.L. Richards were up for a mere 30min. Their Beaufighter (V8705,"Q") had been scrambled at 17.40, vectored on to 320° by "SYRUP" and got an AI contact near Ravenna. Despite throttling back and climbing, they still overshot. Requesting the controllers' help at 18.00 they were told that "China 28" had a contact and were ordered due north before being sent on to 220° four minutes later. Then:

> Two bursts were fired from dead astern of Beaufighter. Nav/Rad heard the firing.
> First burst passed under the port wing, second burst hit aircraft. Pilot dived steeply
> away and called up for emergency landing as he was slightly injured in the neck.

After ten months of combat against one another, almost three more would pass before No. 600 Squadron and NSG 9 exchanged fire again.

On the 21st, Deutsch and Nawroth (E8+HL) took off at 17.30, followed a minute later by Wintermayr and Hofmann (E8+RH) who were to use EGON. Hans Nawroth has understandably vivid memories what followed:

> [To avoid] being picked up by English radar, we flew at low level from Villafranca to Bologna and then climbed to 3,000m. From there we flew on to the target area or were guided there by the EGON system. As were were spiralling up so comfortably, I saw another Ju 87 [coming] from the eastward (which was already in darkness) directly under us. It was already too late and the Ju below struck us.
>
> I can never forget the sight of *Uffz.* Karl Hofmann – overcome with fright, you might well say [and] certainly I would have felt no different – curled up and covering his head with both arms. Hans Deutsch subsequently dropped his bombs [an AB 500 with fragmentation munitions and four containers of 1kg incendiaries on Castel del Rio from 2,000m] and we were back again in Villafranca.
>
> Our machine had been hit hard in the collision with Carl Wintermayr. Shortly before landing, Hans Deutsch told me he was going to jettison the landing gear since he didn't know if one of the tyres might be damaged. This he duly did and we made a belly landing that went off well. So about half to three-quarters of an hour later, an Italian turned up at the aerodrome carrying an undercarriage leg and saying one of our planes had lost it.
>
> As I found out later, Wintermayr's aircraft was badly damaged … in one of its wings and elsewhere. Hofmann's MG 81Z was bent right out of shape, the two

A Luftwaffe Unteroffizier sits on one of the 3.7cm Flak guns defending Villafranca aerodrome. At the right are two Italian Hiwis (volunteers), in the background gutted hangars. Both the gun barrel and the metal box at the rear of the emplacement have been painted to camouflage them.

barrels in a half-circle pointing upward. From the damage you could see how lucky we two crews had been...

Remarkably, Wintermayr and Hofmann flew twice more that night, albeit in other aircraft. Kehrer and Eck (+CL) also flew three sorties:

17.37-19.20:	Leaflets in areas Fontanèlice and Firenzuola. Strafed lorries.
20.45-22.00:	Bombs on Fontanèlice and Castel del Rio. 1 lorry shot up and set on fire.
22.52-00.05:	Incendiary bombs on Monte [illegible]

Messerschmidt and Hettling (E8+LK) and Müller and Lotsch (+K) flew from Ghedi at 17.33 and 17.35 respectively against the village of Grizzana Morandi (BO), south of Bologna. A second attempt by the former crew ended after 11 minutes when E8+KH's electrics failed, while von Grone and Lenz (+HK) flew sorties to the area south east of Vergato and to the Futa Pass.

According to the Allies, the night's events unfolded as follows:

17.35:	P-61 of 414th NFS in contact with a hostile for 4 minutes, 25 miles north of Florence.
18.09:	Florence, Army on red alert as radar stations report eight hostile aircraft in Bologna-Florence area.
18.10:	Bombs dropped in the vicinity of Castiglione (L-7310), resulting in 15 casualties.
18.11:	Window and bombs reported at map reference L-9231.
18.19:	Strafing at L-8712.
18.25:	"All clear" in Florence.
21.09:	Strafing reported at L-9219.
21.10:	Army above 44° North on red alert.
21.17:	Bombing reported at L-8712.
21.23:	Strafing reported at L-9522.
21.51:	"All clear" in Army area.
23.45:	Bombing reported at L-9531.

The anti-aircraft gunners engaged no enemy aircraft until 18.45, then at 19.15 a crew from 600 Sqn. reported seeing one shot down by light AA over the River Reno. The only known NSG 9 loss was from 2. *Staffel*, Ju 87D-5 WNr. 142082 crashing along the Castenédolo-Montichiari (BS) road while returning from its mission. This was caused by engine trouble reported as "probably attributable to enemy action" and both *Fhr.* Bernd Jungfer und *Uffz.* Fritz Geide were injured. Werner Lotsch recalls that Jungfer had already bailed out twice at night along with his gunner. Incidents where an aircraft was lost but its crew emerged unhurt are the hardest to pinpoint from surviving records and it is possible therefore that Jungfer's jumps account for two of the several night fighter and AA victory claims yet to be matched with a German loss.

On 22 January, Thunderbolts of the American 350th FG attacked Villafranca and claimed four Ju 87s destroyed. Nevertheless, between 22.00 and 00.40 on the night of 22/23 January, seven Junkers dropped anti-personnel, high explosive and incendiary bombs along Highway 9 between the River Senio and Faenza: no casualties were reported but one or two vehicles were damaged. Fischer and Staudt (E8+FL) bombed moving lorries at Castel del Rio but broke off a second sortie when their generator failed. Flying his last two sorties in Italy, 2./NSG 9's *Lt.* von Grone (E8+FK) claimed a direct hit on a bridge north of Castiglione. The *Gruppe* did not go into action again until the 28th: Deutsch and Nawroth (E8+DL) loitered for a while south of Bologna but finding no break in the weather eventually dropped their bombs from 3,000m through solid cloud. Kehrer and Eck (E8+EH) again used EGON in their attack on Fontanèlice; Stollwerck (in a new E8+AL with *Uffz.* Rafael Szyglowski) bombed Faenza while Fischer and Staudt's (E8+FL) targets were Allied positions in the mountains south east of Imola (BO). These attacks broke with the pattern of recent nights by getting underway much later, from about 20.20.

Meanwhile, in Silesia the pilots of 1. *Staffel* were continuing their training on the Fw 190. Most of the flights had been extremely brief and were recorded simply as "conversion" but as the course progressed, they had come to include orientation, low flying, bomb release from low level, high altitude flight (up to 8,000m) and practice dives. All this was rudely interrupted by the Red Army, as Willy Ferling relates:

> 20 January, School flees from Schroda to Berlin-Staaken. (Russians firing on the airfield, catastrophic state of affairs, burning aircraft etc.). First attempted take-off at 12.15 [in Fw 190F-8 "22"] aborted after 10 minutes with engine trouble. Second try at 14.20 successful. 15.12, landed in Staaken [after a 300km flight].

Horst Greßler:

> Schroda airfield was being fired on by Russians. We had to quit the base in full flight. We headed for Berlin-Staaken.

Other units could not escape Schroda so cleanly: 9./SG 77 reported blowing up five of its Fw 190F-8s in the face of the approaching tanks; *Uffze.* Heinz Niemann and Helmut Hemann of 3./NSG 4 had been stranded by instrument failure but managed to get their Ju 87D-3 (WNr. 31141, 1K+BM) away although it was some days before they could rejoin their unit.

Despite frequent Allied bombing, once it arrived in Staaken the NSG 9 contingent began learning to fly the Fw 190 by night. In Ferling's case this took a week and 25 flights, the longest of them lasting 10 minutes. Also in training at Staaken during January was *Fhj.Fw.* Franz Züger. Another former instructor, already well acquainted with the Fw 190 in the ground-attack and *Wilde Sau* roles, now he was learning to become a *Nachtschlachtflieger*. Züger flew practice bombing sorties first by day and then at night to a range at Jüterbog, south of Berlin. After his training school had been pitched into action in early February against Russian bridgeheads on the Oder, he too would be posted to NSG 9. *Feldwebel* Paul-Ernst Zwarg was to arrive by a somewhat different route:

> I was a flying instructor with FFS [Pilot School] C20 — subsequently B20 — in Rosenborn, near Breslau [now Wroclaw, Poland] … All the B and C schools were disbanded since the war situation was so bad and bombers no longer operated. Only the Ju 88, Fw 190 and Messerschmitt types were flying, by night.
>
> After the school was disbanded in 1944, we instructors came to units that could fly the Fw 190 day fighter by night. After converting on to the Fw 190 we practised night operations at Copenhagen in Denmark. So I came [from SG 111] to 1. *Staffel* NSG 9 on the Fw 190.

Dirk Bunsen had finished his course at Air Warfare School 12 in mid-January (as had Helmut Schäfer) and, after two weeks' home leave, was making his way back to Italy. Having missed out on Fw 190 training, he found himself reassigned from 1. to 3. *Staffel*. His journey exemplifies some of the difficulties under which the Germans in Italy were labouring:

> The rail journey terminated in Bolzano (viaduct blown up). At night, waiting for hours in an enormous hall. Then someone called, "There's a bus going to Trento!" Moving

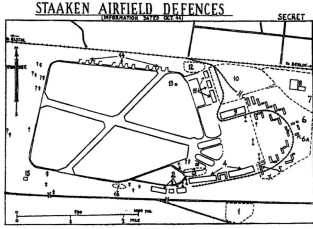

STAAKEN AIRFIELD DEFENCES
(INFORMATION DATED OCT. 44)
SECRET

When the Red Army's January 1945 offensive forced 1./NSG 9's pilots out of Schroda, they finished their conversion to the Fw 190 at Berlin-Staaken. This plan was drawn by RAF Intelligence based on inormation from a prisoner who had been there until the previous October. The vertical arrows represent Flak machine-gun posts, the crossed arrows 2cm cannon. Hangars are at 2, 4 and 11; the HQ building at 5 and the base commander's house at 15.

W.Nr.581632 (in white)

slowly and cautiously the vehicle felt its way through the starry, freezing night down the military road along the River Adige. Because of the air raids, we spent a day and half a night in the sub-basement of the *Fascio* Building in Trento. I finally got to Verona in the early hours, after crouching from midnight to 04.00 on the ice-cold, draughty flatbed of a truck. In the soldiers' hostel on Corso Cangrande (which ran from the bombed-out station to the Arena) I sank into a dreamless sleep under three woollen blankets until 11.00. During the day, stroll around Verona; late afternoon, by suburban railway to Povegliano [Veronese] where the *Capitano* and his staff were based at that time in the *Scuola Comunale* [town school].

In Povegliano, Bunsen was billeted with the family of a pharmacist.

… A couple of days later we moved to the *Kasino* in Villafranca, the requisitioned home of a lawyer whose plaque still hung on the street frontage. At the rear… was an enclosed garden [where] at the end of March we dug foxholes on account of the increasing air raid alerts (Radio: *Apparecchi nemici vengono verso Verona!)*[1]

On the 28th, Peter Stollwerck logged an attack on vehicle columns near Castel del Rio. Raids on the night of 29/30 January involved groups of two or three aircraft (as estimated from the receiving end) spread over the nine hours from dusk to 03.00. The first mission set out a little too early for comfort. Second Lieutenants Clark Eddy and Richard Sulzbach of Silver Section, 346th FS, 350th FG were (as Eddy wrote to Hans Nawroth in 1994) on dusk patrol, "hoping to locate your Ju 87s, as you had been hitting our troops at dusk on a pretty regular basis." Acting on information from Signals Intelligence, "COOLER" had vectored their P-47s toward various northbound bogeys but with no success. It was 18.00 when, five miles north of Bologna, low on fuel and heading for home, the Americans spotted 1,500ft above and to the west of them, seven Ju 87s "clearly outlined in the last light of day." The following account draws on Clark Eddy's 1945 diary and (words in italics) his letter of 1994:

We climbed at 180mph and as we were silhouetted against the ground, we were unseen until we opened up on "tail end Charlie." *The sky was lit up with our tracers.* Dick and I both got in solid bursts and he was seen to crash. After having followed the first plane down a short way, we chandelled up to find another bandit behind us. When we came head on he turned and did a wing-over. We were both shooting at him all the time. Our bursts were good but we did not observe any crash as we immediately turned to protect our tails.

We saw the wreckage of one in the snow on the ground and believed we probably downed another. Score: one Ju 87 destroyed, one Ju 87 probable. Hoping that 5th Army can confirm the probable.

It was Peter Stollwerck's E8+AL (with a *Hptm.* Jahn in the backseat) that they had chased down: he jettisoned his bombs but took hits from infantry fire. Although the German crews were from 3./NSG 9, their aircraft came from all three *Staffeln*, for example: E8+EH (Kehrer and Eck), E8+BK (Deutsch and Nawroth) and E8+FL (Fischer and Staudt). Nawroth tells how:

> Over the Bologna area we had contact with two enemy fighters, Spitfires, one of which opened fire on us. I returned fire and must without question have hit it to judge from the tracers. Since they were armoured along the sides, it couldn't have caused any damage.

From Clark Eddy's viewpoint:

> Your gunners made every effort to shoot us down but fortunately for us your 9mm machine-guns had too short a trajectory even to reach us. We suffered no hits. Our 50 caliber machine-guns were much more powerful and had a much flatter trajectory, as was so evident in the darkness.

From the Allied side the engagement was seen as a great success, moving F/O Runciman of HQ 62 Fighter Wing to write to White Fighter Control:

> Air warning has been excellent … It is hoped that [you] will give a repeat performance of the job done on the night of January 29th during which one enemy aircraft was destroyed, one claimed probable and one damaged by the Dusk Patrol.

In fact there is no record or recollection on the Germans' part that any of their number was shot down. Herbert Kehrer:

> I still remember that mission well. I can say with 100% certainty that all the aircraft came back, we had no losses.

Deutsch, Fischer, Stollwerck and Wintermayr jettisoned their bombs but Kehrer went on to attack long-suffering Loiano by EGON, reporting heavy and light *Flak* in the target area. Their encounter with the P-47s did not excuse the crews from further missions that night: Stollwerck and E8+AL flew another three with Szyglowski as *Bordfunker*; Kehrer and Eck went out again at 20.10 for another EGON sortie, this time against Fontanèlice; Deutsch and Nawroth followed suit, dropping an AB 500 and four SD 70s from 3,000m.

Taking off again at 20.35, Harry Fischer and Heinz Staudt reported night fighters over the target and took a hit in their radio mast. This damage was probably from AA fire since none of the four defending Beaufighters and one Mosquito of 600 Sqn so much as made a contact. Fischer went out again in the same aircraft (E8+FL) at 23.30 and this time was attacked near Villafranca; Heinz Staudt's radio failed and they aborted, landing after 24 minutes in the air. The 416th NFS had four Mosquitoes on intruder missions in "the area of Milan and West of Milan" which — apparently unaware of the alarm they had caused this Ju 87 crew — reported only the destruction of 12 motor and six horse-drawn vehicles. Fischer and Staudt's fourth take-off of the night came at 01.50 to raid Loiano; Deutsch and Nawroth also took part and used the same weapons, guidance and attack altitude as they had over Fontanèlice five hours earlier. The Allies had their own perspective on all this activity:

> From 1800 until 0215 hours enemy aircraft were reported in groups of 2 to 3 in the LEGHORN [Livorno], BOLOGNA, IMOLA, FORLI areas. They were believed to be JU-87s. Flares were dropped in the LEGHORN area at 0215 hours, guns were attacked 20 miles south of BOLOGNA at 1815 hours, the road straffed at L-7512 at 2115 and 1 bomb dropped at 2117 at M-009175 damaging 1 M/T but causing no casualties.

A few days later, a MAAF Field Intelligence unit recovered four unexploded SD 10A anti-personnel bomblets from an AB 500 canister that had fallen on a hillside at 00.25 on the 30th.

ABOVE: *Lieutenant Clark. Eddy of 346th FS claimed a Ju 87 of 3./NSG 9 damaged at last light on 29 January 1945. This photograph was taken after he had shot down two Italian Bf 109s on 2 April 1945. His P-47D was named "Chickenbones."*

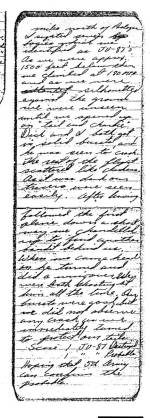

BELOW: *Lieutenant Clark Eddy's diary records his and Lt Richard Suzlbach's interception of a group of Ju 87s from 3./NSG 9 on 29 January "1944" (1945 in fact).*

RIGHT: *By the end of January 1945, the De Havilland Mosquito was serving with three RAF and one USAAF squadrons in Italy. The type's claims against NSG 9 amounted to one Fw 190 destroyed and one damaged, neither of which is recalled by Gruppe veterans. In return, Fw. Werner Hensel claimed a Mosquito shot down on or about 20 April 1945.*

RIGHT: *Unteroffizier Rafael "Rolf" Szyglowski of 3./NSG 9 flew as Peter Stollwerck's Bordfunker in January 1945, after Stollwerck's regular back-seater, Franz Fischer, was injured on the 20th.*

LEFT: *Victory Board of the 346th Fighter Squadron, 350th FG. Entries 31 and 32 are Ju 87s of 3./NSG 9 claimed by Lts Eddy and Sulzbach on 29 January 1945.*

BELOW: *On 29 January 1945, Peter Stollwerck logged an encounter with "Night fighters (Spitfires)" which pursued his aircraft to ground level and forced him to jettison his bombs. These were in fact the P-47s of Lts Eddy and Sulzbach of the 346th Fighter Squadron, day fighters on a last light patrol.*

| 31. | -"- | -"- | 29.1. 1945 | 1712 1820 68ᵐ | . | Villafranca Raum Bologna Villafranca. | Nachtjäger (Spitfire) Treffer durch eigen. Infanteriewaffen. | Kampfeinsatz HKL Nacht auf Lonato. Wegen Nachtjägeran- griff u. Verfolgung bis in Boden- nähe Bomben im Notwurf u. Feindflug abgebrochen | Hptm. Palm |

On 29 January, a paper was issued by *Oberstlt.* Hallensleben, commanding NSG 1 and NSG 2 in western Germany. This discussed the introduction of the "Egon double control procedure", drawing on a "consolidated report of theoretical and practical operational tests and operational experiences of NSG 9" which apparently ran to 19 pages or more. Hallensleben suggested that reliance on the manual processing of electronic data (in the form of radar returns) and the relaying of spoken instructions meant that the system's theoretical potential could not be realised in practice. For NSG 9's operations, fine control plotting was done with 1:2500 scale maps of the target area but these took a considerable time to prepare and so were only practicable for fixed targets selected well in advance. While the radars used were capable of producing plots accurate down to 25 metres, handling these was, according to Hallensleben:

> ...impossible. For instance, if an average speed of 360km per hour is assumed for an Fw 190, that means that the aircraft flies 100 metres in a second. Even at the best, however, and with good liaison between the first and second control position, plots can only be passed through at the rate of one a second. This means that only distances to the nearest 100 metres can be reported [and] with the normal measuring scale ... of the Freya [radar] it is only occasionally possible to measure to the nearest 50 metres. The degree of accuracy which is given by this can be shown on a map of 1:100,000.

With its heavy commitment against supply routes through mountain passes, NSG 9 was engaging immobile targets on a front currently in effective stalemate. It may also have been the case that the slower speed of its Ju 87s was allowing the *Gruppe* to plot more accurately but controllers in Italy had also contended with the Focke-Wulf during *Einhorn's* deployment and would shortly be handling the type again.

January, during which NSG 9 had reportedly flown just 90 sorties over six nights, ended with notice from *Komm. Gen.* that: "In future special instructions for marking [the] front line for safe carrying out of night ground attack operations will no longer be given. Most frequent possible marking of front line by white Verey lights to be requested from beginning of operation." But it would be 11 weeks before any of the crews mentioned above flew again and Volkmar von Grone would leave NSG 9 entirely:

> We could all see that the end of the war was coming. Early in 1945 I caught hepatitis and was admitted to the *Wehrmacht* hospital at Gardone on Lake Garda, a welcome opportunity to catch my breath for once. There, one fine day, we had a visit from the Italian *Duce*, Mussolini, accompanied by two adjutants. The door of my room opened and there appeared before me an amazingly small figure with an impressive Caesar's head. With a powerful handshake, he awarded me – amongst other things – the Italian gold pilot's badge which I was very proud of.
>
> With my convalescence at an end, so too was my Italian interlude. I got myself transferred to the Berlin front to be nearer my family...[2]

---

1. "Enemy aircraft heading for Verona!"

2. He joined NSG 8 which began transferring from Norway to Wunsdorf on 16 January and, after rest and refitting, operated against Soviet foces threatening Berlin before disbanding at Hohn in Schleswig-Holstein in May 1945.

The Night Fighter Problem

> There has been considerable interest … at DAF in possible new methods of radar control of German night fighters. I wish they might be able to lure some of them sufficiently far south to fall into our hands.
>   (Capt Truman M. Webster of MAAF Prisoner Interrogation, 31 March 1945)

Reports of night fighter sightings or attacks, whether single- or twin-engined, were far from unusual over northern Italy in the early months of 1945. Allied aircrew and their commanders believed they faced a genuine threat but the problem for the present-day researcher lies in reconciling these eyewitness reports with the *Luftwaffe's* order of battle. That NSG 9's Fw 190s flew night fighting sorties — albeit not with the upward firing guns reported by some Allied bomber crews — is certain and there is testimony from the immediate postwar period, by *Gen.* von Pohl and officers of his Staff, that Bf 109s were likewise employed. In 25 years' research into the *Aeronautica Nazionale Repubblicana*, authors Ferdinando D'Amico and Gabriele Valentini, have found no indication that the Italian fighter *Gruppi* ever operated during the hours of darkness, nor has this author found any Signals Intelligence reports of nocturnal R/T traffic from Italian fighters. The only other Bf 109 unit in Italy was NAG 11, based at Campoformido-Udine. There is precious little information to be had on this *Gruppe,* so the employment of its aircraft to hunt by night cannot be ruled out and indeed No. 600 Squadron's diarist noted on 24 February 1945 that, "enemy night fighters are suspected to be operating, possibly from that area [Udine]. Nine Bostons are missing and some … report seeing enemy night fighters."

As far as reports of Ju 88s are concerned, March/April orders of battle show just two in Italy, both of them T-3 reconnaissance models, aircraft normally armed with but a single rear-firing machine-gun. The dozen or so Ju 188s of FAG 122 and *Kommando Carmen* also come into contention. In other theatres their square fin/rudder assemblies often led to their being confused with the Ju 88G series during night encounters; they carried more guns, one in a turret, and stood a correspondingly greater chance of doing serious damage to a big bomber. However, while they may have opened fire on Allied aircraft they encountered, there is no evidence from German sources of their being sent deliberately to engage the enemy. The 1945 war diary of 2.(F)/122 survives and none of its Me 410s flew anything but daylight reconnaissance missions. No Signals Intelligence material seen by the author describes R/T traffic between any twin-engined aircraft and a ground station that so much as suggested night fighting.

The present work does not attempt to record every reported night fighter encounter over Italy in 1945, concentrating rather on those where Fw 190s were identified or fire was exchanged.

BELOW: *The Ju 188s of 4. and 6. (F)/122 may have given rise to the many reported encounters with Ju 88 night fighters over Italy in 1945. This is one of five said to have reached Innsbruck after withdrawing from Bergamo: it carries the "P" code letter of 6. Staffel and is fitted with FuG 200 anti-shipping radar. Note how this aircraft stands on firmer ground than the Fw 190s pictured at Innsbruck in later chapters.*

ABOVE: *NSG 9's Focke-Wulf 190s were used as auxiliary night fighters in the closing weeks of the war. Here, two Americans examine the starboard wheel well of Fw 190F-9 WNr. 440340 at Villafranca after the Axis surrender. In the background stands a USAAF B-25.*

"Down to the dregs"

Do you know, they're actually using trained pilots as infantry?
(*Fw. Kaspar Stuber of 1./NSG 9, covertly recorded on 12 December 1944*)

February saw more movement than action as far as NSG 9 was concerned. The transfer of Stab/NSG 9 from Bovolone to Villafranca was announced on the 2nd and the following night it was planned to ferry a Ju 87 to Vicenza. On 7 February, *Flg.* Wolfgang Holtz and *Uffz.* Kurt Wagner ferried Ju 87 "A" from Vicenza to Villafranca and over the next ten days they practised night landings, bombing and navigation. Newly arrived with 2. *Staffel* in Ghedi, *Lt.* Karl Reglin was similarly occupied. On the 9th, Willy Ferling arrived in Riem, his Fw 190 conversion complete, but had to wait four days before continuing his journey:

> Ferried a Ju 87 [WNr. 130897] over the Alps to Villafranca. Absolutely dreadful flight: no wireless operator, no radio contact, darkness coming on, fuel getting down to the dregs. Fireworks from the aerodrome saved machine and pilot. Fortunately, back with the old crowd and comrades … getting totally plastered.

In Riem, Ferling had met 1./NSG 9's new *Staffelkapitän*, *Hptm.* Willi Wilzopolski who was also due to ferry a machine to Italy. Wilzopolski brought with him what one former comrade characterises as "a political influence."

On 15 February, one of the *Gruppe's* first Focke-Wulfs was ferried to Villafranca along with two Ju 87s (one of them probably flown by *Ofw.* Horst Greßler) and a supply return was submitted mentioning Fw 190 ground attack aircraft. Decrypted two weeks later, this gave MAAF its first confirmation that NSG 9 was getting the type, although Signals Intelligence had had its suspicions since the 19th:

> The most interesting development in north Italian R/T was the interception of a new type of German traffic towards the end of the month… It was considered that perhaps a new fighter-bomber unit was being formed … or that it was possibly intended to replace the Ju 87's of N.S.G. 9 with Fw 190's, but on the 27th at any rate, if not on the 22nd, activity by the German aircraft in question seemed to be of the night-fighter type.

The main control station involved in all this was *HEIDE* (="heath") and aircraft callsigns were ULRICH-ANTON, ULRICH-BERTA and so through the phonetic alphabet to HEINRICH.

On 19 February, Holtz (promoted to *Gefreiter* that day) and Wagner made a *Feindflug* in E8+JL, with two more the next night. On the 20th, around three aircraft were active during the morning with R/T traffic apparently referring to the jettisoning of bombs near an airfield at 10.45. From 19.30-20.30, Willy Ferling flew Fw 190 E8+CB on a night fighter sortie, something his conversion syllabus had definitely not covered. Summing up the value of these operations he remarked to the author, *"Wir sahen nichts"* ("we

---

FOCKE-WULF Fw 190F-8

Wing span:	34ft 5.5in (10.5m)
Weights:	8,330lb (3,786kg) empty; 11,905lb (5,400kg) take-off weight
Power plant:	1 x BMW 801D-2 developing 1,730hp (F-9: BMW 801F-1, TS or TU of 2,200hp)
Max speed:	325mph (520km/h) at 19,000ft (5,800m) with bomb load
Climb:	16min to 21,250ft (6,500m)
Ceiling:	23,800ft (7,250m)
Range:	485 miles (775km)
Armament:	2 x 13mm MG 131 fixed above engine; 2 x 20mm MG 151 fixed in wing roots; 750kg max. bombload (typically 1 x 500 or 250kg on centreline and 4 x 50 or 70kg on wing racks)

Described by one veteran as «Das Nachtgespenst» (the Night Ghost), this Ju 87D-3 was draped in white sheets for effective snow camouflage. It was photographed on the perimeter of the "campo di fortuna" (makeshift landing ground) of Thiene on 5 February 1945.

Photographed between 6 and 11 February 1945 on the landing ground at Thiene, near the Flying Control hut, most of this group braving the snows are unidentified. Fourth from left is Ofhr. Dirk Bunsen, followed by the Flugleiter himself (an Oberfeldwebel from Bremen, aged about 40) and Uffz. Eduard Kimmel (a gunner with 3./NSG 9). At the right are two Italian civilian workers. The Flugleiter's dog is held by the third man, while between him and Bunsen a church spire can be seen, possibly that of Rozzámpia (VI) on the field's south eastern perimeter.

didn't see a thing"). A Focke-Wulf was ferried to Villafranca that night and could perhaps have been the German aeroplane overheard homing and short of fuel from 20.07–20.25 or that experiencing undercarriage trouble between 21.21 and 21.27.

Next morning, radio traffic was heard relating to three or four "German fighter-bombers" on what was interpreted as a bombing exercise near Lake Garda. They were warned of approaching Allied fighters and told to land or evade. At 07.34 one had reported undercarriage trouble and been told to crash land. "German fighters" were also detected in the Villafranca–Vicenza area at 08.06. It was much the same on the 22nd when 276 Wing logged three instances of German aircraft on night flying training around Villafranca and Ferrara, one of them being directed to lose height and then alerted to Allied intruders over its base. In all probability this was Willy Ferling, up in Fw 190 E8+GH from 16.15-16.51 on a practice bombing sortie. He recorded an attack by eight Thunderbolts, his arithmetic and aircraft recognition spot on. The P-47s were machines of the 66th FS sent to dive-bomb Villafranca. Over the target, their formation leader spotted a red smoke pot at each end of the runway and then, at 3,000ft and heading north over the field's southeast corner, an Fw 190. The Americans jettisoned their bombs and gave chase but the Focke-Wulf was lost in the ground haze and fog. Possible night fighter activity overheard on this date consisted of radioed reports about flares and bomb bursts. Heavy bombers of the RAF's 205 Group raiding marshalling yards at Padua did sight three bogeys including a Bf 109 classed as "not aggressive."

One of the more succinct examples of the propaganda dropped on Allied troops in Italy.

During the morning of the 23rd, radio traffic had been heard from Fw 190s thought to be on a training flight and from 16.05 from "German fighter-bombers" in the Lake Garda area. Two of these landed a little after 16.24, reporting fuel shortage and engine trouble. With Allied fighters reported coming in from the west, the Germans were told to disperse and to fly low over an airfield. These intercepts correspond with the experiences of eight 57th FG P-47s about to dive-bomb Villafranca when they saw "four Me 109s" flying south at low level over the field. After bombing, they sought these hostiles in the thick haze without success. Once again, Willy Ferling was involved. He was up on a *Rottenflug* (flight with a wingman) from 16.10-16.33 in Fw 190 E8+EH but did not report any encounter with the Americans.

Another four Fw 190s were later overheard on a "night training flight", Ferling logging a night fighting sortie from 18.50-19.20 in E8+FH, which he was forced to break off due to engine trouble. The 1./NSG 9 listed an Fw 190F-8 (WNr. 584549) as 30% damaged at Villafranca through a "technical deficiency" but it is not possible to say whether this was Ferling's aircraft or one of two that had been overheard reporting trouble earlier in the day.

From the traffic on the 27th it was ascertained that night attack aircraft were active, callsigns having changed to VIOLINE-DORA, -EMIL, -FRITZ etc. (="Violin-D", -E and -F). From 17.35–18.15 "German fighters" were practising formation flying over the Po Valley and were heard again from 19.38–21.06 in action against Allied bombers in the Verona-Ferrara area. No. 276 Wing recorded R/T traffic from the engagement, including references to flares, an Allied formation and orders to attack. Aircraft of 205 Group were attacking the Verona West marshalling yard and reported that "fighters were again active", with 14 sightings in the target area, two brief encounters and a Liberator of No. 2 Sqn SAAF holed by an unidentified single-engined aircraft. An Fw 190 of 1./NSG 9 crashed at Villafranca during the day, according to a signal sent two days later but, unusually, not decrypted until 18 March.

In a letter to *Ob.SW* on 28 February, *Komm. Gen.'s* Operations Officer, *Major i.G.* Walter Hutmacher, set out a plan to store up fuel for a programme of 14 days' flying in the event of "large scale operations" by the Allies: his calculations included 222 cubic metres of B4 to permit 21 *Nachtschlacht* sorties each night. That day, MAAF reconnaissance reported 14 Ju 87s in Villafranca's northern dispersal area. During the night, station HEIDE 1 was heard passing plots to HEIDE 2 on the position of aircraft VIOLINE-HEINRICH etc. and, "due to R/T reception [these] FW 190's were identified as N-F's and GA in North Italy" while at 22.10 an aircraft believed to be single-engined bombed and strafed at map reference L-8812, the Raticosa Pass.

An unusual achievement received recognition in the section of *Komm. Gen.*'s monthly intelligence report devoted to the *Flak*: 3./NSG 9's shooting down of an aircraft with small arms fire. Harry Fischer was there when this episode had its origins:

> When the *Amis* attacked an obscure ammunition dump and kept coming back, we got the job of fetching two aircraft cannon from the Breda works. Accompanied by my wireless operator, Heinz Staudt, we set off with bikes and trailers trough the partisan territory between Vicenza and Thiene. In Thiene we took charge of the cannon and they were set up on a hill not far from where the *Gruppenstab* was billeted … mess personnel were detached to the hill top.

Dirk Bunsen continues:

> I can tell you the following about the "Monte Mamaor *Flak* Platoon": 6km WNW from Villafranca a hill rises about 50m above the plain, between the River Mincio in the west and a narrower watercourse in the east, the so-called Monte Mamaor[1]… It was home to an ammunition dump consisting of 10-15 munitions sheds set at 70m intervals along the path winding up to the summit.
>
> From the beginning of March 1945, American Thunderbolts were in the habit of attacking these huts and using them for target practice. Unpleasant, especially so in view of the fact that *Gruppenkommandant* Frost had his Staff Quarters in Custoza Castle, 2 or 3km to the east. (Shell fragments are supposed to have carried as far as his balcony). So the nearest of his three *Staffeln,* the 3. in Villafranca, received orders to fit out a *Flak* platoon to protect the ammunition dump, using aircraft cannon mounted on tripods … from a neighbouring hill to the east. The guns were emplaced in pits 3m in diameter and 1.5m deep. Apart from the 2cm cannon, there were 1.7cm twin MG's. I was to command this 20-man platoon. We slept in a grape grower's barn or in his barrel store…

ABOVE: *Monte Mamaor's 192m (600ft) peak offered a commanding position. Ofhr. Dirk Bunsen scans the skies while an Italian Hiwi (Volunteer Auxiliary) mans the twin 1.7cm BREDAs. Despite his earthbound assignment, Bunsen still wears his flying jacket.*

ABOVE: *Ofhr. Dirk Bunsen and an Obergfreiter manning twin 1.7cm BREDA machine guns of 3./NSG 9's Flak Platoon on Monte Mamaor, set up to protect a nearby ammunition store. The small placards set around the gun pit indicate compass bearings, enabling the gunners to respond swiftly to aiming commands.*

> At the beginning of March ... the battery had a brilliant success right away. The Kitchen Bull [Mess Sergeant] — of all people — had brought down a Thunderbolt. Early one morning [the Thunderbolt] had made a low pass over one of the ammunition sheds ... opened fire and blown it up. Perhaps the Thunderbolt was caught in the shock wave (having said that however, I don't wish to denigrate the Kitchen Bull's contribution by any means!). The burned out remains of the machine lay exactly 300m along a bearing of 20° from the ammo bunker. Near the aircraft we found the pilot's body ... I took over command of this bunch about two days later...

Hans Nawroth adds:

> I can remember the Thunderbolt being shot down. The *Flak* had had new armour-piercing shells for some time. Besides, it wasn't long before search aircraft were circling overhead. We said at the time, "this is a service that takes care of its people."

The victim was 1/Lt Maurice L. Asbury of the 346th Fighter Squadron, 350th FG, his aircraft a P-47D-28-RE named "Curly Mohammed" (s/n 44-19581, squadron markings "6A6"). Asbury had led his four-plane "MINEFIELD GREEN" section off from Pisa at 16.00 to dive-bomb Ghedi, 2./NSG 9's base. With that part of the mission accomplished they had flown east to look for some ammunition dumps about which they had been briefed. They had caused fires and an explosion in a dump just south east of Valeggio before, as Asbury's wingman, F/O Alfred A. Kowalski related:

> Lt Asbury, seeing ammo revetments all over the area, told Lt [Robert S.] Davis and his wingman [2/Lt Martin S. Domin] to work over the ammo dump due east of the one we first started on. When we approached our ammo dump, Lt Asbury spotted another very large ammo hut, so the both of us closed in on it. At the moment he was over it, it blew up as a result of his straffing. He was at about 2200 feet and I was at about 2500 feet at the time of the explosion which went up to about 4500 feet. I saw his aircraft do two violent snaps to the right and straighten out for a second or two. At that moment I observed that he didn't have any horizontal stabiliser or elevators. His aircraft then went tail over nose and exploded as it hit the ground. I immediately contacted Lt Davis, and told him about Lt Asbury and that I was hit by the explosion also.

Davis and Domin then escorted their comrade home, as the former explained:

> I thought Kowalski's plane was very seriously damaged and the best thing to do was to get him home. It was not until we were crossing the Po Valley that I flew close to Kowalski to examine his plane ... [which] had many holes in the underside and had lost hydraulic fluid but [he] did a good job of bringing it back and making a no flap landing [at 17.30]. Lt Domin had been hit by flak at Ghedi, but hadn't mentioned it until we were south of Highway 9.

Although to judge by their reports the three surviving Americans did not even notice any *Flak* around the dump, according to Dirk Bunsen the German "sharpshooters" were awarded the EK II. Life on the hill had other compensations to offer besides medals:

> When we moved in [the farmer] drained one of his barrels and continually offered us red wine ... Sometimes I sat with the family in the evening. They told me of their woes ... their eldest son belonged to the Badoglio Army and ... after they were disarmed, he had been taken into German captivity, put to work in Essen during the air raids of 1944/45 and been killed there.

NSG 9's strength on 1 March 1945 was:

	Aircraft			Crews		
Stab	1	(1)	Ju 87D-5	1	(1)	Training
1.	7	(4)	Fw 190	13	(12)	re-equipping
2.	10	(9)	Ju 87	10	(6)	
3.	15	(13)	Ju 87	13	(11)	

In March, NSG 9 was a little more active than it had been during February. At 22.00 on the 1st, a single aircraft was reported to have strafed near Highway 65 and Allied night bombers reported 12 sightings of single-engined aircraft, some of which may have stemmed from the *Gruppe's* tentative forays into night fighting.

At 18.10 on the 3rd, two Fw 190s took off from Villafranca. They were flown by *Hptm.* Willi Wilzopolski, the new *Kapitän* of 1./NSG 9 on his first operation in Italy (WNr. 583576) and Willy Ferling (E8+FH). Their target was the village of San Clemente (BO), in the mountains south south east of Bologna. Ferling comments:

> Radio landing and guidance system tests were always necessitating special missions by NSG 9's pilots and wireless operators. I think the operation by me and Wilzopolski from Villafranca on 3 March 1945 should be seen in this light. For example, radio contact between pilots was something completely new for us.

This innovation was to prove lethal, as MAAF Signals Intelligence tracked the pair's progress from shortly after the time they left the ground. Two P-47s of the 347th FS ("Screaming Red Asses") had already been up for an hour, piloted by Lt Sigmund Hausner and his wingman, F/O "Deb" Wylder, who takes up the story:

> We took off about 1700; our code name was Midwood Copper. The weather was clear where we were flying at 12,000 feet, but there was heavy haze beneath us. We patrolled south of Bologna just north of the bomb line.

ABOVE: *Clearing away the wreckage of 1/Lt Maurice L. Asbury's P-47, s/n 44-19581, "Curly Mohammed" of the 346th Fighter Squadron, 350th FG. The squadron's black/natural metal chequer pattern can be seen on the rudder. Asbury was killed on 27 February 1945 when the tail of his aircraft was blown off. Although the Germans credited the victory to the Monte Mamaor Flak Platoon, Asbury's comrades believed he was caught by the explosion of the ammunition store his flight was attacking.*

```
2.) Flakartillerie.
    Der Feind verlor bei Luftangriffen im eigenen Bereich und beim
    Durchflug in das Reichsgebiet durch die Flakartillerie und ohne
    erkannte eigene Waffenwirkung insgesamt 142 (88 - 32 - 22)
    Flugzeuge.
    Die Anzahl der Abschüsse gliedert sich wie folgt auf:
    Flakartillerie . . . . . . . . . . . . . . 1o4
    Heereseinheiten . . . . . . . . . . . . .   2
    Marine-Flak-Art. . . . . . . . . . . . .   21
    dch.Handfeuerwaffen (3./NSG 9) . . . . .    1
    Abgestürzte u.notgelandete Flzg.
    (ohne erkannte eigene Waffenwirkung) . . . 14
                                              ─────
                                               142
```

LEFT: *A situation report records 3./NSG 9's achievement in shooting down one aircraft "with small arms" during March 1945.*

RIGHT: *Flight Officer Delbert E. Wylder of the 347th Fighter Squadron, 350th FG, USAAF. On 3 March 1945, "Deb" Wylder and Lt. Sigmund Hausner intercepted the Fw 190s of Hptm. Willi Wilzopolski and Lt. Willi Ferling of 1./NSG 9.*

The "Screaming Red Ass", emblem of the US 347th Fighter Squadron. The background is blue, outer ring red and cloud and lightning white.

At 18.22 the two Focke-Wulfs were heard crossing the Po, prompting ground controllers to alert the patrolling Thunderbolts. Wylder:

> At about 1820, Hausner called me to indicate it was getting dark and we should start back to Pisa. Only a few moments later, the radar controller "Cooler" reported that two bandits were 20 miles north of Bologna, headed south west at 8,000 feet, and vectored us toward them.

In what the CO of 62nd Fighter Wing later hailed as "a superb performance", the RAF's No. 10 Field Signals Unit and radar station US 3001 had between them given the fighters 13 minutes' warning. The trap closed on Wilzopolski and Ferling at about 18.35. Wylder continues:

> We came down from 12,000 feet into the haze, and I moved closer to Hausner so I wouldn't lose him in the darkness. We had gathered quite a bit of speed coming down so fast, and when we saw them, we were coming up on the left one very fast. The one on the right was somewhere 100 yards or so on my right - I could see him by peripheral vision. As we had approached them, "Cooler" switched us to another radar control, "Rhubarb." As I said, we were coming up on them very fast, and I was worried that Hausner might run up on him. Then, Hausner said, "It looks like a P-47." And it did to me too, from the rear. In another second or two, he opened fire. The tracers looked strange in the dark. Then there was a small explosion, and Hausner, coming up on it fast, almost ran right through the explosion, the German plane split-essed, and Hausner pushed forward hard on the stick and nosed straight down. Evidently the force of the explosion, plus the violent manoeuvre was too much, and the P-47 tumbled end over end.
>
> I watched both aircraft until they disappeared in the dark, and then saw a fairly white parachute blossom out. I didn't know who was in the parachute. I also saw two explosions when the Fw 190 and the P-47 hit the ground.

RIGHT: *Leutnant Willy Ferling of 1./NSG 9, who witnessed the shooting down of his new Staffelkapitän, Hptm. Wilzopolski by a USAAF P-47 on 3 March 1945 during a range-testing operation for the EGON radio-directed bombing method.*

It was Hausner who had bailed out, while Wilzopolski was killed and his Fw 190 completely destroyed with its bombs still aboard. Ferling, who had been in voice contact with his leader until shortly before they were attacked, radioed in at 18.41 that the *Hauptmann* had probably been shot down by Allied fighters.

Fifteen minutes after that he was signalling his intention to land and duly put down in Villafranca at 19.03, concluding his final combat mission. Wylder knew nothing of this and the defective fuel warning light burning in his cockpit since take off now began to seem less of an irritation and more of a threat:

> My eyes had been fixed on what was happening, and I suddenly realised there was another German in the air with me. I looked in the direction where it had been, over to my right, but there was nothing there that I could see. I called "Cooler", and they vectored me until they lost the other bandit. That was not very long. The controller asked me to continue patrolling the area. It was then quite dark, and I could see very little outside the cockpit … especially with the red fuel light shining, and was very nervous, I reached out and broke the bulb, a rather stupid thing to do. However the German pilot had not seen Hausner coming, and I wanted to see as much as I possibly could. It was a pretty eerie feeling, being up there with a German airplane. Neither one of us could have seen the other until the last moment.

Although Ferling had by now managed to evade and drop his bombs over the front line before turning for home, Wylder was not alone:

> I heard either Rhubarb or Cooler talking to, I thought, me. The controller indicated that the bandit was flying at my altitude at a certain number of degrees, mostly north. I looked at my compass and that was my heading, so I changed direction, 15 degrees to the right. The radar controller reported that the bandit had just turned 15 degrees to the right. Once again I changed direction. Again the controller responded. The tension increased quite a bit as I realised that one of our night fighters … was on my tail. I immediately reported all this to the radar controller. There was silence and then the controller said, "Midwood Copper 2" you may return to base." I was more than happy to do so, and made a night landing, bouncing quite a bit, at 1900 hours.
>
> … I think I sweated more during that mission than on any other two or three put together.

Wylder's report, taken together with Signals Intelligence information ensured that Hausner was credited with an aircraft destroyed rather than a "probable." While one German attack had been headed off, a third aircraft also picked by radio monitoring reached Pisa just after dusk, as the diary of the 347th's Oscar M. "Cactus Jack" Wilkinson records:

> Gerry bombed us tonight. It was the first time I had heard bombs from ground. Our field threw up a lot of flak.

The bombs fell west of the road bridge over the River Arno rather than on San Giusto airfield and little damage was reported. This sortie did not feature in the German morning report of 4 March (decrypted on the 9th) which mentioned only "…two night ground attack aircraft … range test of EGON control. Losses: … one Fw 190 shot down by Allied fighters." Neither was there anything to corroborate the report by a 205 Group Liberator that while in its target area at 23.29 on the 3rd, it had evaded a single port–starboard pass by an Fw 190.

The story of the Wilzoploski's loss as it reached NSG 9 was that the American who downed him had himself fallen victim to German *Flak* and that "he was said to be a coloured man." While there were certainly African-American pilots in Italy, the USAAF of that era was racially segregated and the 347th was a white unit. Hausner was in fact of Polish parentage and had flown as a volunteer with the RAF before America entered the war and then with a B-24 unit before joining the 347th FS in October 1944. Not knowing his true fate, the Squadron's newspaper "De-Nuss-Ance." printed this tribute:

ABOVE: *The diary of Lt Oscar H. "Cactus Jack" Wilkinson for 3 March 1945. He records the encounter between Lts Wylder and Hausner and "a couple of Gerry" (Lt. Willy Ferling and Hptm. Willi Wilzopolski of 1./NSG 9) and the fact that "Gerry bombed us tonight."*

BELOW: *Leutnant Willy Ferling's five Fw 190 flights with NSG 9: on the second he was attacked by eight Thunderbolts over his own base; the fourth was broken off with engine trouble and the fifth (on 3 March 1945) saw his leader shot down. In fact on this last occasion, there were only two Thunderbolts not the three recorded in his log.*

Spectators at a football match at Villafranca airfield in early March 1945. From left: unknown (wearing Spanish Cross), Flugleiter Ofw. Dzykowski, Ofhr. Dirk Bunsen, Fhj.-Ofw. Carl "Sepp" Wintermayr, Fw. Soukopp of a Propaganda Kompanie.

Colourful, aggressive and possessing a warm personality, Hausner centered all of his attention upon flying with an amazing singleness of purpose. Predicting, as late as an hour before his last mission that "his number was up", he vowed not to return to America until the Germans were humbled. Because of extreme personal reasons, his desire for vengeance against the Hitler men knew no bounds. He held decorations from the Polish, British and American governments.

After capture, Hausner was taken first to Verona and thence to a compound in Nürnberg. The third of his escape attempts succeeded and he amazed Squadron comrades who had "given him up as a goner" by walking into the Ops-Intelligence room one day, "grinning like a clown."

On the 6th, two Fw 190s flew an armed reconnaissance in the Bologna area, making three strafing runs along Highway 6, south of the city. The German documentary source for this mission does not specify the unit concerned and omits known NSG 9 activities. Since one of NAG 11's Fw 190A-8s was damaged due to pilot error during the day it seems likely that it was the *Nahaufklärungsgruppe* carrying out not only these attacks but similar ones involving four aircraft on the 9th. On the latter date one of 1./NSG 9's Fw 190s (WNr. 584577) belly-landed at Mantua on a training flight, incurring 10% damage.

That night, Lt Beattie's Liberator Mk. VI of No. 31 Sqn SAAF ("Y") was attacked five times by an unidentified single-engined aircraft near Ostiglia. The first pass damaged the mainplane, the second the bomb bay and nose. None of the bomber's gunners was able to bring a weapon to bear during any of the attacks and it was thought upward firing guns had been used during the second of them. After jettisoning its bombs, the Liberator flew back to Falconara on three engines and with air gunner W/O Symes slightly wounded. "Y" was subsequently entrusted to Neil Galloway of 2 Wing Repair and Salvage Unit:

> We... undertook to repair the (extensive) damage to Yoke – especially the port wing where a 30mm cannon shell had exploded in the main wheel-bay, partially destroying the main spar as well as the electrical junction box for Nos. 1 and 2 engines.
>
> We got her back in the air in three weeks, despite gloom and doom predictions from various Engineer Officers who doubted the repairs to the spar. Fortunately, a Boeing-trained engineer from 773rd Bombardment Group of the U.S.A.A.F (we shared Celone with B. 17's) approved our repair methods and came along on the test flight to prove his faith!

The next night attack operation came on the 11th, when fragmentation bombs were dropped 25km south of Bologna at first light. On 12 March, Lt. Rowan's Liberator (KH248, "T") of "B" Flight, No. 178 Squadron was returning from the marshalling yards at Padua:

1957hrs, 44 59N, 12 05E, 9,000 ft – aircraft believed Fw.190 came in starboard quarter and closed to 200 yards. Liberator opened fire at that distance – three second burst. Tracer seen to ricochet. Aircraft dived steeply to port then lost to view. Claim damage to enemy aircraft.

On the 15th, reconnaissance recognised seven Ju 87s at Ghedi and 19 at Villafranca. From 19.45 on the 18th, MAAF Signals Intelligence listened as a lone German night fighter was guided on to Allied bombers. Many of 205 Group's Liberator crews saw both fighter flares and a Fw 190 in the target area (the marshalling yards at Vicenza) but according to the radio traffic the German was unable to find the Allied formation. His mission was aborted at 20.08 and he was ordered to land at Villafranca, setting down at 20.27. No more was heard of NSG 9 for the remainder of the month.

Dirk Bunsen (right): "…one Sunday in March 1945, Helmut Schäfer visited me with his girlfriend, Gina." This photograph was taken among the Flak emplacements at Monte Mamaor (twin BREDA machine-guns at left).

On 6 February, two groundcrew had been transferred from 2./NSG 9 at Ghedi to 90. *Panzergrenadier Division*, only to desert on 23 March. They told Allied interrogators that 1. and 3. *Staffeln* were in the Verona area and attributed the *Gruppe's* recent lack of operations to fuel shortages. The prisoners however "failed to mention the recent conversion of NSG 9 from Ju 87's to Fw 190's, which another PW has reported." By now *Hptm.* Reither had been posted to Berlin (see page 112) and on 24 March Dirk Bunsen was detached from his *Flak* platoon to San Michele Extra (VR) for a week-long course on the *Panzerfaust* shoulder-launched anti-tank rocket. When an air force's technical personnel are being drafted as foot soldiers and its pilots learn to use close-quarter infantry weapons, its prospects are bleak. Accordingly, Bunsen and his fellow trainees were also treated to rousing speeches and more subtle propaganda intended to bolster their will to resist.

Non-flying employment was also being found for some of 3./NSG 9's *Bordfunker*. Hans Nawroth:

> In March 1945, operations were severely curtailed since there was little aviation spirit to be had. Apart from that, there were officer candidates who must have combat flights. Accordingly several air-gunners were posted to Germany: Berlin, *General der Schlachtflieger*, then on to Gardelegen. After that, to the front as paratroops. I came to the Western Front.

Nawroth was accompanied by fellow 3. *Staffel* member, Franz Till. Rudi Sablottny too had been posted away in February to serve as an infantryman in what he terms the "final defensive battle."

---

1. Monte Mamaor's peak is 192m above sea level.

"The first Mosquito didn't see me"

…Low-level attack with guns (20m over enemy territory)
(*Leistungsbuch of Lt. Peter Stollwerck, 20 April 1945*)

O n 1 April, NSG 9 informed the *General der Schlachtflieger* that its 2. and 3. *Staffeln* had an average strength of ten crews each and that owing to the surrender of personnel (presumably those "combed out" for infantry service) neither was fully operational. It was therefore proposed to amalgamate them and bring them up to strength, so releasing yet more ground personnel. Meanwhile, the continuing hiatus in operational flying meant that complements remained stable in the early part of the month at 27(25) Ju 87s and 11(9) Fw 190s; *Komm. Gen.* had two Ju 87D-5s and two Fw 190Fs in reserve on the 1st while by the 4th this pool had gained another six Focke-Wulfs. Inactivity also led to talk, as Dirk Bunsen relates:

In April, rumours passed among us that we [would have to] defend the southern part of the east front, [that is to say] Hungary.

Even if NSG 9 was stood down from raiding, Allied bomber crews were still shooting at night fighters. South east of Trento at 21.40 on 2 April, the rear gunner of 231 Sqn's Liberator "J" fired six short bursts at a Bf 109 seen 400yds astern and climbing to attack. Two nights later, there was a short and inconclusive encounter between a Liberator and an e/a over the Brescia West marshalling yards.

With the Italian front quiet — at least compared to the avalanches engulfing the Reich — NSG 9 risked being stripped of technical aid as well as ground crews. On the 4th, *Komm. Gen.* signalled that the *Gruppe's* EGON *Trupp* (platoon) was being sent to Kamenz, Saxony and that loading would start in Villafranca in two days' time. Also on the 4th, Dirk Bunsen, fresh from his anti-tank course, took up a new assignment:

A similar *Flak* detachment [to that at Monte Mamaor], near Highway 62, the Mantua-Villafranca road, immediately south of the little village of Mozzecane (VR), 8km south of Villafranca …
Three Breda aircraft cannon of 1.7 or 2cm calibre, each on a tripod, that we emplaced in cylindrical holes in the ground, 1.6m deep and 3m in diameter.
Apparently we were supposed to stop oncoming Americans (tanks?!) with 2cm cannon. Accordingly, tank barriers were constructed out of thick baulks of timber and sand-filled barrels at the entrance to Mozzecane. At night we let a press-ganged Italian civilian guard them.
One midnight, drunken German paratroops got rowdy on their way home, grabbed his cap and threw it in the brook that ran nearby, as the Parish Clerk complained to me next day.

The Americans launched an offensive toward La Spezia on the 5th, signalling an end to the stalemate in Italy. It was reported "very early" on the 6th that Udine I and II had been bombed by Flying Fortresses, with two Fw 190s among the aircraft damaged. These were probably machines of NAG 11, of whose Focke-Wulfs we shall hear more. On 9 April, Eighth Army assailed the Senio and Santerno River lines, overwhelming the German fortifications with the help of the Strategic Air Force. Next day, P-51s claimed the destruction of 7 Fw 190s on the ground but even so, that night RAF Signals Intelligence again heard a pair of Fw 190s on a night fighter sortie.

With the Allies about to debouch across the Po Valley, the time had arrived for *Gen* von Pohl to commit his remaining reserves of aircraft and fuel and so NSG 9 returned to action. Taking off at 04.58 on the 11th, "Sepp" Wintermayr and Karl Hofmann dropped bombs south of Lugo and Herbert Kehrer and Alfons Eck were on a mission in Ju 87 E8+NH from 05.07-06.20. Their target is not recorded but around this time they were again dispensing propaganda:

ABOVE AND BELOW: *Death or "Gloria"? British soldiers examine both sides of a propaganda leaflet of the type dropped by NSG 9 in from the winter of 1944 onward.*

ABOVE: *Invitation: this German propaganda leaflet, dating from January 1945, appears to herald the delights of the Po Valley. The woman was believed by Luftwaffe airmen to be modelled on one Gloria, the most alluring prostitute in Bologna. NSG 9 dropped hundreds of thousands of such leaflets over the Allied lines. In April 1945, the Americans would cross the river about where the fisherman is hauling in his catch and these crossings would be NSG 9's last target.*

RIGHT: *Threat: the figure of Death triumphantly holds American and British helmets aloft as he punishes an attempted assault crossing of the River Po.*

Then there was the "Gloria Series" — she was supposed to be the most attractive prostitute in Bologna. I still remember one of the last leaflets, when the front was already over the Appenines: "The Po is waiting for you." A front-line soldier is balancing on a tightrope across the Po, some are already lying dead in the water and in the background someone is enjoying himself with Gloria.

That evening, about 15 Fw 190s and Ju 87s were active by Allied reckoning. Two Focke-Wulfs were heard on an operation from 18.19–19.19 GMT; a target near Bologna was raided; there was bombing and strafing around Ravenna and Messerschmidt and Hettling (Ju 87D-5 E8+AK) flew a mission from Ghedi between 22.32 and 24.00.

On defensive patrol that night was a Mosquito Mk. XIX (TA133, "X") of No. 600 Squadron, crewed by F/O's D.S. Denby and C.H. Raisen. After a fleeting contact near Bologna, they soon had another north of Imola (BO). Closing to 800yds, they got a visual on a single-engined aircraft and, moving closer, identified it as a Ju 87 at an altitude of about 3,500ft, weaving so violently "that it was as well that he was clearly silhouetted against the light portion of the western sky". Three bursts of cannon fire produced no obvious hits but they "saw flashes from the rear of JU. 87 … presumed this to be return fire", although no tracers were apparent. As Denby opened fire again, the Junkers "whipped over to starboard in a peel-off and was lost to view" and to radar at 20.48.

Despite the transfer orders of a week earlier, NSG 9 had not re-entered the fray without EGON support, as the Allies noted when examining captured.radar stations in May:

> A station at Este [MERIDIAN at Monselice (PD)] had been used in conjunction with a mobile Freya at Kustozza near Bovolone [Custoza (VR)], for the purpose of night strafing in the Po Valley, using the *Zwei Standlinie Verfahren*. In this method the range of the leading aircraft was measured from both stations simultaneously and the values passed to the control station at Bovolone which would thus be able to maintain continual supervision over the position and course of the aircraft. Instructions were passed to the a/c over the R.T. set FuG 16ZS.

German radar stations in Italy were operated by *Luftnachrichten Regiment 200* (those in the Verona area by its III. *Abteilung*) but NSG 9 also had its own signals elements. At Custoza, subordinated to the *Gruppenstab*, was *Ln. Zug (mot.) NSG 9* while under it, at Villafranca, was *Ln. Funknav. Trupp (K) (mot.) 1*. The location of the former and the name of the latter both suggest their involvement in the EGON system.

On 12 April, a pair of Focke-Wulfs was heard in the Ferrara area between 10.53 and 11.05 GMT (two hours behind local time), probably the "two Fw 190s with orange cowlings" which jumped an F-5C at 25,000ft over Corbola (RO), this reconnaissance version of the Lightning evading without damage. Since this was the main east coast battle area and in broad daylight it is likely that these were aircraft of NAG 11 running into an American counterpart. At 08.30 on the 13th, *Komm. Gen.* announced that he intended dusk-dawn Ju 87 and Fw 190 operations from Villafranca on the front of LXXVI. *Panzer Korps*. Suiting the action to the word, sorties duly went in against targets in Eighth Army's zone. From 20.00–21.39, three aircraft were operating with EGON and at 19.08 the second of these was called by both its plotting station and main control without response. It is now possible to see what may have happened to it.

Near Alfonsine at 20.30, S/L G.W. Hammond and F/O L.R. Moore were on defensive patrol in a Mosquito Mk. XIX west of Ravenna when vectored toward a bogey heading south east at 9,000ft. They obtained simultaneous visual and AI contact with two climbing, single-engined aircraft approaching from 10 o'clock and passing about 2,000ft overhead:

> Turned hard onto 160° and climbed after the bogies. Had no difficulty in closing the range and climbing to their height.

At 12,500ft near Alfonsine (RA):

> Closed to 1000yds and identified targets as being F.W. 190s. The leader was about 75 yards in front of the No. 2 … flying straight and climbing, the No. 2 was weaving very slightly.

Hammond was able to keep his targets silhouetted against the bright portion of the western sky as he closed into 350yds and:

> … opened fire on the leader from dead astern and very slightly below. Saw strikes on

the F.W. 190, a good concentration that caused bits to fly off the e/a. What appeared to be a long-range tank centrally-underslung, burst into flames. There was an explosion as the e/a turned over to starboard and went straight down, still burning. Last seen, this aircraft was disappearing into 10/10 cloud at 7000ft. and on fire.

This F.W. 190 is claimed Destroyed

The Mosquito then turned his attention to the No. 2, who had been slightly out to starboard. The e/a turned to port in a dive, and then reversed into a dive to starboard, afterwards heading Northwards. The Mosquito followed him down at 360 I.A.S. gaining slightly. The E/A entered cloud at 7000ft. but the Mosquito maintained A.I. contact closing steadily from 2½ miles.

Flying in cloud, contact was maintained by AI alone although the Mk. X set had by now started giving a blurred picture, attributed by Moore to the very high engine revs maintained during the chase. Range was closed to 1,000 yards:

> … just coming out of cloud to get a quick glimpse of the e/a who was now flying above cloud at estimated 320 m.p.h. Closed the range to 500 yards on A.I. Came up out of the cloud and closed to 200 yards. Opened fire, seeing strikes on the starboard wing. At this moment the reflector sight switch went into the "off" position due to the vibration caused by the cannons firing.
> Continued the burst by firing in the general direction of the e/a and moving the nose up and down. The e/a then entered 10/10 cloud and broke away to port.
> Mosquito did a quick orbit, getting a momentary A.I. contact at 5 miles … last seen … going north.

This F.W. 190 is claimed DAMAGED

Although No. 600 Sqn. would have contacts on five more nights, this combat was both its and (reputedly) the RAF's last in Italy. It is notable too for an unusually protracted chase, a consequence of the aircraft types involved being more evenly matched in performance than hitherto. Both sides were being controlled from the ground initially and the second German could conceivably have received warnings that Hammond and Moore were still after him. That a target could be stalked successfully through solid cloud at night shows just how far airborne radar had come by April 1945.

The identity of the German pilots involved in this action has yet to be established. Willy Ferling, on being shown a copy of Hammond's combat report, assured the author that after the death of *Hptm.* Wilzopolski on 3 March, «*wir hatten keine Verluste mehr*» – "we [in 1./NSG 9] had no more losses." The evidence of the radio traffic does however suggest that, if not actually shot down, the Focke-Wulf's radio may have been disabled or it may — as was not uncommon — have dropped below the controllers' radar horizon.

On the 14th, at least two *Nachtschlacht* aircraft were active in the Lake Comàcchio area between 20.14 and 21.35 while the next night 276 Wing listened in as an aircraft with instrument problems homed on its airfield in the Ghedi-Villafranca area, bombs still aboard. It jettisoned its load near home base and landed at 21.53. There were between five and ten sorties flown on the night of the 16th (Kehrer and Eck in E8+NH aborting theirs soon after take-off) with a further flurry just before dawn, a pattern repeated over the next four nights. On the 16th, MAAF Signals Intelligence recorded an EGON attack in progress:

> 18.48   Nero-Anton from REGENT: twice Lisa
> Nero-Anton from REGENT: once Rolf
> Nero-Anton from REGENT: duck, 4 minutes
> Nero-Anton from REGENT: again a bit Lisa
>
> 19.00   Nero-Anton from REGENT: duck, 50 seconds
> Nero-Anton from REGENT: target dead ahead of you
> Nero-Anton from REGENT: kettledrum, kettledrum
> Nero-Anton from REGENT: attention, release now
> Nero-Anton from REGENT: I can't visit you at present
> Nero-Anton from REGENT: you are too low. Source 320

19.10   Nero-Anton from REGENT: I am visiting you again

Watch out for little owl
Marie 100: you are right in front of the railway station.

Understanding EGON		
Rakete	Rocket	Take-off
Ich besuche Sie	I'm visiting you	Assuming control from ground
Karuso	Caruso	Course
Lisa	-	Left 5°
Rolf	-	Right 5°
Ente	Duck	Target
Pauke	Kettledrum	Bomb-release signal imminent
Quelle	Source	Bearing to base
Kleine Eule	Little Owl	Hostile night fighter
Marie 100	-	Distance to base, 10km
Bahnhof	Railway Station	Home base

On the 17th between 20.09 and 20.31, three aircraft were detected on what may have been an EGON mission but they were forced to abort by instrument problems. Soon after sunset, two German aircraft strafed targets including a landing ground in the Ravenna area and although a Mosquito chased one, it could not overhaul it in the climb. From 02.05 on the 18th, two or three unidentified aircraft followed an A-20 from Ostiglia to the bomb line, staying with it for 50 minutes and making two passes without firing. An A-26 reported being followed in the same vicinity at almost the same time then, at 03.24, four aircraft dropped bombs in the Portomaggiore-Argenta (FE) region, all of them returning to Villafranca. Another was plotted in that general area at 05.15.

Radio traffic that evening pointed to four aircraft active around Bologna under EGON control, strafing and bombing from 20.32-21.44 (local time) and another reaching its target south of the city at 23.00. This last may have been Herbert Kehrer and Alfons Eck's Ju 87 (E8+NH) which was in the air at the relevant times and bombed Marzabotto (BO) by EGON before shooting up artillery and searchlight emplacements. The night's rash of incidents is vividly conveyed by MATAF's Intelligence and Operations Summary:

> Hostile picked up at 20.30 VILLAFRANCA area. Headed South to area S. of BOLOGNA. At 21.25 a Fw 190 strafed at L-6030, 1 E/A reported to have strafed at L-852310 or 2312. Straffing was reported at L-6229 and L-6626 at 23.15. A-20 was attacked once 15 miles W. of FERRARA at 00.47, no damage to A-20. 2 E/A unidentified dropped 1 x 500lb. on Highway 64 at L-638184 and 2 x 500 on Highway 64 at L-613157. E/A circled PORETTA and dropped 1 x 500 and strafed in vicinity of VERGATO at 21.15. No damage or casualties reported. Bombs estimated to be 250kg type.

At 05.15 and 05.20 respectively, two crews of No. 256 Sqn, F/L N.A. Beaumont and F/O G. Seed (Mosquito Mk. XIII, MM534/JT•C) and S/L G.M. Smith DFC and F/O H.J. Wilmer DFM[1] (Mosquito Mk. XII, HK508/JT•A) had taken off on armed reconnaissance of the battle line, north to the River Po. Two or three kilometres north of Ferrara, Seed reported how he:

> Observed HK508 to strafe two stationary M/T at M.2191, leaving one in flames and one smoking. Aircraft MM534 straffed same M/T, leaving both in flames. After straffing run … HK508 broke off to the the south and MM534 broke off to the north. Scant 40mm flak was observed to come up from the area but HK508 was not seen to be hit. Called up and asked him if he was alright. Reply was, "OK, flying 180°." Aircraft was then observed at 200ft flying south. About 60 seconds later pilot of HK508 called up saying, "Navigator has just baled out" and on request of the pilot of aircraft MM534 this message was repeated. Orbitted area 5 miles south of Copparo [FE], where aircraft HK508 was thought to be. Called up several times on R/T but no reply was received. Nothing seen on ground. Aircraft MM534 returned to base and landed at 06.30 hours.

The RAF's Air Historical Branch has this to add:

> Our records show that the Pilot ... Sqn Ldr G M Smith DFC died when the aircraft crashed, and that his Navigator, F/O Wilmer DFC managed to survive, after making a successful parachute descent. F/O Wilmer sustained only minor injuries and was captured on the evening of 19 April 1945, and taken to a camp at Brunico [(BZ) where he] remained until his release on 4 May 1945, with the arrival of Allied troops.
>
> After liberation F/O Wilmer confirmed that at approximately 06.00 hrs on 19 April 1945 ... after attacking some motor transport in the vicinity of Ferrara ... their aircraft had been hit by anti-aircraft fire. Investigations made by No. 256 Squadron at the crash site of an aircraft found at Map Reference M.153854, 1 mile South of Ferrara, identified it as a Mosquito belonging to [the] Squadron. An undischarged 250lb bomb suggested that it was the aircraft of S/L Smith as the two other No 256 Squadron Mosquitos missing in the area had not been equipped with bombs[2]. Locals were questioned concerning this incident who confirmed the fact that a crew member had been seen to bale out, and that the other had been killed with the aircraft.

A possible explanation for the loss of HK508 lies in the experiences of 1./NSG 9's Werner Hensel:

> ...Flying back from a bombing attack, I shot down a Mosquito with my Fw 190.[3] Around 03.00 hours I crossed Lake Comàcchio at low level, heading for Villafranca. At my back, the sun was coming up over the Adriatic. I knew from our ground radio station that two night fighters were coming toward me on a reciprocal heading. We met not far short of Ferrara. Apparently the first Mosquito didn't see me, it flew right over my head. In combat with the second Mosquito, I set its port engine on fire. It crashed near Ferrara from an altitude of 200m and immediately went up in flames. None of the crew tried to bail out.
>
> After I landed in Villafranca, *Major* Frost sent our Maintenance Technical Sergeant from the ground echelon out to the crash site with a car and he confirmed my report. On account of this, just before the end of the war, I was promoted to *Fahnenjunker-Oberfeldwebel*.

Although many elements of the above accounts — location, altitude, number and type of aircraft — match up, it cannot be said with certainty that "A-Apple" was Hensel's kill. The German pilot originally recalled the date as "early in April" but so far as is known, NSG 9 flew no raids during the first third of the month. Hensel revised his estimate after being reminded by his son that the date of a letter home about the victory suggested it would have taken place on or about 20 April. The timing of 03.00 seems unlikely to be correct because first light, which he mentions, would have been around 06.00. In conversation with the author in June 1997, Hensel stated that he clearly — "one hundred percent" — saw the USAAF's star and bars insignia on his victim. With each retelling he has become more certain that 20 April was the date but no twin-engined American aircraft is recorded as lost then, only an A-26 of 47th BG damaged by *Flak* during the night of the 19/20th. If it was an American aircraft then it must have been one of the three 416th NFS Mosquitoes that failed to return from a strafing mission in the dawn hours of the 22nd. Although these too are understood to have fallen to *Flak* and their patrol area was in Map Square F (which did not reach as far south east as Ferrara), the USAAF lost no others of the type over Italy during April.

Whatever the exact circumstances, Hensel's achievement clearly made an impression. When MAAF Intelligence questioned captured *Luftwaffe* officers (including Rupert Frost) after hostilities ceased, they were told:

> Me 109 or Fw 190 aircraft were not used as night fighters except in emergency, and Fw 190's had only recently been employed on this task. Three such missions accomplished during the last two weeks [of the fighting], claimed two four-engined bombers and one Mosquito.

General von Pohl wrote in his postwar recollections:

> The great speed of the Fw 190 made it practically unassailable by opposing night fighters — indeed, as the shooting down of a Mosquito by a *Nachtschlacht* 190 at the beginning of 1945 showed, in an encounter [it was] even superior.
>
> [It also served as] an auxiliary night fighter over Upper Italy, making use of the day fighter control organisation.

His staff officers told their interrogators that:

> Neither in its new capacity of NS [i.e. *Nachtschlacht*] aircraft, nor as a defensive
> night fighter in Northern Italy, could the Fw 190 be utilised to the full, however, due
> to the growing fuel shortage.
>
> …Egon enabled the controller to warn airborne NS aircraft of the presence and
> whereabouts of Allied night fighters, and order last-minute changes of course. In the
> case or the Fw 190 the NS aircraft would sometimes be directed on to a hostile,
> with a view to turning the tables on the night fighter.

Lieutenant Leo A. Gertin of 319th FS, 325th FG was testing a Mustang near Florence between 16.00 and 17.30 on the 19th when he encountered an Fw 190, both pilots attempting head-on passes against one another before the German broke for home at low level. Gertin followed and shot him down as he tried to land at an airfield near Verona. While the Fw 190's destination may suggest NSG 9, its *modus operandi* does not: the *Gruppe* neither flew in broad daylight nor ventured more than a few kilometres behind enemy lines while NAG 11, which may still have retained some Focke-Wulfs at this stage, did both.

Harry Fischer and Franz Fischer's Ju 87 (E8+FL) took off from Villafranca at 20.57 that evening but they were attacked by a night fighter while still over the airfield, suffering instrument failure and breaking off their sortie. The crews of the two Mosquitoes which 416th NFS had sent into enemy airspace would surely have been delighted had they known this, for all they could report was:

> No incident occurred on … Intruder Patrols over GHEDI and VILLAFRANCA
> aerodromes.

From 20.48-22.07 that evening, two "German ground attack aircraft" were operating over the north western edge of Lake Comàcchio, one unidentified type being reported by a Baltimore of 253 Wing as dropping flares and strafing both shores at 21.25. Another unidentified machine was seen in the same vicinity at 23.20, possibly Ju 87 E8+NH (Kehrer and Eck) which was in the air from 22.57–00.06, bombing Argenta by EGON and strafing gun emplacements and roads in grid square MA2, the area immediately to the west of the town, across the River Reno. Liberator "J" of No. 70 Squadron fired on a Bf 109 that night, the bomber's crew believing they hit it; three or four minutes later, another e/a was seen astern which followed the Lib through a corkscrew, closed in and then dived away without firing. Hits were claimed on this one too.

On the 20th, Allied reconnaissance aircraft spotted eight Ju 87s at Villafranca and two in Ghedi's north western dispersal area. *Fähnrich* Helmut von Mitterwallner and *Gefr.* Lotsch transferred Ju 87D-5 E8+BK to Bovolone that evening, *Ofhr.* Messerschmidt and *Uffz.* Hettling following in E8+AK. An ULTRA decrypt of a message from *Komm. Gen.* timed at 11.30 on the 20th gave 1. *FJ Div.* defending Bologna notice of dusk–dawn ground attack operations for the coming night and NSG 9 put in about five sorties south of the city. *Feldwebel* Paul-Ernst Zwarg of 1./NSG 9 was one who took part:

> I flew several ops with Fw 190 "FH" against positions in the vicinity of Bologna,
> toward the Futa Pass. My last mission took place without a gunsight (it couldn't be
> swapped or repaired).

Other NSG 9 aircraft were flying in a defensive capacity. That night's target for seven Liberators of No. 205 Group was the railway bridge over the River Adige at Parona di Valpolicella (VR). Apart from the *Flak*, "the *Luftwaffe* appeared to make a last despairing effort to oppose the attack", a sequence of assaults by Ju 88s and Bf 109s between 21.45 and 22.08 being reported by the bomber crews. Over the target, a Liberator of No. 2 Squadron (SAAF) reported attacks by four twin-engined types and a Bf 109, claiming strikes on the latter. Also:

> Flying back over Ferrara at 22.08, aircraft "<u>C</u>" of 31 Squadron [SAAF] was at 9,000ft
> when its crew reported a Bf 109 crossing from port to starboard dropping a flare as
> it went. The fighter attacked from the port quarter. The tail turret was hit and the
> gunner, W/O I.N. Brown received multiple lacerations and burns to his face, head,
> shoulder and right thigh. The controls to Nos. 3 and 4 engines and the aileron were
> shot away and the beam gunner baled out during the engagement.

The Squadron's Operations Record Book adds more details:

> …After leaving the target, Lt. Tresize was attacked consistently by an unidentified

aircraft, an ME.109 and a JU.88. The aircraft received several hits, particularly in the empennage, the tail gunner, W.O. Brown, I.N. being wounded and thrown from the turret into the aircraft, which was by then on fire. The beam gunner W.O. Tarr was also wounded and in the confusion baled out. He has subsequently returned to the Squadron and tells an interesting story of evasion. Considerable credit is due to the crew as a whole, who showed great calm throughout and particularly to the second pilot Lt. Lagesen who beside extinguishing the fire, rendering first aid to the wounded and assisting the pilot with an extremely difficult landing also manned the beam gun and obtained probable strikes on the Ju 88.[4]

Minutes later, Allied Field Signals Units heard two Fw 190 pilots on R/T, claiming to have shot down a Liberator over the Adriatic. None of the author's contacts with NSG 9 veterans has elicited any memories of this particular action although theirs is the only unit in Italy known to have attempted any night fighting this late in the war. Neil Galloway recalls how:

"<u>C</u>" was also damaged in April but repairs were not undertaken because, by that time, the end of the war in Europe was on the horizon and only our "low time" Libs were to be fitted out to fly the Hump [Himalayas] into China, (which exciting prospect was blown by the atom bomb).

At 21.00, aircraft believed to be Fw 190s bombed in the valley of the River Setta, east of Marzabotto (BO) and an hour later an unidentified aircraft flying east at 9,000ft, north west of Mantua was picked up by at 2 miles range by a Mosquito. The night fighter gave chase for 15 minutes but lost contact south of Bologna: although making 280–300mph, it was unable to overtake the hostile, "which easily maintained lead while taking evasive action." Peter Stollwerck, bombing and strafing round Argenta was harried by night fighters "from take-off to landing" and his radioman, *Ofw.* Hartmann, engaged one with E8+AL's rear guns. Kehrer and Eck's E8+NH was up at 22.38, using EGON to bomb Sasso Marconi (BO) before shooting up artillery positions in "map quare FD8", the area near Calderino (BO), a short distance to the northwest. At 23.30 an aeroplane was plotted going south at 8,000ft near Loiano and at the same time troops in that area reported being bombed and strafed. Two more aircraft were active between 04.50 and 05.39, reporting "*Ich habe abgeworfen*" (="bombs gone") at 05.03.

On the night of the 21/22nd, two aircraft were over their target at 21.12 and A-20s reported being fired on by a lone, unidentifed type at five different grid references between 21.25 and 23.00. South of Chioggia (VE), a Baltimore sighted an Fw 190 at 4,000ft and 800yds astern but evaded. Kehrer and Eck of 3. *Staffel* were operating for an hour from 02.32 but — and perhaps this is symptomatic of the disintegration overtaking the German armed forces in Italy — logged no details of their target.

Villafranca was partly obscured by cloud when MAAF came to photograph it on 22 April but coverage of the northern dispersal area revealed five Ju 87s, two "probable Ju 87s" and two single-engined fighters. In fact the Gruppe's official strengths and locations that day were:

Stab/NSG 9	Villafranca	1(0)	Ju 87D (trainer)
1./NSG 9	Villafranca	3(2)	Fw 190A-8
		4(4)	Fw 190F-8
2./NSG 9	Ghedi II	3(3)	Ju 87D-3
		7(7)	Ju 87D-5
3./NSG 9	Villafranca	6(6)	Ju 87D-3
		10(7)	Ju 87D-5
Total crews		39(27)	

As we have seen, some of 2./NSG 9's aircraft were by now in Bovolone, however. The three Fw 190A-8s seem likely to have come from 2./NAG 11 which had recorded 3(2) of the type on strength on the 9th but now had none. This impression is perhaps lent weight by the fact that *Seenotostaffel '20* (which later ceded its aircraft to NAG 11) had lost WNr. 734006 on 16 February while 734014 and 734018 (E8+BB) were found by the Americans at Villafranca. Readers will note that the presence of *Stab/NSG 9* markings on the latter and on Willy Ferling's E8+CB (see page 151) is not explained by this order of battle.

The RAF rated the night of 22/23 April as the peak of the current phase of *Nachtschlacht* activity, one estimate crediting NSG 9 with 30 sorties in the area round Bologna. From 2./NSG 9, *Ofw.* Artur Heiland and *Gefr.* Werner Lotsch flew a 70-minute mission from Bovolone starting at 21.30, against the Via Emilia west of Bologna, in the face of light and medium AA fire; Messerschmidt and Hettling flew

Straßenjagd: A British Army lorry on fire following a Luftwaffe attack during the final offensive in Italy. NSG 9's aircraft would come down as low as 20m to make their strafing runs against convoys of lorries.

four (the first in Ju 87D-5 E8+AK, the rest in D-3 E8+LK); Wintermayr and Hofmann (E8+EL) made three sorties against the Bologna–Modena highway. Fifth Army HQ was strafed around midnight by a single aircraft which attacked from 400-500ft but there were no casualties; 4–5 aircraft strafed II Corps HQ from 20.55–23.11 and again no casualties were reported. Grid references L-8050, 8040, 9040 and 9050 were bombed (SD 2 "butterfly bombs" fell on motor transport near Budrio (BO) for example) and Highways 64 and 65 south of Bologna were strafed. The radio monitoring picture was of a single sortie early in the evening thought to be a weather reconnaissance while soon after a pair of aircraft appeared to abandon their mission. Eight hostiles were detected between 22.09 and 23.13, one being about to bomb at 22.20 and another nearing its target at 22.41. Seven aircraft were homing in the hour after midnight and six bombed by EGON between 02.31 and 03.49. Having changed over to Ju 87D-5 E8+BK, Heiland and Lotsch logged an EGON mission from Bovolone lasting from 01.30–02.55, to drop incendiary bomb containers on Bologna, strongly defended by AA fire. *Komm. Gen.'s* daily report for 23 April, signalled to *Luftflotte 6* in Bavaria, speaks of 21 sorties to bomb and strafe targets along the front south of the Po, with losses of "1/90 missing." Whether this signifies the loss of an Fw 190 is unclear.

Harry Fischer wrote in 1992 that both his original air-gunners had been lost while flying with other pilots. On this night one of them, *Obgfr.* Heinz Staudt, was flying with 21 year-old *Fhr.* Karl-Heinz Liebmann: they took off from Villafranca for Bologna but were never heard from again. Hans Deutsch with a new *Bordfunker*, Fritz Scharmüller, flew a one-hour sortie in E8+EL from 22.03 (his first flight since 30 January) dropping bombs on roads south of Bologna. Relieved of his ground defence duties, Dirk Bunsen also took part, finally getting his chance to fly a mission after seven months with NSG 9:

> Very short, rather superficial briefing. No definite target was given, just the cue "roads south of Bologna, leading down from the Appenines." Hardly enough for you to mark the positions of the most important visual beacons for the return flight to Villafranca on your 1:500 000 map…
>
> *Uffz.* Bürger from Danzig was radio my operator… Mission: bombing of roads leading from the Futa Pass, south of Bologna (Highway 503) – a vague target that was barely illuminated by the moon and therefore very hard to find.

First, the crews had to get to their aircraft:

> From 21 or 22 April we were no longer quartered in the city of Villafranca but in the village of Povegliano [Veronese], 5km further to the east south east… As far as I recall, we were fetched by lorries and brought from Povegliano to the landing ground near Sommacampagna [VR]. Since some of the aircraft stood way off along the perimeter — widely dispersed — on the last evening we made a farmer who happened to be passing take us there with his horse and cart!

After flying five sorties that night:

> I was picked up somehow, in a car or small lorry that took me the 8km back to
> Povegliano in the small hours, there to sink into a "deathlike" slumber that lasted
> until one o' clock in the afternoon.

Near complete Allied reconnaissance coverage of Villafranca on the 23rd revealed five Ju 87s and ten single-engined fighters in the dispersal areas. For the dusk–dawn period of 23/24 April, *Komm. Gen.* envisaged night ground attack by Fw 190s and Ju 87s from the Verona area on Fourteenth Army's front in the zone Viadana (MN)–Modena–Mirandola (MO). Around San Benedetto Po (MN), the US 10th Mountain Division had forced a crossing of the river under fire and set up pontoon bridges:

> Late in the afternoon of 23 April, the 85th [Mountain Infantry Regiment] commenced
> its crossing of the river at Camatta [MN] ... The 3rd Battalion led off, reached the
> other shore and established their beachhead by 1830 hours... The night had brought
> scattered enemy resistance and some strafing by enemy planes...

Dirk Bunsen was flying one of those "enemy planes":

> After my first take-off I had to turn back again right away: the airspeed indicator
> wasn't indicating anything! A landing without the ASI was too risky for me. Cause of
> the defect: the groundcrew had forgotten to remove the watertight cover from the
> pitot tube that projected from the wing's leading edge. So, fresh start to carry out
> the mission "bombardment of the enemy crossing points (pontoon bridges) over the
> Po at San Benedetto Po." Again it was hard to discern details...

From 2./NSG 9 in Bovolone, Messerschmitt and Hettling in Ju 87D-5 E8+BK harassed the same target, landing in Vicenza at 21.45 before moving on to Thiene at 05.15. MAAF estimated that as many as 20 sorties took place altogether.

The proximity of American ground troops finally forced NSG 9 out of Villafranca. Dirk Bunsen:

> On [this] second night, [my] sorties (perhaps it was only three) finished earlier and
> we waited, drunk with sleep, in the Flying Control buildings the two or three hours
> until first light... to begin the transfer flight to Vicenza or Thiene.
>
> In the narrow space behind the armour plate (situated between the pilot and
> gunner) flew not only the radio operator but also the crew chief. Our baggage (the
> rectangular airman's rucksack) we placed in a transport container slung beneath
> the fuselage, which looked like one of the first Zeppelins from before the
> First World War...

He recalled to the author in 1996 that he remained in Vicenza barely long enough to be waved off again by the control tower and that:

> This flight from Villafranca to Thiene, with a short touchdown en route at Vicenza,
> was my last.

Stollwerck and Fischer had flown missions to San Benedetto and nearby Bondeno (FE) that night then at 04.20 they too transferred to Vicenza, again with two passengers aboard. On landing, their Ju 87D-5 (WNr. 132230, E8+AL) ran into a bomb crater, stood on its nose and stayed there for the rest of the war. Harry Fischer and *Uffz.* Bürger flew direct from Villafranca to Thiene without mishap. A MAAF reconnaissance of Villafranca at 16.05 reported the northern runway blown up by mines while the main field remained serviceable; in the north dispersal were a Ju 87 and seven other single-engined aircraft.

The Diary of Thiene Parish records for the 24th that: "On the airfield there are more than 30 aircraft, German bombers of various models" and how at 16.00 a column of 100 weary men arrived with three lorry-loads of bombs. Not all the crews had transferred to Thiene that day, as Herbert Kehrer attests:

> On 25 April 1945 we had to evacuate Villafranca since the front line had already
> reached the Po.

Nevertheless, Kehrer and Alfons Eck flew another two missions from their old base (from 23.30–00.28 and 01.10–02.55) before flying E8+NH over to Thiene at 04.30 on the 25th. An even later departure, according to his *Flugbuch*, was that of Willy Ferling, reunited with gunner Bruno Grüning in Ju 87 E8+DL. They supposedly transferred at 20.20 that evening but it is likely that the time was incorrectly logged, since by then troops of the US 85th Mountain Infantry had taken Villafranca:

ABOVE: *Lt. Peter Stollwerck of 3./NSG 9 stood Ju 87D-5 WNr. 132230, E8+AL on its nose when he ran into a bomb crater while landing at Vicenza at 04.45 on 24 April 1945. Crowded in with him were Bordfunker Franz Fischer and two ground crewmen.*

BELOW: *Also discovered at Vicenza by the Allies was this Fw 190F-9, WNr. 440323, E8+MH. The inspection panel for the radio compartment has been cannibalised another aircraft with a different style of Balkenkreuz.. Unfortunately, no photographs of an Fw 190F-8/R1 (E8+EH) found at the same airfield have yet come to light.*

Company C pushed on to the 1st Battalion objective, the large Villafranca Airport. By 1700, 25 April, the airfield was entirely in the hands of the battalion and the CP [command post] was established across the highway east of the field. This terminated a rapid foot march, against opposition, of 25 miles in less than 20 hours… The closing curtain to this action came at 2200, in the form of a German Volkswolf 190 which landed on the north end of the airstrip. The plane, apparently out of gas, was captured intact but the pilot escaped into the nearby woods.

The "Volkswolf" was an Fw 190 F-9, WNr. 440340, which, like some of its sisters found in Innsbruck (and WNr. 440341 in Neubiberg), bore no unit markings. Its pilot has not been identified.

NSG 9's arrival in Thiene had not passed MAAF by, as their airfield reconnaissance report for the 25th noted:

> Villaverla/Thiene, southern perimeter: 8 Ju 87 and 1 single-engined aircraft; south west dispersal, 11 Ju 87.

That night, two P-61s from 414th NFS strafed the airfield but German activity seems to have been very limited: one hostile was reported over F.5814 and at 20.20 a Mosquito made a contact which then evaded it. A 233 Wing Baltimore approached head-on by a Ju 87 south west of Monsélice (PD) likewise managed to evade. Also at Monsélice sometime on the 25th, EGON guidance had come to an end when radar station MERIDIAN was stripped and destroyed, probably by its operators. The system's other (mobile) Freya had pulled out of Custoza by the time the Allies arrived and may have been the one found after the war "in road order" in the equipment assembly area at Caldaro (BZ).

According to the Thiene Diary, aircraft took off at 21.30 to bomb targets along the Pc, one returning an hour later only to be destroyed in a crash near the local church. Heinrich Leinberger remembers this incident:

> On the last mission against a crossing over the Po [we encountered] very heavy anti-aircraft fire which seriously damaged our machine. After this operation a machine overturned on landing at Thiene airfield, killing the crew.

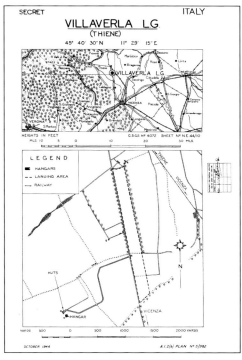

Werner Lotsch had taken off on his 89th and final mission at 20.30, with Horst Rau as pilot. Their target had been crossings over the Po east of Ostiglia where they had encountered light, medium and heavy *Flak*:

> We were just back from our op [landing at 21.25], had taxied to dispersal and were stood on the wing of our Ju 87 [D-3, E8+EK]. Another machine came back and floated in for a landing. I watched a normal approach, soft touchdown and — after 50–100m — two or three hops. The tail went up and they overturned. We ran to assist but the cockpit canopy was flat and the crew were dead, probably from broken necks.

Herbert Kehrer:

> We'd transferred from Villafranca early on, since the front had already reached the Po. We didn't reckon on any more combat missions now. Nevertheless, that evening [*Oblt.*] Müller was tasked with attacking the Po crossing south of Mantua. I got the order to attack the crossing early the next morning.
>
> On the evening of 25 April we were sitting right near the airfield, eating a duck that Alfons Eck had supplied and got the farmer's wife to roast. It was well after 21.00 when we saw Müller come back from his mission. Later on, when we got to the field they told us that [he] had overturned on landing. Overturning a Ju 87 was always fatal for the crew. He must have been hit during the attack, with "only" his tyres shot up. If only one tyre had gone *kaputt*, he would have done a "circle dance" and they'd have had a good chance of coming out of it alive.
>
> Müller's death affected me a lot. He joined us as a young *Leutnant*, was very popular, native of Breslau. One instance: it was in Cavriago, I'd received two letters and a telegram telling me that for four weeks I'd been the father of a son. I generally had to fly a weather reconnaissance before the evening mission — after twilight there was often thick haze in the Po Plain. That evening I declined [and] *Lt.* Müller offered to make the flight... that was how he "baptised" the child. We drove back to quarters and celebrated... It hurts when I think about him. We flew a lot of missions together and the last one really was his last.

Friedrich Müller had turned 33 the previous day while his crewman, *Obgfr.* Lothar Görtz, was 21. Both were members of 2./NSG 9 and now lie in the Costermano (VR) military cemetery.

Ernst Messerschmidt's target that night was the Mantua area while Carl Wintermayr's log records, "04.20–05.09... Ostiglia, bombs on the bridgehead" and Alfred Kunzmann writes simply, "I belonged to those units that flew the last missions against the Po bridges, from Thiene..."

Horst Greßler recalls:

> After several operations [in an Fw 190 from Villafranca] we transferred to Thiene. From there I flew a few more missions over northern Italy. Due to a damaged machine, I had to make an emergency landing on the airfield perimeter. For me that was an end to flying in Italy, I simply no longer had an aircraft.

Herbert Kehrer:

> I flew the last mission, at 04.28 on 26 April. Flew south from Thiene until [we were] across the Po, then west and attacked the crossings heading north without inflicting too much damage, I hope. That's how I see it from today's standpoint.

During the day, New Zealand troops reached the River Adige in the northeast and the Allied advance cut the Axis forces in Italy in two. The situation was clearly past saving and on the 27th the Germans set about the destruction of stores, documents and installations at Thiene. The Parish Diary records that the *Platzkommandant* donned civilian clothing and made good his escape. *Leutnant* Peter Stollwerck wrote in 1946:

> ... vehicles were packed to the limit with weapons, ammunition and baggage. Anything superfluous was either burned or swiftly exchanged for good salami. With raised voices, drivers and passengers were allocated to the individual vehicles and aircrew brought to Flying Control. Parting from *"nostra piccola bambina (con bambino)"*[5] Marcella and the other Italians was quick and painless, though beforehand they all used to tell us they'd follow us to the ends of the Earth.

LEFT: *Fw 190F-9, WNr. 440340 landed at Villafranca at 22.00 on 25 April 1945, soon after the US Army captured the field. Its arrival was such a surprise that the pilot made good his escape. The aircraft had no unit markings.*

BELOW: *How Fw 190F-9 WNr. 440340 came to lose its cockpit canopy is not known but efforts have been made to protect the interior with a tarpaulin.*

BELOW: *This view of WNr. 440340 shows to advantage the broad chord airscrew of the Fw 190F-9 as well as its bomb racks, cannon and machine gun armament.*

Before we took off for Innsbruck, our *Kommandeur* gave a fiery speech during which he prophetically uttered sad words about "probably the last flight of NSG 9" and then announced (incomprehensibly for me at that time) that personally he was going to choose the harder and more dangerous journey overland. Events proved him right. The rest of us believed in our childlike way that the hardest and thorniest flight of our lives lay before us. About all we spoke of was baling out.

Burdened down with our impossibly numerous pieces of baggage, we took off one after another as each became ready, with long intervals between us. In ML ([Dirk Bunsen's] bird a while previously?) I climbed into the clouds to the safe height of 4,000m and set course. A "pleasant" flight, permanently in cloud with no information on the winds at altitude or the weather at our destination. But then could it have been otherwise?

A few minutes before my ETA, a gap opened in the clouds which I couldn't go through fast enough for my liking. Beneath me I could see the badly damaged Brenner line and, up in front, Innsbruck. Calmly and without apprehension I sought out the correct field west of Innsbruck and made my last — textbook — landing with everything neat and trim.

Although I'd been almost the last to take off, I could only make out two or three *Ju's* that had landed ahead of me. I was soon to learn the reason: at the time of my landing some fighters had made the Innsbruck area unsafe and caught some of us. I think nine aircraft were missing.

Ofw. Horst Rau (a *Bundeswehr* helicopter pilot, postwar*)* set down his account on 2 May, just days after his more eventful trip:

…*Oblt.* Schewen of 2./NSGr. 9 ordered me to ferry Ju 87 E8+EK from Thiene … to Innsbruck … to escape the threatening enemy advance. Apart from myself, about 18 aircraft (around 12 Ju 87s and six Fw 190s in all) got the take-off order toward midday.

The general weather situation made considerable demands on the crews' flying skills in order to accomplish a safe crossing of the Alps. Over Thiene there was 6–8/10 cloud cover at 800–900m and above that, at 1,200m, 9–10/10. At that time there was solid cloud over the Alpine area and München reported 10/10 with its base at 800m.

I was ordered to break through the cloud cover over the airfield and — above or in the clouds — fly to München by dead reckoning without sight of the ground. There, without any kind of electronic aid, I was supposed to go back down through the clouds, sight ground, get my bearings and fly back along the Inn Valley to Innsbruck-East.

I and my radio-operator, *Obgfr.* Rudolf Ende, took off at 12.25. After flying through the first cloud layer, I established that my turn and bank indicator had gone u/s. Considering that I had to fly blind for the greater part of the way, I decided to turn back and land. At 12.35 I landed back in Thiene.

When the 2. *Staffel* workshop chief had established that there was no longer any possibility of exchanging the indicator, *Oblt.* Schewen ordered me to ready my aircraft to be blown up and for me and my wireless operator to set off overland for Innsbruck.

Meanwhile however, *Ofw.* Gräßer landed his machine, likewise reporting instrument failure. Therefore it became possible to install his turn and bank indicator in my aircraft and the artificial horizon from an unserviceable plane was put into Gräßer's.

Although retrained on the Fw 190, on this occasion Günther Gräßer was flying a Ju 87D-3, +DL[6]. He and Werner Lotsch had turned back with compass failure. After landing and swapping instruments, at 12.45 they tried again for Innsbruck, only to lose both compass and artificial horizon this time. Nonetheless, they decided to carry on:

Solid cloud cover — attempt to climb through a gap into the clear, blue sky fails — blind flying in the clouds — all of a sudden a whistling noise growing ever louder — recovery of the diving aircraft. Emerge from the cloud base on our backs with the woods overhead. Pilot catches the aircraft and recovers the situation, low over the woods of the pre-alpine region. A renewed attempt through a gap in the clouds succeeds — northward at 5,500m over a thick cloud layer with sun at our backs.

LEFT: *"After setting off explosive charges in the driver's cab, the motor oil caught fire and slowly ate through the engine bearers. Like a world-weary, grief-stricken creature, the bird… allowed its head to droop."* One of NSG 9's Ju 87D-5s at Hötting, June 1945. Unusually for NSG 9, this aircraft lacks wheel covers.

RIGHT: *This Ju 87D-5 on the southern perimeter at Hötting has particularly heavy dark meander camouflage applied to its lower surfaces.*

LEFT: *This shot shows to advantage the long-span wings of the Ju 87D-5 and the characteristic upper surface camouflage of NSG 9. A JV 44 Me 262 sits in the distance. This is the southern part of Hötting airfield, in the bend of the River Inn which runs between the field and the first range of hills in the background.*

RIGHT: *Partially hidden in a barn at Hötting, this Ju 87D-3 bears a yellow "G" on its port wheel cover, suggesting its full code is E8+GL. On the bomb rack is an uncapped transport container, used by crews to ferry their personal effects when changing base.*

Some didn't make it to Innsbruck. Dumped at München-Riem along with three Fw 190s and a Do 335, Ju 87D-3 E8+DK of 2./NSG 9 was photographed in the summer of 1946. At some stage, it has sustained damage from small-calibre bullets. Exposure to the elements has erased any trace of meander camouflage and parts of the wing are down to bare metal. Still present are a toned down fuselage cross, partial white Mediterranean Theatre band and the four character code. There are also traces of an overpainted factory callsign. This may be the aircraft in which Uffz. Kurt Urban flew 5 missions in September 1944.

We don't know where we are — suddenly the clouds part — about 10km east of a city — Innsbruck? Too good to be true — we fly on with the ground in sight — church with two towers — München. We fly south along the River Isar in the direction of Innsbruck. Four Mustang fighters appear but luckily they don't see us, they have another target in view.

The valley of the Isar grows narrower [so] we turn around — too dangerous. We look for an airfield around the city of München [which is] destroyed, we see nothing but ruins with the exception of the *Liebfrauenkirche*! We see an airfield and land. Four fighters appear on the horizon — the four Mustangs? We jump down from the wings and run from our *Ju*. We look around — four Me 109s, that's lucky.

The time was 14.55. After 130 minutes over the mountains, without proper instruments, in "the worst weather conditions" Gräßer and Lotsch had landed safely at Oberwiesenfeld, München's civil airport of the interwar period and nowadays the site of the city's Olympic Park.

We return now to Horst Rau in Thiene:

When I'd made sure that my [replacement turn and bank] indicator was working, I took off for the second time at 12.50. I came through the clouds and at about 13.10 and 3,000m set course in a gentle climb. Over the central Alps, the cloud ceiling got higher, so that at 4,500m I was forced to fly blind some of the time. My wireless operator suffered from oxygen shortage more than I did.

At 13.40, I lost control of my aircraft while flying blind. I couldn't control it and ended up falling at 20m/sec. Mustering all my strength however, I was able to restore normal flying attitude according to the instruments and continue blind flying. I now flew temporarily at between 4,600 and 5,000m above and within the clouds and oxygen shortage again made itself unpleasantly apparent. At 14.00 and flying completely blind, I lost control of my machine again. The aeroplane was totally out of control but once more, with the utmost concentration and summoning up all my flying skill, I was able to save the aircraft and crew from imminently being smashed to pieces in the Alps.

I regained control and after about 20 minutes' flying time, I sighted the ground again, toward 14.20. I lost height right away and established that underneath me was the River Inn. In the Bavarian mountains there was 4/10 - 6/10 cumulus at about 2,000m. At 14.20 over Rosenheim I established my position from landmarks and flew up the Inn Valley at low level toward Innsbruck.

At 14.30, between the clouds, I saw two fighters flying above me. I alerted my wireless operator and we took defensive measures. A fraction of a section later I realised that one of the fighters was attacking another Ju 87.

The fighters were F-6s of the Ninth Air Force's 15th Tactical Reconnaissance Squadron (XIX Tactical Air Command), flown by 1/Lt Haylon R. "Joe" Wood and 2/Lt Maxwell E. Chambers, heading back to their base at Fürth, near Nürnberg. They claimed the destruction of three Ju 87s at 14.15, two by Wood alone, one shared between them. Wood described the engagement to American author, Tom Ivie:

> My wingman … and I had been assigned the mission of checking the area south of München, a valley leading to the Brenner Pass… The mission was uneventful until we were emerging from the pass just west of München and suddenly a fighter pilot's dream unfolded some 2,000ft to my front at 6,000ft altitude, heading in the opposite direction - three Stukas. Two were in close formation and one 500ft aside…

In his encounter report written at the time, Wood mentioned that he was in the area of the US Army's forward troops and that the Ju 87s were climbing, probably — as he mistakenly surmised — pulling out after bombing.

> I seemed breathless, but I could hear myself on radio instructing my wingman … 'Take it easy son, just stay tucked in, don't fire until I do, and take dead aim.'
> I opened fire at 300yds and the lead Stuka exploded into flame and crashed into the ground.

The identity of the stricken aircraft has not been established, although it is known that Wintermayr and Hofmann (E8+EL) sighted the Mustangs but arrived safely in Innsbruck.

Wood's elation at his success comes through in his description to Tom Ivie over 30 years later:

> Pulling up from the dive we throttled back, dropped 30 degrees of flaps and started slowing our aircraft to 190mph in order to set up for the big kill … this was really something … I had shot down two German fighters previously … becoming an ace if I destroyed these three.

Reverting to his encounter report:

> The section then did a 180 and I was in position for a dead astern shot on the second enemy aircraft. I opened fire at 200 yards, firing a two-second burst, air speed 150mph, and the E/A started smoking badly and its landing gear fell off. He went into a tight turn to the left and then crash-landed and burned. Photo taken for confirmation.

Herbert Kehrer had taken off from Thiene in E8+PL at 13.00 and was 95 minutes into his flight:

> We'd no map of Innsbruck, no weather [report] from Germany, it was raining in Thiene. We'd prepared ourselves for bailing out, not combat and the gunner never got a shot off. From Mr Wood or Mr Chambers I took hits through the right wing. Luckily they only perforated my kitbag and not the tanks, so I was able to jettison the undercarriage and make a smooth belly landing.

The "gunner" was his long-time backseater, Alfons Eck:

> Some American Mustang fighters still had ammunition to spare and brought us down over the picturesque little town of Kufstein-Oberaudorf. With undercarriage jettisoned, fuselage turned into a sieve by bullets and wings in similar state we ended this, our life together, with a near-fatal trip on to a meadow between two closely-spaced mountain ridges. End of a life of adventure? What a mistake: it was just about to start…

1/Lt. Haylon R. Wood, USAAF of 15th TRS, Ninth Air Force. "Joe" Wood claimed three of NSG 9's aircraft shot down over Austria on 27 April 1945. He was never credited with them, earning a reprimand for departing from his reconnaissance duties instead.

ABOVE: *The F-6 in the background, 5M*W, s/n 32574, is Lt Wood's Millie… In the foreground, S/Sgt Lesher relaxes on the wing of another 15th TRS aircraft.*

ABOVE RIGHT: *Twins, Osa and Ora Tyra pose in front of Lt Wood's F-6, Millie, My Baby, And Me.*

Wood now went after the third Ju 87. Horst Rau related how:

> I went right down on the deck to get myself as much out of the enemy fighters' sight as possible. At the same moment I was attacked from behind and above by the other hostile machine and fired upon. My wireless operator returned fire immediately, simultaneously giving a commentary on where the enemy's shots were going. I flew violent evasive action and came through the fighter's first pass without taking any hits. Meanwhile I could no nothing to prevent the second machine also attacking me and scoring some hits, cutting off my radio and especially the intercom to my wireless operator. Now I was deprived of this invaluable aid and was offered up practically defenceless to the two fighters that, from 20m distance, I could now recognise as American Mustangs.

We return to Wood's encounter report:

> After breaking off the encounter with the second E/A I found the third Ju-87 directly ahead and closed to 100 yards before firing a one-second burst. Pieces fell off the enemy aircraft and he started smoking. I then pulled up and Lt. Chambers came in and closed to 200 yards before firing a long burst. The E/A started smoking very badly. I then closed and opened fire at 200 yards, closing to 50ft at which time the E/A straightened up and jettisoned its canopy. The Stuka then went into a spin at 500 feet. Two airmen bailed out and hit the ground just as their chutes were opening. Chambers confirmed all three victories.

No longer bound by the conventions of military reporting, Wood was able to offer Tom Ivie a more colourful account:

> After a chase around church steeples, crags etc. which lasted about 10 minutes, I opened fire and saw pieces fall away and it began smoking just as I pulled up. At this point Chambers hit it with a long burst and just as my guns emptied the crew of the Stuka jettisoned their canopy. Suddenly from an altitude of no more than 100ft the pilot pulled straight up, and as I side-slipped to avoid hitting him I could almost see the color of the tail-gunner's eyes as he crouched in his seat, about to jump. I thought aloud, "you poor devil, don't bail out at that altitude." But bail out they did. One chute opened full apparently, and I observed its occupant scurry into the nearby woods. the other chute opened only partially, and I'm quite sure the flyer attached to it was killed. A photo taken by my vertical camera later revealed what appeared to be — or obviously was — a chute and a body sprawled on the ground.

"I'd brought along a bicycle"

Those elements of NSG 9 that could get there regrouped on the landing ground of Innsbruck-Hötting[1], a 1,000 x 300m grass strip a little to the west of the city between the Innsbruck-Telfs road and the River Inn. The *Gruppe* immediately set to work restoring its operational capability, organising camouflage, aircraft servicing, supplies of bombs and everything else it needed to rejoin the fight:

> ... in the firm expectation of flying some more missions ... subsequently we got the order from the *Gruppe* to transfer to Sluderno, an airfield in Italy. Meanwhile however, it snowed all day without a break and the already soft field at Innsbruck got completely saturated. Taking off was out of the question.

Sluderno (BZ) was the most northerly fully operational air base in Italy and had been *Komm. Gen.'s* original choice of aerodrome for the *Gruppe* in the event of a general withdrawal of the Italian front to the so-called Pre-Alpine Position. It seems therefore that someone was even now trying to redeploy units to their intended locations. If NSG 9's flying days were at an end, the war was not. Peter Stollwerck continues his account:

> We saw exciting days in Innsbruck: jet fighters landed in large numbers and made headstands, one after another.

Alfred Kunzmann too remembers that, "...there we encountered the first Me 262s" although neither he nor his comrade seems to have known that these were part of *Genlt.* Adolf Galland's JV 44 which after evacuating München-Riem was now scattered between Hötting, Ainring, Salzburg-Maxglan and Prague. Returning to Stollwerck:

> The Army in Italy surrendered on 1 May; the Yanks were coming ever closer from Garmisch-Partenkirchen way. Feverish vehicle traffic became noticeable on the roads into the lonely mountains. Huge crowds of people were constantly pressing into the rations depot in Innsbruck.

Back in Thiene, NSG 9's rear party under the command of the recently appointed NSFO, *Lt.* Fritz Resch, had gathered a selection of vehicles for their own journey north: a Büssing lorry, an Italian SPA "desert vehicle" and an Opel Olympia car. A heavily armed group set out, led by a *Feldwebel* of the technical staff, as Horst Greßler describes:

> Our two [goods] vehicles were laden down with rations and armament. There was a 2cm cannon mounted on the SPA and we had all kinds of small arms, grenades and munitions to hand. The Büssing carried mainly men and women signals auxiliaries.

Münchem-Riem soon after the war ended. Among the variety of aircraft gathered together in front of the airport buildings is a Ju 87. This may be E8+DK, a "stray" from NSG 9's retreat to Innsbruck, which ended up on Riem's scrapheap.

ABOVE: Among the alpine flowers on the banks of the River Inn, this Ju 87D-3 carries unusual third and fourth code letters that appear to be a black "C" and a white (or yellow?) "L". This may therefore be the E8+CL flown to Hötting by Willy Ferling and "Bruno" Grüning. In the background are an Fw 190 of 1./NSG 9 draped with a camouflage net and two Me 262As of JV 44. The overhead wires show that these aircraft are dispersed away from the main landing field.

ABOVE: Ju 87D-3 E8+GL of 3./NSG 9 lies half-concealed in a barn at Innsbruck-Hötting. American troops have arrived and the men of NSG 9 have taken to the mountains prior to heading for home as best they can.

ABOVE: Ju 87D-3 "yellow D" (E8+DL) seen at Innsbruck-Hötting in June 1945, an unidentified object resting beneath it. Detail of the meander pattern on the cowling suggests that this may be WNr. 3-1257, pictured on page 75.

LEFT: One of NSG's Ju 87D-5s abandoned in a meadow on the northern edge of Innsbruck-Hötting airfield, summer 1945. In the background is an Me 262 of JV 44, while the line of trees marks the road from Innsbruck to Telfs.

RIGHT: *The south western perimeter of Hötting airfield. To the left, behind the sparsely camouflaged Me 262, is a Ju 87D-3 of NSG 9 while to the right is a Ju 87D-5 wrecked by its owners. Unlike the aircraft on page 175 (top) this machine appears to have its wheel covers in place. Its pale blue undersurface camouflage has been supplimented for night operations with cloudy patches of dark grey. Behind the electricity pylon is a glimpse of the River Inn.*

LEFT: *This view of Ju 87D-3 E8+GL shows to advantage the white segment on the front part of its spinner. Carried by many aircraft of NSG 9, the significance (if any) of this marking is not known.*

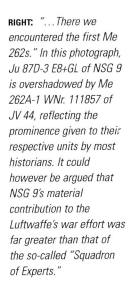

RIGHT: *"…There we encountered the first Me 262s." In this photograph, Ju 87D-3 E8+GL of NSG 9 is overshadowed by Me 262A-1 WNr. 111857 of JV 44, reflecting the prominence given to their respective units by most historians. It could however be argued that NSG 9's material contribution to the Luftwaffe's war effort was far greater than that of the so-called "Squadron of Experts."*

Their route took them from Thiene though Bassano del Grappa (VI), Feltre (BL) and Belluno, then on to Cortina d'Ampezzo (BL) and Dobbiaco (BZ). At this time they believed the remnants of the *Gruppenstab* to be in Brunico (BZ), about 14 miles further along the Pusteria Valley. Since there was a general expectation that the partisans would have mined the mountain roads, Greßler formed an advance guard and three days into their journey the Opel did indeed hit a mine. Thankfully no one was hurt although the vehicle had to be abandoned. Greßler again:

> We billeted ourselves for the time being in a disused sawmill... Here our Austrian comrades took their leave of us to head for home on foot. Our quarters lay about 500m from the Brunico-Dobbiaco Highway. Since we had sufficient food, for the first time we could wait a while and see how things turned out. The partisans in Dobbiaco were preoccupied with one another: first the Reds were in the Town Hall, then the Greens.
>
> About a week went by like this, until one night I was woken from my sleep by a rumbling noise... Great masses of American tanks were rolling by along the highway. Now the war really was over for us.

Leutnant Resch's group had been overtaken by a Regimental Combat Team of the US 88th "Clover Leaf" Division. American troops advancing north and south through the Brenner Pass met early on 4 May and similar link-ups were soon made in the neighbouring passes, leaving no way out of Italy for the many Germans still there. After aborting his flight to Austria, Helmut Schäfer had found 3./NSG 9's ground echelon "already sitting on the vehicles", set off with them and was taken prisoner by the Americans in the Alps near Bressanone (BZ).

On 5 May, the following NSG 9 aircrew remained in Italy according to the personnel roster of *Komm. Gen's. Italien's* Quartermaster:

	Pilots	W/T Operators	Gunners
Stab	-	1	-
1. *Staffel*	5	-	-
2. *Staffel*	2	2	1
3. *Staffel*	1	-	2
4. *Staffel*	-	-	8

Any resemblance between these figures and reality seems questionable when NSG 9's men and women were scattered across the map from Thiene in the south to München in the north and mostly out of contact with one another, let alone von Pohl's HQ in Bolzano, where a MATAF liaison party arrived at midnight on the 5th to oversee the surrender of the *Luftwaffe* in Italy. As for 4./NSG 9, this roster is, so far as the author is aware, the only place such a unit — if indeed it existed — has ever been mentioned.

Meanwhile, the *Spieß* (senior NCO) of 3. *Staffel* had been trying to make it over the Alps in a worn-out, overloaded lorry which finally broke down on the rugged mountain roads. Cut off from the main body of the *Gruppe*, he was fortunate in encountering an army vehicle — described as a Lancia "mountaineer" — whose driver obligingly ditched his load of gas protection gear over the mountainside in favour of taking the *Spieß* and all his men and baggage (including the contents of the Orderly Room). With difficulty, they made their way through the Brenner Pass and other control points to Innsbruck. To their amazement they were the first and only vehicle from the *Gruppe* to have made the crossing, learning days later that the others had been diverted to Sluderno, presumably in the expectation that the aircraft would be joining them there.

Meanwhile, imagining that soon they would be "somewhere up in the mountains, with the *Capitano* at our head, fighting out a lone partisan war", 3. *Staffel* busied themselves with acquiring rations and diesel for their vehicles.

On 2 May, the Austrian Resistance had moved to seize control of Innsbruck and by now military authority had broken down in the city. The local army commander, *Genmaj.* Böhaimb, and his staff had been captured; the radio station proclaimed revolt and civilians and Austrian-born *Wehrmacht* troops alike were rallying to the red/white/red "Free Tyrol" banner. Now, a last Ju 87 *Nachtschlächter* arrived on one of the city's airfields: 1./NSG 4's *Fw.* Faber had volunteered in March 1945 for a "self-sacrifice" mission against the Soviet-held Oder bridges but had been returned to his unit shortly afterward. When his *Staffel* disbanded in Travemünde on the Baltic, this pilot managed to fly safely home to Austria, along with his wireless operator.

Next day, the first American artillery shells fell near Hötting airfield; that evening, a battalion of the US 409th Infantry Regiment was in the city centre raising the Stars and Stripes and being hailed as liberators. Peter Stollwerck:

LEFT: *An Fw 190F-8 with a blown canopy. The underwing cross (type B4) seems to have been applied to bare metal, after which camouflage paint has been put on around it. In the background are a severely damaged Me 262 and a US Army truck.*

ABOVE: *The rusting half of an AB 500 cluster-bomb container found at Thiene after NSG 9 had departed for Innsbruck.*

ABOVE: *In the south western corner of Hötting airfield, an unmarked Fw 190F of 1./NSG 9, its late-model blown canopy lying across its tail. Some attempt has been made to camouflage the aircraft with branches. In the background is an Me 262A of JV 44 and beyond it, across the River Inn, the white tower of the Emmaus Church in the village of Völs and the conical peak of the Blasienberg.*

RIGHT: *An Fw 190F-9, to judge from its broad chord airscrew blades. It carries type B4 and H5 crosses but once again no unit markings. Note how the aircraft (like the other Focke-Wulfs pictured here) has bogged down to its axles in the soft ground that characterised Hötting airfield.*

Horst Rau filed his "Report on the shooting down of a Ju 87 by two American Mustang fighters" on 2 May 1945, recounting his experiences at the hands of Lts Wood and Chambers on 27 April. By now, NSG 9 was in Innsbruck, its dissolution just days away.

```
Horst Rau,
Oberfeldwebel,
1.N.S.G.9.                              O.U., 2. Mai 1945.

     Bericht über den Abschuß einer Ju 87 durch zwei
            amerikanische Mustang-Jäger.

Am 27.April 1945 bekam ich von Oblt.Scheven von der 2.N.S.G.9 den
Befehl vom Flugplatz Thiene(Italien) das Flugzeug Ju 87 Kennzeichen
E8+EK nach Innsbruck-Ost zu überführen,um es dem drohenden feind -
lichen Zugriff zu entziehen.Außer mir bekamen noch etwa 18 Flugzeug-
führer der N.S.G.9 gegen 12 Uhr mittags Startbefehl.(Insgesamt etwa
12 Ju 87 und 6 FW 190).
```

We held a council of war, decided to wait until morning, take to the hills with bag and baggage and let events take their course. So we scrounged an old abandoned bus that … could no longer shift under its own steam and hitched it up to our Lancia…

They left as planned, with rations (including over 600 loaves), weapons, ammunition, kit and 30 or 40 men. The party's store of personal baggage was so great that some had to be entrusted to the care of strangers near their quarters in Innsbruck. There had been one other job to be done before they left:

…we'd blown up, shot up or rendered unusable our trusty old mills[2]. It was a sorrowful parting from our birds and one I'll never forget. After setting off explosive charges in the driver's cab, the motor oil caught fire and slowly ate through the engine bearers. Like a world-weary, grief-stricken creature, the bird — looking so ready for action otherwise — allowed its head to droop slowly [at first] and then ever faster forward. So flying, the best part of the war years for me, came to an end.

The NSG 9 party headed north east for Kufstein, the Lancia towing not just the bus but five cyclists on long ropes and one of these outriders fell en route, seriously injuring his arm. Kufstein held out no lasting safety, since it was in the path of another prong of the American advance and little of the Inn Valley remained unconquered. Stollwerck described, "…a witch's cauldron, everyone going wildly hither and thither, if only to grab the best spot" and so the group decided to get as far up into the Kaiser Mountains as they could, which elicited:

A really brilliant performance from both driver and vehicle. A lot of the time we were on narrow, precipitous mountain roads with not 5cm leeway at the sides but despite it all we and the bus came through safely. I'd never come across such a steady hand and practised eye as that driver had.

Near Walchsee, a forester offered them the use a lonely cabin set high in the mountain pastures and that evening, former mountain infantryman Carl Wintermayr led a group up there in a climb not without its difficulties. The following morning, the rear party tried to get the Lancia a bit further on but the back wheels slid off the track into a ditch and its cargo had to be carried to the last farm before the cabin, either in ground sheets on the men's backs or by whatever wheeled conveyances they could organise. Binoculars revealed American tanks driving the length of the Inn Valley and scout cars already probing uncomfortably close. This spurred repair work on the lorry and toward evening they got it going once more, only to bog down again soon after. Installed in their eyrie, Peter Stollwerck related how, by contrast to so many of their compatriots elsewhere:

…we had everything the heart desired, right down to *vino rosso*. The men's bearing and morale were splendid. We celebrated our last evenings together… During this time, Grüning turned out to be an outstanding cook and the finest dishes followed, just one on top of another. Unfortunately it was too much of a good thing for everyone and all complained of loss of appetite. Is there anything so hard to bear as a complete surfeit of everything edible?

During the night of 3/4 May, German forces evacuated Kufstein. What remained of 16. *Volksgrenadier Division* had been pulled back by *Ob. West* from Scharnitz through Innsbruck for deployment round Kufstein and the division now withdrew to the area south of Bayrischzell, where it surrendered to the

US 36th Inf. Div. on the 5th. In Innsbruck on the same day, *Gen.* Brandenberger, CO of the Nineteenth Army, formally surrendered all German forces in the Tyrol and Vorarlberg. For NSG 9's remnants in Austria the party was over:

> Gradually our situation deteriorated. The *Amis* announced through loudspeakers that all soldiers found still bearing arms would be shot as partisans and aside from that you couldn't trust the locals. So we slowly divested ourselves of both weapons and uniforms... the first Yank appeared at our farmer's [place], all by himself, and ordered us to come to the camp in Kufstein right away. Luckily he was amenable to discussion and gave us until the following morning. Holtz, who from his time in the USA was able to converse fluently with the American, was God's gift as far as we were concerned... Each day he went down into the "lion's den" to assess the situation and ascertain whether there was any possibility of us getting home.
>
> The Orderly Room prepared the most beautiful discharge papers, the NCO accountant shared out the last of the pay and a group of experts got the Lancia roadworthy. The men's talent for organisation was amazing: some could no longer be distinguished from innocuous Tyrolean farmers. From the proper little hat down to the walking stick, many already had a complete civilian outfit. The first Austrians and Bavarians who lived nearby set off for their homes on 6, 7 and 8 May.

Harry Fischer, his home city of Berlin now occupied by the Red Army, was another who chose not to hang around:

> Up above Kufstein, on the *Zahmer Kaiser* [mountain], I agreed with Alfons Eck to go with him to Tengen, his home [right next to the Swiss border]. I'd brought along a bicycle in my machine [and] had a civilian suit, tailor-made in Villafranca. Getting past the *Ami* check points was a piece of cake: I stopped a woman I met, swapped my military greatcoat for her luggage rack and so I had a good means of transport. I had my parachute with me too ... That was worth its weight in gold because later on, at the Schliersee Theatre, I swapped a couple of panels for white linen from which I had a pair of trousers made. The rendezvous with Alfons didn't come off and so I pressed on alone.

Alfons Eck had missed this appointment thanks to "three American military policemen, armed to the teeth" who removed him and Herbert Kehrer from the villa where they had spent the eight days since crashlanding at Oberaudorf on 27 April. Eck noted that the MP who relieved him of his EK I seemed prouder to wear it than he himself had ever been. Up in the mountains, Heinz Buß's group divided up the personal effects of those, living and dead, who had not reached Austria. As Peter Stollwerck described it to Dirk Bunsen:

> The large number of bombed-out people and evacuees who'd gathered round our truck for the occasion were made a gift of our comrades' best and frequently most personal possessions — your rucksack amongst them. I can still picture how someone went off overjoyed with the lovely red leather shoes you'd had made in Villafranca ... many valuable things were shared out there. But the people were sensible and didn't grab at the stuff, [they] asked for what they needed from among the different items, agreed amongst themselves, were grateful and very pleased.

Wolfgang Holtz, accompanied by *Capitano* Buß and Stollwerck, spoke personally to the Military Governor of Kufstein but was unable to secure an official permit for the NSG 9 party travel home in their lorry. So, on the morning of the 9th, about 30 men and their kit set off "unofficially" in the Lancia in the hope of getting a bit nearer home before what seemed their inevitable imprisonment:

> Enormously apprehensive... we sat quiet as mice in the back of the lorry and didn't dare peep out from behind the tilt. The *Cap.* at the wheel, Holtz as interpreter and the *Spieß* as driver's mate. After only a short ride, behind a bend in the road, the first Yankee sentry was suddenly standing in front of us. Our hearts sank into our boots... We tied the most beautiful bandages of parachute silk around our heads, necks, arms and legs and travelled in the guise of wounded airmen en route to hospital. The American pointed the way to his District Commandant and let us drive there alone. We preferred not to find [it] and carried on a few towns further.

> Our morale and spirits returned, then once again a sentry suddenly stood before us. All of Holtz's persuasiveness went for nothing. The sentry installed himself on the running board and rode with us to his CO [in] a big American vehicle park. We had to switch off the engine and wait for ages. Holtz negotiated for an eternity but came back, beaming, with a tiny slip of paper, the permission to pass through this District.
>
> …Black sentries stopped us on a few more occasions and demanded watches but let us drive on until we were stopped outside the aerodrome at Erding and brought on to the base. We saw our daring journey coming to an end but even so we were pleased that we'd at least put such a stretch of the homeward trip behind us. We waited over an hour in the lion's den, seeing how soldiers were grabbed, their kit searched and they were marched into the camp. It looked like good old Holtz had failed this time. At last however he came out of the guard room and gave us the sign to drive on.

This first day's travel took them as far as Landshut in Bavaria before they decided to call a halt. The lorry was driven up to a barn and camouflaged "like in the old days", while its occupants hid themselves amongst the straw. Two Americans were quartered in the farmhouse, so only Holtz could risk a scouting trip, from which he returned downcast. All the bridges over the Isar had been blown, the one crossing was a temporary bridge erected by the Americans in Landshut itself. This however was closely guarded and barred to all civilian traffic. There was talk of splitting up and hiding out with farmers or perhaps trying to get further alone and on foot but in the end Buß rallied his troops to take the risk of carrying on:

> Early next morning, the nearer we got to the bridge … the more tense we became. We scarcely dared draw breath. Shortly before the bridge the *Cap.* suddenly turned right, into a side street. He'd spotted that one of the bridge sentries had our lorry specially in his sights and was staring supsiciously… We drove round a few blocks of houses to regain the main road where endless streams of vehicles with black drivers were travelling in both directions. The *Cap.* took his place in the line, sat up in the driver's seat chewing gum like a real Yankee and drove unmolested over the perilous bridge.

Now using back roads, the Lancia began to emit a disquieting noise and its reverse gear stopped working but in the event a minor repair sufficed. The next obstacle was the Danube and here again all the bridges had been blown, necessitating their entering the city of Ingolstadt. The road took them directly to Manching aerodrome, site of a large PoW camp but the guards evinced no interest and waved them on. Ingolstadt's traffic police did the same but then the bridge sentry suddenly signalled a stop and ran to his telephone. After some anxious moments it turned out that traffic on the bridge was one-way only and they were simply being held up while a batch crossed over from the opposite bank.

Emboldened, they joined the long convoys on the main highway, stopping for the night in a village near Ansbach "whose commissar-like mayor", a former Polish farm worker, "terrorised the whole village." In dealing with this man, Holtz and Buß posed as Americans although the latter's English sufficed only to add "Oh, yes" at the end of Holtz's sentences. Holtz took his leave of the group in Ochsenfurt and, according to Herbert Kehrer, "the general opinion was that we wouldn't get much further without him." Kehrer and a gunner got out at Würzburg and stayed the night with an elderly couple in the suburbs. Tobacco bought a ride on a milk lorry to Haßfurt (where the gunner's family had been evacuated from East Prussia). Trading more tobacco and his Italian *Lire* for a bicycle, Kehrer set off for home on Monday, 13 May. His mood was good and the weather perfect but within an hour he was picked up by Americans in Zeil am Main and, despite his discharge papers, spent two years as a prisoner.

The rest of the party had reached Buß's home village near Heiligenstadt on 11 May, with a joyous reunion for the *Capitano* and his wife. Heinz Buß kept the Lancia and, with Bruno Grüning (who also lived locally) as driver's mate, used it to start a successful haulage business. Next day, Peter Stollwerck celebrated his 26th birthday with Willy Ferling in the Buß household, resuming the long walk home on 13 May:

> …I should never have tried anything on a date like that. Toward evening a farmer's wife betrayed us to the Americans and we were taken prisoner. At first [they]

handed us over to Poles who sifted all through our kit for anything usable… We were shoved into a damp cellar with a bunch of other troops and shipped off next day to Osterode… Out of about 70 people, Ferling, myself and two more were — thanks to our discharge papers — the only ones allowed to travel on…

On 18 May, after another four days' footslogging, Stollwerck reached Hildesheim to find his home basically intact, albeit minus its roof.

…A few days later I was working in my old bank like before the war, like nothing had happened. I had the same people around me, who didn't appear to have changed: they had the same jobs, told the same jokes and moaned about the dreadful situation and the necessity that dared raise them out of their accustomed rut!

After parting from Buß's group, Werner Hensel's discharge papers cut no ice with the Allied troops who stopped him. The impression of authority conveyed by his *Oberfeldwebel's* rank and medals saw him placed in charge of a group of prisoners building a bridge at Mainz under the direction of the Americans. Conditions there were not harsh and Hensel remembers how the prisoners breakfasted on ham and eggs like their captors.

On 2 June, a soldier's body was found in a roadside stream at Hohenfeld, just outside Kitzingen. He had gunshot wounds to the head and was reckoned to have been lying in the water for about 14 days. A 20-year old evacuee from Saarbrücken told the *Gendarmerie* how one evening around two weeks previously, she and a friend had been out walking and picking meadow flowers. On the way home she had seen an American military vehicle stop and set down a German officer. He was bareheaded, carried no baggage and seemed to be in pain. He asked her directions to "Military Hospital 54" (which she was unfamiliar with), saying he had come from the prisoner of war camp in nearby Ochsenfurt and that the Americans had left him by the road to await their return. In the course of their conversation she learned that he had a wife and children and he asked her to convey his greetings to a *Hauptmann* in Ochsenfurt if she had the chance. At 20.15 she took her leave but after going about 100m was able to observe the American vehicle return and stop a short distance from the officer who sat at the roadside by the stream and the poplars. One of the Americans got out carrying a rifle and the vehicle headed off for Kitzingen. She continued on her way and had just reached the railway bridge when she heard a shot. Turning, she saw the G.I. standing close by the German and, believing he had shot the prisoner, ran for home. The murdered man was Wolfgang Holtz who had flown with great distinction for Germany, only to be imprisoned and stripped of his rank by those who ruled his country and who had lived and worked for years among Americans, only to be killed by one of them in peacetime. Holtz is remembered with enormous affection and gratitude by the comrades he helped bring home from Austria to Germany through so many hazards and obstacles.

Harry Fischer got across the Inn on a ferry and near Schliersee was taken in by a schoolteacher, *Frau* Pachmeyer, who treated him like a son. He made three round trips to retrieve supplies from NSG 9's abandoned stores before the ferry stopped running. He worked in a smithy and then a paper mill belonging to the Pachmeyer family until Christmas 1945, when he made an illegal crossing of the reinstated Austrian-German border to smuggle his wife and son back from Berlin to Oberaudorf (the village where Kehrer and Eck had been shot down). His next job, lasting a year and a half, was to test-fly surplus aircraft which the Americans were selling off to various European countries. Fischer was drawn by the news that his former employer, *Deutsche Lufthansa*, was being reborn in Frankfurt but family ties militated against his going to the USA for the requisite training. Back in Berlin just in time for the blockade, he worked for the French as a diesel vehicle mechanic at the new Tegel Airport. Noticing that the droves of shift workers required by the airlift were lacking news, he arranged for his wife to sell papers and magazines, a line of work the couple were to follow for the next 35 years. Having flown

By 6 November 1946, Horst Greßler had served 280 days as a Mechanic Staff Sergeant with the British Army, his character "exemplary." The list of personal effects on the left hand page at least shows that, unlike so many NSG 9 prisoners, he was not robbed of his possessions.

ABOVE: *After NSG 9, Ofw. Horst Greßler's next unit was 610 German General Transport Company, part of the British Royal Army Service Corps. This document sets out what pay he has owing for the period September 1945– March 1946. However Greßler states that the pay was of little consequence, since the prisoners were making so much money selling Army petrol on the black market.*

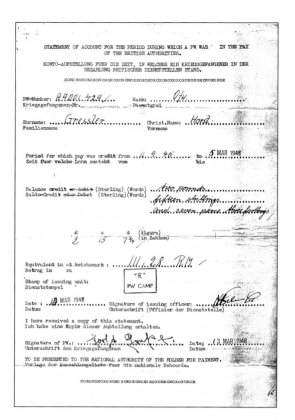

transport and cargo gliders with the *Luftwaffe*, in peacetime Fischer was to co-found the Lilienthal Gliding Club of Berlin with which he still flies each summer.

In Italy — after a captive odyssey taking him from the northern Alps to the Gulf of Taranto — Horst Greßler too worked in a motor pool, with 610 German General Transport Company of the British Royal Army Service Corps. The Company had about 400 German officers and men on strength alongside a small British nucleus and was one of many such PoW units in Italy, so ubiquitous that the graffiti claimed, "British officers and German prisoners rule the roads of Italy." They began by bringing loads of timber down from the mountains then moved to Bari (BA) where they ferried supplies from the docks to British units; next they went up to Mestre (VE), running transport convoys through into Austria. Greßler served 280 days with the British Army as an "exemplary" Mechanic Staff Sergeant. His discharge came on 6 November 1946 and he was released into the Russian-occupied zone of Germany. After several weeks "quarantine" he was allowed to return home in February 1947. Helmut Schäfer was transferred from American to British captivity in Rimini, acquiring a taste for afternoon tea with milk (of necessity, the Tommies not imagining there was any other way to drink it) which has stayed with him to this day.

Franz Fischer made his way home from the Austrian mountains, sometimes in a lorry but mostly on foot. A year later, along with almost three million other ethnic Germans, he was expelled from what was now Czechoslovakia again and has lived in Germany since 1946.

Hans Nawroth's career as a paratrooper had been brief:

> Retreat from Montabaur into the Harz [Mountains]. Taken prisoner by the Americans on 22 April 1945. Collecting camp at Helfta near Eisleben: 55,000 men in the open air. Transferred at Whitsun to Naumburg/Saale, released on 28 June 1945.

Dirk Bunsen remained in Thiene's Civic Hospital for about two weeks before being transferred to the military establishment in Vicenza which was now guarded by Americans. Toward the end of May, he was moved yet again, to Galliera (BO) before being discharged to a camp for wounded PoWs along Highway 103 on the northern outskirts of Modena. Early in July, with the Brenner rail line working again, he was shipped from Verona to Bad Aibling airfield, near Rosenheim in Bavaria. Here, as in other camps, the Americans — whether overwhelmed by sheer numbers or reacting to the horrors they had uncovered in liberating Ohrdruf, Dachau and Mauthausen — left their captives in the open, under persistent rain and with little to eat. Bunsen and others avoided starvation by volunteering to clean the quarters of African-American soldiers. After about three weeks, he was transferred north to a British-run camp at Wunstorf and markedly contrasting treatment: adequate rations, waterproof four-man tents and white tape in place of barbed wire. He was there four days before being trucked over to Münster and, on 29 July 1945, was set free to walk home.

Entering American captivity, Alfons Eck was allowed, as an airman, to keep his kit bag. The 500 cigarettes this held bought him morphia pills for his toothache in Rosenheim, materials to build a shelter from the summer heat at Ulm and water purification tablets that saved him from the dysentry raging through the camp. In transit from Ulm to Heilbronn, Eck's guardian angel paused to catch its breath, as he put it, and his kit and remaining cigarettes went missing. Shipped into France, he was put to work as a woodcutter. Near Blois, he and Albert, a Hamburg lawyer, dug 200 holes for a roadside avenue of trees which still stands. As *Prisonnier de Guerre* 51852 he played in a swing band (acquiring the nickname "Saxophone") and formed a symphony orchestra in the camp. A fellow prisoner tried to get himself transferred to work for the French Circus Amar for which he had been a banker before the war. The circus duly asked for him but he was rejected by the authorities as a Nazi fellow-traveller and so recommended his friend "Saxophone" in his stead. On 8 January 1948, Alfons Eck stepped out of the camp gates and into a chauffeur-driven Cadillac. For the next 22 years the address he registered with the police would be 120 avenue des Champs-Elysées, Paris. Beginning as a cashier he rose to become Circus Director, touring Europe in a luxurious caravan and socialising with filmstars and royalty.

Paul Sonnenberg was not released from British captivity in Egypt until late in 1948, a prisoner twice as long as he had been an airman.

In the postwar years, as Europe was rebuilt and freedom of movement was restored — in the west at least — many NSG 9 veterans revisited Italy, to pay their respects at the graves of old friends and look up families with whom they had been billeted. Returning to Innsbruck in April 1946 to retrieve suitcases he had left there a year before, Peter Stollwerck made a different sentimental journey:

...to see the pitiful remains of the planes that we destroyed there.

NSG 9 has disbanded and ex-Uffz. Karl Hofmann pauses in Wiesenbronn, Lower Franconia during the long hike home from Walchsee in Austria.

---

1. Also known as Innsbruck-West and now the site of Innsbruck-Kranebitten internatonal airport.

2. The men of the Luftwaffe affectionately dubbed their aircraft "mills" or "birds" just as the RAF had "crates" and "kites" and the USAAF "ships."

Postscript
NSG 9 Veterans

Werner Lotsch (crashed, 30 September 1944; suffered chest and facial injuries).

RIGHT: Harry Fischer (shot down by Spitfires, 31 August 1944; crashed and suffered facial injuries)

BELOW: Alfons Eck and Herbert Kehrer (shot down by Mustangs, 27 April 1945).

Veterans of NSG 9, family members and friends at their 1997 reunion in Krauschwitz. Kneeling at the front is Rudi Sablottny (left).

Heinrich Leinberger

Willy Ferling

Horst Greßler (shot down by a Beaufighter, 1/2 June 1944; crashlanded his burning aircraft with a bullet wound to his shoulder and injuries from glass splinters).

Helmut Schäfer

Eduard Reither (7 April 1916 – 18 August 2000).

Hans Nawroth (injured his left hand and knee bailing out following attack by a Beaufighter, 6 July 1944) and his wife Hanni.

Dirk Bunsen (ambushed by partisans, 26/27 April 1945; suffered a fractured skull).

Werner Hensel (shot down, 1/2 August 1944; bailed out and evaded capture, walking 25km to German lines) and his wife Isolde.

Markings and Camouflage of Nachtschlachtgruppe 9

*I*f markings are defined as paintwork intended to make an aircraft recognisable, camouflage serves the contradictory purpose of making it harder to see. To an extent, NSG 9 was systematic in its application of both, especially on its Ju 87s, but inevitably there were aberrations and there remain a number of gaps in present-day knowledge. This section should of course be read with reference to the illustrations throughout this book and — since the author makes no claims of infallibility — to the reader's own judgment.

Identification Codes

Under the *Luftwaffe's* standard four-character system, NSG 9 was assigned the unit code "E8." Although there are some reports of aircraft without this code, this may simply mean that it was obscured when the *Gruppe's* characteristic night camouflage was applied.

The "E8" code was painted in black, to the left of the fuselage *Balkenkreuz* and in characters one fifth the size of those to the cross's right. These compromised a coloured letter designating the individual aircraft and a black one representing its *Staffel* or *Stab* affiliation. According to a prisoner shot down in early July 1944:

> …[on] all planes in the *Gruppe* … the recognition signs are outlined in white against the dark fuselage.

This was before either the *Stab* or 3./NSG 9 came into being and, as we shall see, the latter at least departed from this standard. Markings of the *Gruppe's* constituent elements were as follows:

***Stab*/NSG 9** (codes E8+_B): In the absence of photographic evidence, one might infer that the *Stab's* few aircraft carried a green letter outlined in white. However, a "very thoroughly destroyed and burned" Ju 87 at Villafranca is recorded as E8+MB with the "M" in yellow. Without knowing the precise state of this marking — was the "B" intact or could a damaged "L" have been misconstrued for example? — it is impossible to be sure. Unfortunately, no reference to colour is made in respect of any other abandoned *Stab* aircraft.

1./NSG 9 (codes E8+_H): Individual letter in black with a narrow white outline on Ju 87s and Fw 190s. There is no photographic or other evidence to disprove or confirm that the same applied to this unit's Ca.314s or CR.42s — nor any reason to doubt it — but Fi 156 E8+YH carried a plain black "Y" in early 1944. On Ju 87s, the aircraft's letter was often repeated in white on the port wheel spat, enabling a parked or dispersed machine to be identified from the front, obviating the need to walk around or duck under the wing to read its fuselage codes.

2./NSG 9 (codes E8+_K): Individual letter in red with a narrow white outline on CR.42s and Ju 87s alike. Although CR.42s E8+JK and +FK, at the bombed Torino Factory in late April 1944 had a thin black outline to their individual letters, this could simply have been a guide to the painter, and they may have been awaiting application of the white outline. The crudely applied numbers on these aircraft were probably put there for the factory's purposes. Horst Greßler's E8+BK, pictured around the same time, has the white outline. There is no evidence to confirm whether the individual aircraft letter was painted on the wheel spats of Ju 87s but the reasons for doing so would have held good, whatever the *Staffel.*

2./NSG 2 (code D3+_K): this *Staffel's* Ju 87s were unusual in apparently carrying their "D3" unit code in small *white* letters and (probably) a red individual letter. Each aircraft bore on its rudder a large white number corresponding to the alphabetical position of its individual code letter. In the mud of the Eastern Front, wheel spats were often removed; in Italy they were used and the aircraft's number was repeated on the port one.

3./NSG 9 (code E8+_L): The *Staffel* letter was in yellow with no outline. In Italy the rudder number was removed or disappeared under night camouflage, while that on the wheel spat persisted for a while before being supplanted by the aircraft's letter, apparently in yellow.

Special Paintwork

The emblem of NSG 9 was a black shield with a white ghost carrying a bomb. According to veterans, this badge was applied only to vehicles, never to the *Gruppe's* aircraft.

Two ULTRA decrypts from April 1944 set out the regulations governing the marking of Italian aircraft operated by the *Luftwaffe.*

KV 1979: [23 April 1944] *Komm. Gen. der Deutschen Luftwaffe Südost* ordered following recognition colouring for German and Italian aircraft operating in Mediterranean area; underparts of engine cowlings to be painted bright yellow. Round the fuselage a white ring about 50cm wide behind the cross. Captured aircraft to be painted bright yellow. Italian aircraft to be distinguished (comment: details unknown).

KV 2089: Comment to KV 1979: known that orders were (a) for the continuation of existing regulations; (b) identical regulations existed in the Mediterranean in December 1941; (c) in November 1943 captured Italian aircraft were to be used only with cross on wings and fuselage, white ring around fuselage, yellow paint on wing tips 1.5 metres in width.

As the rules under "(c)" were made at almost the same time as the Ca.314 was allocated to 1./NSG 9, it might be expected that they would have been followed in painting the *Staffel's* aircraft. Of the four known photographs of Capronis in the Gruppe's service, one appears to show a yellow wing tip (although well short of the specified width) and no aircraft appears to have yellow beneath its engine nacelles. Horst Greßler writes that:

No Ca.314 aircraft of NSG 9 had any yellow paint on the wings or the undersides of the motors.

One of the machines does show an area between nacelle and *Balkenkreuz*, darker than the background pale grey and only one of them definitely carries a white fuselage band.

Some of the *Gruppe's* Ju 87s were delivered with a white rear fuselage band but this was undesirable for night operations and was soon either removed entirely or camouflaged over to a greater or lesser extent.

The *Gruppenstab's* Junkers W.34, E8+WB probably carried the double yellow fuselage bands associated with blind-flying trainers.

Camouflage and National Markings

Each camouflage colour authorised by the German Air Ministry was allocated a number. Those occurring in this section (with their names and literal English translations) are:

65	*Hellblau*	light blue
70	*Schwarzgrün*	black-green
71	*Dunkelgrün*	dark green
74	*Graugrün*	grey-green
75	*Grauviolett*	grey-violet
76	*Lichtblau*	light blue
79	*Sandgelb*	sand yellow
83	*Dunkelgrün*	dark green

The Caproni Ca.314

The handful of known aircraft appear to be camouflaged in their basic Italian scheme of dark green (*verde oliva scuro 2*) above and light grey (*grigio azzurro chiaro 1*) beneath. One has B3 *Balkenkreuze* on its fuselage and under the wings, another has a non-standard variant of the B2 on the fuselage. None of the photographs shows the unit tactical codes for which there is documentary evidence, nor even a *Hakenkreuz*.

The Fiat CR.42 Falco

When first on strength with NSG 9, these aircraft would seem, from the available photographs, to have been painted in standard Italian dark green and light grey on the upper and lower surfaces respectively. Some examples photographed in the bombed FIAT factory appear to have had black undersides; they have the B5 fuselage cross and one has a white fuselage band just aft.

The original camouflage of the CR.42s was supplemented for night operations by overspraying cloudy patches of brown and either pale blue or pale grey on the upper surfaces and dark green or grey on the undersides. The accuracy of researcher and artist Gabriele Valentini's deduction of this scheme from black and white photographs was later confirmed by Horst Greßler. The crosses carried were the H2a *Hakenkreuz* and B1a *Balkenkreuz* (fuselage), the lower half of the latter tending to become partially obscured when night camouflage was applied. Under the lower wings were B3 crosses and one would have expected the B6 on top of the upper wing but it is worth noting that a Fiat from a *Luftwaffe* training school which crashed in Switzerland had the non-standard B3 in this position (within the still intact outer rings of the Italian *fasci*).

Known 1./NSG 9 CR.42s (and E8+LK of the 2.) had white spinners, those of 2. *Staffel* had red. Some if not all of the *Gruppe's* Fiats seem to have retained their yellow airscrew blade tips, a safety measure used by the Italians (and many other air forces) but never adopted by the *Luftwaffe*.

The Junkers Ju 87D-3 and D-5

Initial deliveries of these types to NSG 9 were in standard 70/71/65 camouflage. That the *Luftwaffe* used a green base colour with a brown overspray (*Sandgelb* 79 or perhaps its Italian equivalent) in the North African theatre is accepted as the well known colour photograph of Hs 129, "red C" at El Aouina, Tunisia clearly shows a brown meander over a green background. The same kind of thing is apparent in monochrome shots of other *Luftwaffe* types in Africa including a Ju 88 and a Fw 58. Even so, the idea that the meandering upper surface overspray that characterised the Ju 87s of NSG 9 was *Lichtblau* 76 is tenacious, although the author is unaware of any contemporary evidence whatsoever to support it. Brown/green camouflage is however well attested from sources other than the latterday interpretation of black and white photography, for example:

- A MAAF intelligence report of June 1944 records that on a dump at Viterbo main aerodrome was the burned and stripped wreck of a Ju 87, coded CP+EH. Its camouflage is described as a green and brown mottle on the upper surfaces and light blue on the undersides. Also present was a set of Ju 87 wings: green and brown upper/blue under.

- Aircraft E8+GK, WNr. 2600 was found at Bovolone and is described as "night camouflage — mottled brown and dark green." That WNr. 2600 began life in standard 70/71/65 camouflage is evident from a series of photographs showing it being towed and manhandled into its dispersal (see page 28).

In July 1944, a prisoner from 1. *Staffel* revealed that, "All planes in the *Gruppe* are painted black, deep brown or grey all over", a description which although not actually incorrect, may have lost something in the translation. A few weeks later, a 3. *Staffel* pilot recounted that, "After arrival from Poland [2./NSG 2] was based first at Caselle ... where the a/c were camouflaged brown." Raising the matter with the first NSG 9 veteran with whom he came into contact, the author was told:

> Actually, all the Ju 87s had the camouflage scheme [like +GK's]...

and

> I have only very few memories of the colours. What I still recall: the upper surfaces including the sides and fuselage were olive green sprayed with a brown. The undersides were entirely *Hellblau* with some kind of grey. This colour was definitely sprayed on to the blue. The object was to provide camouflage when viewed from the ground.

Photographs show that this underwing camouflage varied from a few "tiger stripes" running back from the leading edge to a dense meander pattern obscuring most of the blue paint and national markings.

As with its Fiats, a white spinner tip was painted on 1. *Staffel's* first Ju 87s. Later, many aircraft of the *Gruppe* had a one-third segment of the spinner ahead of the propeller blades in white although it was not uncommon for the camouflage overspray to extend over the spinner, obscuring any markings that may originally have been there.

The Focke-Wulf Fw 190A-8, F-8 and F-9

Found at Vicenza, Fw 190F-8/R1 E8+EH was described as "grey upper and pale blue undersurfaces", suggesting the 74/75/76 camouflage specified for fighter types up until July 1944. At Villafranca, Fw 190F-8 WNr. 581632, E8+DH carried the earlier style H2a *Hakenkreuz* with the B3 both on the fuselage and underwing while the upper wing crosses would almost certainly have been the B6. Given its "old" markings and original canopy, this aircraft probably started out with 74/75/76 camouflage but this was heavily toned down with a dark mottle (probably green) extending right down the fuselage sides. An uncoded Fw 190 at Innsbruck had the upper half of its fuselage in a single dark colour, possibly 83 and the new blown canopy. After computer enhancement of the photograph, the underwing B6a cross on this particular aircraft seems to have been applied to bare metal before the 76 camouflage was sprayed around the outside of it.

The F-9 model, WNr. 440340, arriving at Villafranca at the war's end appeared as follows:

> The aircraft bore no squadron letters or numbers; the upper part of the wings and forward fuselage are dark green; undersides and the entire tail unit are light blue.

This description and the various photographs clearly point to the common late-war Focke-Wulf scheme of 75/83/76; the rear fuselage and vertical tail surfaces in the latter colour with a very light mottling of 83. It is worth adding that WNr. 440341 (found at Neubiburg-bei-München and conceivably a stray from NSG 9) had segmented camouflage on the wings and tail and so it does not require too great a leap of the imagination to infer the same for its immediate predecessor on the assembly line at the Norddeutsche Dornierwerke, Wismar.

The Villafranca machine's national markings were H3 (fin), B4 (Fuselage) and B6a (underwing). The Innsbruck Fw 190s however have the H5 *Hakenkreuz* and F-9 E8+MH (WNr. 440323) at Vicenza exhibited the B6 cross on its upper wing surfaces which it sisters can be confidently expected to have carried also. All known Fw 190s of NSG 9 had plain black or black-green 70 spinners.

The Fiesler Fi 156, Focke-Wulf Fw 58, Junkers W.34 and SAIMAN 202

All these types served with NSG 9 on communication and training duties but Fi 156 E8+YH is the only one of which there is a photograph. It seems to have had the standard 70/71/65 paintwork and carries the H4 *Hakenkreuz* on its rudder. *Balkenkreuze* were B5 (fuselage), B3 (underwing) and in all probability B6 (upper wing surfaces). The other German types probably carried similar camouflage but the appearance of 2./NSG 9's SAIMAN remains a complete mystery.

Allied Victory claims against NSG 9

No.	Date	Time	Location	Type	Claim	Pilot	Nav/Rad	Squadron	Aircraft	Serial	Code
1	01/02.06.44	00:30	L. Vico	CR. 42	dest	Rees	Bartlett	600	Beaufighter VIF	MM905	M
2	02/03.06.44	23:40	N Colli Laziale	Ju 87	dest	Bailey	Wint	600	Beaufighter VIF	ND165	N
3	03.07.44	22:04	SE L. Trasimeno	Ju 87	dam	Ewing	Chenery	600	Beaufighter VIF	V8898	V
4	03.07.44	22:41	NE L. Trasimeno	Ju 87	dest	Ewing	Chenery	600	Beaufighter VIF	V8898	V
5	06/07.07.44	—	NW Ancona	Ju 87	dest	Bretherton	Johnson	255	Beaufighter VIF	—	—
6	06/07.07.44	—	Ancona	Ju 87	dest	Bretherton	Johnson	255	Beaufighter VIF	—	—
7	06/07.07.44	—	SW Ancona	Ju 87	dest	Bretherton	Johnson	255	Beaufighter VIF	—	—
8	06/07.07.44	—	—	Ju 87	dest	Griffiths	Kimberley	255	Beaufighter VIF	—	—
9	06/07.07.44	—	—	Ju 87	dest	McClaren	Tozer	255	Beaufighter VIF	—	—
10	07/08.07.44	—	Ancona area	Ju 87	dest	Reynolds	Wingham	255	Beaufighter VIF	—	R
11	07/08.07.44	—	off Ancona	Ju 87	dest	Reynolds	Wingham	255	Beaufighter VIF	—	R
12	07/08.07.44	02:08	Trasimeno	Ju 87	dest	Jeffery	Brewer	600	Beaufighter VIF	ND320	R
13	10/11.07.44		Ancona	Ju 87	dest	McLaren	Tozer	255	Beaufighter VIF	—	—
14	11.07.44	01:21	NW Trasimeno	Ju 87	dest	Bailey	Wint	600	Beaufighter VIF	ND165	N
15	27/28.07.44	—	Ancona	Ju 87	dest	Reynolds	Wingham	255	Beaufighter VIF	—	—
16	27.07.44	22:45	SW Colli Val d'Elsa	Ju 87	dest	Waitman	Goss	600	Beaufighter VIF	ND162	E
17	30.07.44	23:40	SE Florence	Ju 87	dest	Thompson	Beaumont	600	Beaufighter VIF	MM876	X
18	01/02.08.44	22:13	N Arezzo	Ju 87	dest	Thompson	Beaumont	600	Beaufighter VIF	MM876	X
19	01/02.08.44	22:55	NE Florence	Ju 87	dam	Thompson	Beaumont	600	Beaufighter VIF	MM876	X
20	02./03.08.44	22:34	SW Arezzo	Ju 87	dest	Jefferson	Spencer	600	Beaufighter VIF	MM945	J
21	02./03.08.44	03:00	Livorno area	Ju 87	dest	Crooks	Charles	600	Beaufighter VIF	V8876	A
22	03/04.08.44	22:45	E Arezzo	Ju 87	dest	MacDonald	Towell	600	Beaufighter VIF	ND165	N
23	27/28.08.44	22:30	Arezzo	Ju 87	dest	Thompson	Beaumont	600	Beaufighter VIF	ND165	N
24	28/29.08.44	21:09	SE Pesaro	Ju 87	dest	Judd	Brewer	600	Beaufighter VIF	V8879	D
25	28/29.08.44	22:25	N Rimini	Ju 87	dest	Judd	Brewer	600	Beaufighter VIF	V8879	D
26	28/29.08.44	21:49	NE Florence	Ju 87	dest	Styles	Wilmer	600	Beaufighter VIF	ND170	F
27	31.08.44	07:24	River Po	Ju 87	dest	Dixon	—	241	Spitfire VIII	MT634	RZ•U
28	03/04.09.44	00:08	NW Rimini	Ju 87	dest	Judd	Brewer	600	Beaufighter VIF	ND147	Q
29	03/04.09.44	00:20	SW Rimini	Ju 87	dest	Judd	Brewer	600	Beaufighter VIF	ND147	Q
30	04.09.44	04:05	W Rimini	Ju 87	dest	Burke	Whaley	600	Beaufighter VIF	ND172	B
31	04.09.44	04:07	SW Rimini	Ju 87	dest	Cole	Odd	600	Beaufighter VIF	V8891	M
32	04.09.44	23:05	W Rimini	Ju 87	dest	Rees	Bartlett	600	Beaufighter VIF	ND162	E
33	04.09.44	23:15	W Rimini	Ju 87	dest	Rees	Bartlett	600	Beaufighter VIF	ND162	E
34	05.09.44	02:31	SW Rimini	Ju 87	dest	Davidson	Telford	600	Beaufighter VIF	ND320	R
35	10/11.09.44	03:12	SW Rimini	Ju 87	dest	Thompson	Beaumont	600	Beaufighter VIF	MM876	X
36	03/04.10.44	20:19	SE Cesena	Ju 87	dest	Styles	Wilmer	600	Beaufighter VIF	ND170	F
37	23/24.11.44	17:18	E L. Comacchio	Ju 87	dest	Smith	Dunford	600	Beaufighter VIF	KV912	B
38	28.11.44	17:15	Forlì	Ju 87	dest	Archer	Barrington	600	Beaufighter VIF	BT299	T
39	01.12.44	17:03	Faenza	Ju 87	prob	Baits	Lothian	600	Beaufighter VIF	KV972	G
40	01.12.44	17:05	Faenza	Ju 87	dam	Baits	Lothian	600	Beaufighter VIF	KV972	G
41	22.12.44	20:19	N Forlì	Ju 87	dam	Rees	Beaumont	600	Beaufighter VIF	—	Q
42	22.12.44	20:40	NW Forlì	Ju 87	dest	Rees	Beaumont	600	Beaufighter VIF	—	Q
43	22.12.44	21:26	E Bologna	Ju 87	dest	Rees	Beaumont	600	Beaufighter VIF	—	Q
44	22.12.44	21:30	Asola	Ju 87	dest	Jones	Rudovsky	414th NFS	Beaufighter VIF	—	—
45	20.01.45	17:48	NE Forlì	Ju 87	dest	Coleman	Frumar	600	Beaufighter VIF	V8734	M
46	20.01.45	17:58	NE Fusignano	Ju 87	dest	Coleman	Frumar	600	Beaufighter VIF	V8734	M
47	29.01.45	18:00	N Bologna	Ju 87	dest	{Eddy	—	346th FS	P-47D	—	—
48	29.01.45	18:00	N Bologna	Ju 87	prob	{Sulzbach	—	346th FS	P-47D	—	—
49	03.03.45	18:35	S Bologna	Fw 190	dest	Hausner	—	347th FS	P-47D	42-27293	—
50	13.04.45	20:37	Alfonsine	Fw 190	dest	Hammond	Moore	600	Mosquito XIX	TA123/g	H
51	13.04.45	20:37	Alfonsine	Fw 190	dam	Hammond	Moore	600	Mosquito XIX	TA123/g	H
52	27.04.45	14:15	Oberaudorf	Ju 87	dest	{Wood	—	15th TRS	F-6C	35274	5M*W
53	27.04.45	14:15	Oberaudorf	Ju 87	dest	{Chambers	—	15th TRS	F-6C	—	—
54	27.04.45	14:15	Oberaudorf	Ju 87	dest	Wood	—	15th TRS	F-6C	35274	5M*W

NSG 9 Aircraft Lost or Damaged

Date	Time	Location	Cause	Pilot	Crew	Staffel	Aircraft	WNr	Code	Claim
10.01.44	13.55	Udinè	Training acc.	Horn (KIFA)	Dopatka(KIFA) Wendler (KIFA) Hopp (KIFA)	1.	Ca. 314	12740	E8+EH	
10.03.44		Ciriè	Accident	Pallas (KIFA)	—	2.	CR. 42	90831	—	
24.03.44		Perrero	Op. acc.	Müller (KIA)	—	2.	CR. 42	90845	—	
28.04.44		Nettuno	AA	Müller (KIA)	Teichert (KIA)	1.	Ju 87D-5	141024	E8+FH	
02.05.44		SW Tuscania	Op. acc?	Zierkowski (KIA)	Beier (KIA)	1.	Ju 87D-5	141022	—	
02.05.44		N Tarquinia	Op. acc?	—	Filß (WIA)	1.	Ju 87D-5	131604	—	
06.05.44		N Palestrina	Op. acc?	Deffner (KIA)	Kaczorowski (KIA)	1.	Ju 87D-5	141004	—	
14.05.44		Cassino	NF?	—	Strube (MIA)	1.	n/a	—	—	
14.05.44		Cassino	AA?	Schönauer (WIA)	Schmidt (WIA)	1.	—	—	—	
22.05.44		Caselle	Training acc.	Martini (KIFA)	—	2.	CR. 42	90881	—	
02.06.44	00.30	Fabrica	NF	Greßler (WIA)	—	2.	CR. 42	—	—	1
09.06.44		Caselle	Accident	Oefele (KIFA)	—	2.	Ju 87D-3	100090	—	
02.07.44		Forlì	Op. acc.	Büttner (KIA)	Pendel(KIA)	2.	Ju 87D-3	1244	—	
03.07.44	21.49	Ravenan?	Engine fire	n/a —	n/a —	1.	Ju 87D	—	E8+VH	
03.07.44		Florence	Collision	Kapahnke (KIA)	Happe (KIA)	2.	Ju 87D-5	141010	—	
03.07.44		Florence	Collison	Jaegers (KIA)	—	2.	Ju 87D-5	140994	—	
05.07.44	00.00	Loreto	AA	Begemann (PoW)	Lehr (MIA)	1.	Ju 87D-5	140999	E8+OH	
05.07.44		Loreto	AA damage	Pieper	—	1.	Ju 87D-5	—	E8+CH	
06.07.44		Loreto	NF	Ackermann (WIA)	Kasper (WIA)	2.	Ju 87D-3	100335	—	5/6/7
06.07.44		Loreto	NF	Itzstein (WIA)	Rumbolz (WIA)	2.	Ju 87D-3	100382	E8+NK	5/6/7
06.07.44		Loreto	NF	Böwing —	Nawroth (WIA)	2./2	Ju 87D	—	—	8
07.07.44		Mondolfo	NF	von Bork (KIA)	Tröster (KIA)	2.	Ju 87D-3	1266	—	10/11/12
07.07.44		Castelfidardo	NF	n/a —	Ballok (WIA)	2.	Ju 87D-5	141722	—	10/11/12
07.07.44		Osimo	NF	Mokrus (MIA)	Wagner (MIA)	1.	Ju 87D-5	141029	E8+HH	10/11/12
10.07.44	02.30	N Ancona	NF	Wolff (PoW)	Lankes (PoW)	1.	Ju 87D-5	141025	E8+GH	13
26.07.44		Ancona?	?	Schwøbe (MIA)	Schlichting (MIA)	1.	Ju 87D-5	141738	E8+EH	
26.07.44	23.00	Reggio	Em. landing	Deutsch (?)	Kaufmann (WIA)	3.	Ju 87D	—	D3+DK	
26.07.44		Barco	Em. landing	Brinkmann —	Till (WIA)	3.	Ju 87D-3	212291	—	
26.07.44		Cavriago	Op. acc.	Gieger (KIA)	Gabauer (KIA)	3.	Ju 87D-3	1369	—	
27.07.44		Cerasolo	NF	Waißnor (KIA)	Koch (WIA)	1.	Ju 87D-5	140755	—	15
27.07.44	23.24	Pontedera	NF	Urban (WIA)	Lässig (MIA)	2.	Ju 87D	110459	E8+DK	16
27.07.44		W Modena	?	Spörr (WIA)	Leumann (WIA)	2.	Ju 87D-5	2008	—	
01/02.08.44		SE Florence	"AA" (NF?)	Hensel (RTU)	Laufenberg (KIA)	3.	Ju 87D-3	432614	—	17
02/03.08.44		SW Arezzo	NF	Wolfsen (MIA)	Wilk (MIA)	3.	Ju 87D-3	331120	E8+PK	20
03.08.44		?	?	Fietz (MIA)	Razinski (MIA)	1.	Ju 87D-5	131613	E8+DH	21/22
03.08.44		?	?	Krüger (MIA)	Tscirsch (MIA)	1.	Ju 87D-5	131150	E8+BB	21/22
27.08.44		Fano	AA?	Voss (MIA)	—	1.	Ju 87D-5	141039	—	
27.08.44		[Ju 87 listed as missing. no other details]		—	—	—	Ju 87	—	—	23
28.08.44		E Florence	NF	Brinkmann (PoW)	Scherzer (MIA)	3.	Ju 87D-3	100396	E8+KL	25
28.08.44		?	NF	Fink (WIA)	Zantow —	1.	Ju 87D	—	+GL	26
31.08.44		E Copparo	Spitfire	Fischer (WIA)	Hüssmann —	2.	Ju 87D	—	—	27
03/04.09.44	23.55	Fano	NF	Hug (KIA)	Sonnenberg (PoW)	3.	Ju 87D	—	—	29
03/04.09.44		Borghi	NF	Urban DoW	Schertel (KIA)	2.	Ju 87D	—	—	28/30/31
03/04.09.44		?	NF/crash	—	Möhrke (KIA)	3.	Ju 87D	—	—	28/30/31
03/04.09.44		Cattolica	NF	Böwing (MIA)	Jantos (MIA)	3.	Ju 87D	—	—	28/30/31
03/04.09.44		Arno Valley?	AA damage	von Grone —	Lenz —	2.	Ju 87D	—	E8+HK	
25.09.44	20.24	Villafranca	Landing (15%)	Schäfer —	Hofmann —	3.	Ju 87D	—	E8+DL	
28.09.44		NW Verona	Acc. (non-op.)	Fink (KIFA)	Zantow (KIFA)	3.	Ju 87D	—		
30.09.44		Riccione		Stollwerck —	Fischer —	3.	Ju 87D-3		E8+EL	
30.09.44		San Felice	Acc.	Gerstenberger (WIFA)	Lotsch (WIFA)	2.	Ju 87D-5	131440	E8+FK	
08.10.44		Roverbella	Acc. (non-op.)	Schönauer (KIFA)	Hellmann (KIFA)	1.	Ju 87D	—		
04.11.44	20.19	S Villafranca	Acc.	Zander (KIFA)	Eickhoff (KIFA)	1.	Ju 87D-5	130699	E8+FH	
10.11.44		Loiano	AA damage	Stollwerck —	Fischer —	3.	Ju 87D-5		E8+HL	

Date	Time	Location	Cause	Pilot	Crew	Staffel	Aircraft	WNr	Code	Claim
18.11.44	09.54	Villafranca	Bombing	n/a —	n/a —	?	Ju 87D	—	—	
18.11.44	09.54	Villafranca	Bombing	n/a —	n/a —	?	Ju 87D	—	—	
18.11.44	09.54	Villafranca	Bombing	n/a —	n/a —	?	Ju 87D	—	—	
18.11.44	09.54	Villafranca	Bomb damage	n/a —	n/a —	?	Ju 87D	—	—	
18.11.44	09.54	Villafranca	Bomb damage	n/a —	n/a —	?	Ju 87D	—	—	
18.11.44	09.54	Villafranca	Bomb damage	n/a —	n/a —	?	Ju 87D	—	—	
18.11.44	09.54	Villafranca	Bomb damage	n/a —	n/a —	?	Ju 87D	—	—	
18.11.44	p.m.	Villafranca	Strafing	n/a —	n/a —	?	Ju 87D	—	—	
23.11.44		E Comacchio	NF	Buckow (KIA)	Berkemeyer (KIA)	1.	Ju 87D-5	141018	E8+JH	37
28.11.44		Forlì	NF	Stuber (PoW)	Adami (KIA)	1.	Ju 87D-5	131086	E8+DH	38
28.11.44		Fornaci	Accident	Spörr (KIFA)	—	2.	Ju 87D	—	—	
22.12.44	16.52	S Villafranca	Em. landing	Schick (WIFA)	—	3.	Ju 87D-5	131434	E8+BL	
22.12.44		Lugo	NF	Gerstenberger (KIA)	Mechlinski (WIA)	2.	Ju 87D-5	140747	E8+KK	42
22.12.44		NW Bologna	NF	Kolster (KIA)	Leumann (KIA)	2.	Ju 87D-5	130532	E8+FK	43
22.12.44	21.30	N Cremona	NF	Heiland (WIA)	Ballok (WIA)	2.	Ju 87D-5	140750	E8+JK	44
25.12.44		Villafranca	Taxi acc.	—	—	?	Ju 87D	—	—	
27.12.44		Faenza	AA damage	Deutsch	Nawroth	3.	Ju 87D	—	E8+DL	
20.01.45		NE Fusignano	NF (& AA?)	Stollwerck (RTU)	Fischer (RTU)	3.	Ju 87D-5	140717	E8+AL	46
21.01.45		Bologna	Collision	Deutsch —	Nawroth —	3.	Ju 87D	—	E8+HL	
21.01.45		Bologna	Collision	Wintermayr —	Hofmann —	3.	Ju 87D	—	E8+RH	
21.01.45		Montichiari	Accident	Jungfer (WIFA)	Geide (WIFA)	2.	Ju 87D-5	142082	—	
29.01.45		Bologna	Small arms dam.	Stollwerck —	Jahn —	3.	Ju 87D-5	—	E8+AL	
29.01.45		Fontanèlice	Damage (AA?)	Fischer —	Staudt —	3.	Ju 87D	—	E8+FL	
03.03.45	18.35	Bologna	P-47	Wilzopolski (KIA)	— —	1.	Fw 190F-8	583576	—	49
09.03.45		Mantua	Tr. acc. (dam.)	— —	— —	1.	Fw 190F-8	584577	—	
22.04.45		Bologna?	?	Liebmann (MIA)	Staudt (MIA)	3.	Ju 87D	—	—	
22.04.45		?	?	— —	— —	1.	Fw 190 (?)	—	—	
24.04.45	04.45	Vicenza	Landing acc.	Stollwerck —	Fischer (+2) —	3.	Ju 87D-5	132230	E8+AL	
25.04.45		Po crossings	AA damage	Lindemann —	Leinberger	3.	Ju 87D	—	—	
25.04.45		Thiene	Crash	Müller (KIA)	Görtz (KIA)	2.	Ju 87D	—	—	
27.04.45	14.30	Oberaudorf	F-6C	Rau —	Ende	3.	Ju 87D	—	E8+EK	54
27.04.45	14.35	Oberaudorf	F-6C	Kehrer —	Eck —	3.	Ju 87D	—	E8+PL	52
27.04.45		Alps	Accident	(of 2./NSG 9) (MIFA)	— —	1.	Fw 190		—	

Key: AA = anti-aircraft fire; acc. = accident; dam. = damage; em. = emergency; NF = night fighter; op. = operational; tr. = training.
(KIA) = killed in action; (KIFA) = killed in flying accident; (MIA) = missing in action; (MIFA) = missing in flying accdient; (PoW) = prisoner of war;
(RTU) = returned to unit; (WIA) = wounded in action; (WIFA) = wounded in flying accident.

Date	Staffel	Strength	A/c type	Remarks/Source
31.12.43	1.	12(0)	Ca 314	
31.01.44	1.	13(7)	Ca.314	
29.02.44	NSG 9	25(10)	Ca.314, CR.42, Ju 87	
20.03.44	1.	22(19)		
	2	25(7)		
20.04.44	1.	23(11)	Ju 87	
	2.	20(6)	CR.42	
30.04.44	2.	16(2)	CR.42	Converting
10.05.44	1.	16(12)	Ju 87, CR.42	(Felmy: Ju 87 only)
	2.	15(9)	Ju 87, CR.42	Converting
31.05.44	1.	19(8)	Ju 87	
	2.	18(15)	CR. 42	
	2./NSG 2	18(12)	Ju 87	Transferring to *Luftflotte* 2
10.06.44	1.	20(12)	Ju 87	
	2.	13(7)	CR. 2	Training
	2./NSG 2	15(0)	Ju 87	Converting
20.06.44	2.	9(0)	Ju 87	Converting
	2./NSG 2	15(2)	Ju 87	Converting
30.06.44	1.	22(14)	Ju 87	
	2.	22(11)	Ju 87	Converting
	2./NSG 2	14(2)	Ju 87	Re-equipping
10.07.44	1.	17(8)	Ju 87	
	2.	21(12)	Ju 87	Converting
	2./NSG 2	16(9)	Ju 87	Operational (Smith/Felmy)
20.07.44	1.	16(2)		
	2.	12(8)		
	3.	22(11)		
31.07.44	Stab	0(0)	Ju 87	
	1.	13(7)	Ju 87	
	2.	8(8)	Ju 87	
	3.	18(5)	Ju 87	
10.08.44	Stab	0(0)	Ju 87	
	1.	13(9)	Ju 87	
	2.	6(6)	Ju 87	
	3.	?	Ju 87	
20.08.44	Stab	n/a	n/a	(Felmy)
	1.	11(6)	Ju 87	
	2.	11(6)	Ju 87	
	3.	11(5)	Ju 87	
31.08.44	Stab	1(1)	Ju 87D-5	
	1.	7(4)	Ju 87	
	2.	12(10)	Ju 87	
	3	11(9)	Ju 87	
10.09.44	Stab	1(1)	Ju 87	
	1.	7(6)	Ju 87	
	2.	11(9)	Ju 87	
	3.	7(6)	Ju 87	
20.09.44	Stab	1(1)	Ju 87	(Felmy)
	1.	10(6)	Ju 87	
	2.	12(9)	Ju 87	
	3.	9(7)	Ju 87	
30.09.44	Stab	1	Ju 87D-5	
	1.	10	Ju 87D-5	
	2.	9	Ju 87D-3	
		3	Ju 87D-5	

Date	Staffel	Strength	A/c type	Remarks/Source
30.09.44	3.	8	Ju 87D-3	
		3	Ju 87D-5	
10.10.44	Stab	1(1)	Ju 87	
		2(1)	Fw 58	
	1.	10(8)	Ju 87	
	2.	11(9)	Ju 87	
	3.	11(8)	Ju 87	
20.10.44	Stab	1(0)	Ju 87	
		2(1)	Fw 58	
	1.	10(6)	Ju 87	
	2.	11(8)	Ju 87	
	3.	11(10)	Ju 87	
02.11.44	Stab	1(1)	Ju 87	
		2(1)	Fw 58	
	1.	12(6)	Ju 87	
	2.	11(8)	Ju 87	
	3.	10(8)	Ju 87	
10.11.44	Stab	1(1)	Ju 87	
		1(1)	Fw 58	
	1.	13(11)	Ju 87	
	2.	10(9)	Ju 87	
	3.	11(9)	Ju 87	
23.11.44	Stab & 1.	10(3)		Bovolone (Felmy)
	2.	12(8)		Ghedi
	3.	8(8)		Aviano
30.11.44	NSG 9	18	Ju 87D-5	
		7	Ju 87D-3	
10.12.44	NSG9	24(21)	Ju 87	
20.12.44	NSG 9	26(21)	Ju 87	
31.12.44	NSG 9	14	Ju 87D-5	
		7	Ju 87D-3	
15.01.45	Stab	1(0)	Ju 87	1(0) crews
	1.	—	—	10(1)
	2.	13(11)	Ju 87	12(5)
	3.	10(8)	Ju 87	12(9) (ULTRA BT 3088)
01.03.45	Stab	1(1)	Ju 87	1(1) crews Training
	1.	7(4)	Fw 190	13(12) Converting
	2.	10(9)	Ju 87	10(6)
	3.	15(13)	Ju 87	13(11) (ULTRA BT 6621 & 7402)
01.04.45	Stab	1(0)	Ju 87	
	1.	11(10)	Fw 190	
	2.	10(10)	Ju 87	
	3.	16(15)	Ju 87	Reserve: 2 Ju 87D-5; 2 Fw 190
09.04.45	Stab	1(0)	Ju 87	
	1.	11(9)	Fw 190	
	2.	10(10)	Ju 87	
	3.	16(16)	Ju 87	Reserve: 2 Ju 87D-5/D-3; 8 Fw 190
22.04.45	Stab	1(0)	Ju 87D-5	Villafranca, school aircraft
	1.	3(2)	Fw 190A-8	Villafranca
		4(4)	Fw 190F-8	Villafranca
	2.	3(3)	Ju 87D-3	Ghedi II
		7(7)	Ju 87D-5	Ghedi II
	3.	6(6)	Ju 87D-3	Villafranca
		10(7)	Ju 87D-5	Villafranca
				Total crews: 39(27)

Sources

In the following notes, major national archives are abbreviated as follows:

BA-MA   Bundesarchiv-Militärarchiv, Freiburg-im-Breisgau, Germany
IWM   Imperial War Museum, Lambeth, London
PRO   Public Record Office, Kew, London
USAFHRA   USAF Historical Research Agency, Maxwell Air Force Base, Alabama, USA
WASt   Deutsche Dienststelle (Wehrmachtauskunftstelle), Berlin

Most of this book's information on NSG 9's personnel casualties is derived from the reports held by WASt. Since November 1990, German privacy laws have closed these files to researchers, so I was fortunate that Hans Nawroth already had copies. I was also able to draw on notes taken at WASt by researcher Winfried Bock. My own request to visit in 1990 was refused. For casualties during the final weeks of the war, information came from the memories and some contemporary letters of NSG 9 veterans.

Information on NSG 9's aircraft losses came in the main from the above personnel records, RAF intelligence files and translated German documents (AIR20 class) at the PRO and from the microfilm copies of the *Luftwaffe* Quartermaster General's files at the IWM (the originals were returned to BA-MA in the 1960s). The IWM holds no records for 1944 or January 1945 and only patchy coverage of February and March 1945. Incidents where aircraft were damaged or lost without personnel being injured are accordingly difficult to establish for all of 1944 and much of 1945.

ULTRA material (reports based on decrypted German signals traffic) is held on microfilm at the PRO in class DEFE3. Messages are filed chronologically, are not segregated by service or operational theatre and are not indexed.

RAF formations' Operations Record Books and pilots' sortie reports are held at the PRO but the latter are not complete for all squadrons.

My microfilmed copies of CSDIC and ADI(K) prisoner interrogation reports were obtained from USAFHRA. The ADI(K) material has since been declassified in Britain and is available on paper at the PRO in class AIR40. Some CSDIC material is in the PRO, mostly in class AIR51.

Invaluable information came from the often fragmentary logbooks (*Flug-* and/or *Leistungsbücher*) of Hans Deutsch, Willy Ferling, Toni Fink, Harry Fischer, Theo Hoch, Karl Hofmann, Herbert Kehrer, Ernst Messerschmidt, Karl Reglin, Helmut Schäfer, Peter Stollwerck, Kurt Urban, Volkmar von Grone and Kurt Wagner.

INTRODUCTION: "FROM IMPROVISATION TO WEAPON"

ULTRA KV 5693

Kriegsberichter Gerhard Rauchwetter: *Von der Improvisation zur Waffe ← der Weg der Nachtschlachtflieger und ihr Einsatz an der Südfront* (magazine cutting via Nawroth)
IWM microfilm GER/MISC/MCR 18 (Reel 12): re losses of *Störkampfstaffel Kroatien*

BA-MA RL10/509: *Aufstellung der N.S.G. 9*
BA-MA RL2 III/57: order establishing 1./NSG 9
CSDIC (Air) CMF Report A.583 of 27 July 1945: *"Initiation and Development of Night Attack (Nachtschlacht) by the GAF on the Russian Front"* (Interrogation of *Major* Rupert Frost)
CSDIC A.406 of 16 July 1944: Interrogation of *Oblt.* Rolf Begemann

Gen. a.D. Felmy: *Einsatz der fliegenden Verbände der deutschen Luftwaffe: Südost, 20. Juli 1944* (order of battle)

Personal communications: Herbert Kehrer, Horst Greßler and Volkmar von Grone
Letter, Dirk Bunsen to "Inge", 16 February 1944

Wolfgang Dierich: *Die Verbände der Luftwaffe 1935-45* (Motorbuch Verlag, Stuttgart)
Barry Ketley and Mark Rolfe: *Luftwaffe Fledglings* (Hikoki Books, Farnborough 1996)
Ernst Obermaier: *Die Ritterkreuzträger der Luftwaffe, Band 2* (Verlag Dieter Hoffmann, Mainz 1988)
John Weal: *A Nocturnal Miscellany* (*Air International* magazine, March 1995)

Kupfer statements from "Nahkampfflieger" - discussion exerpt from RLM conference, 10 September 1943, presided by FM Milch, USAFHRC Ref. K113.3019-3

CHAPTER 1: "SUNNY ITALY SEEMED VERY ATTRACTIVE"

ULTRA VL 5804

PRO AIR26/381: Wing 276, Appendices to Operations Record Book
PRO AIR51/267: Extracts from Intelligence Sources
PRO AIR51/289: MAAF HQ Intelligence Section, *Signal AI.366 of 29 February 1944.*
USAFHRC Microfilm roll no. K1028Y, Index 1598, *Von Pohl Memoirs*

BA-MA RL2 III/58: *Az.11b16.18 Nr.7483/44 g.Kdos.(IIA)* (order establishing 2./NSG 9)

Personal communications: Horst Greßler, Volkmar von Grone, Alfred Kunzmann, Hans Nawroth

CHAPTER 2: "SEVERAL FIRES OBSERVED"

ULTRA VL 8381, VL 8427, VL 8854, VL 8708, VL 9381

CSDIC (Air) CMF Report A.342: Pilot of 6./SG 4 shot down 7 February 1944
CSDIC A.360: Pilot of II./JG 77 shot down 27 March 1944
CSDIC A.361: Pilot of 6./SG 4 shot down on 22 March 1944
CSDIC A.400: Captured Document Report, 28 June 1944
CSDIC A.595: *The G.A.F. in Italy (Part 6)*

Ufficio Storico Aeronautica Militare, Rome: Daily Reports to Italian Air Ministry
Lebensabschnittbericht of Volkmar von Grone

CHAPTER 3: "SO ROMANTICALLY LIT"

ULTRA KV 748, KV 3452, KV 1640, KV 1639, KV 1906, KV 1923, KV 2532, KV 2212, KV 2240

AIR20/8534: CSDIC (Air) CMF Report No. A.596 of 19 October 1945: *The German Air Force in Italy*
AIR26/380: ORB Wing 276, 1942-45
AIR27/2062: ORB No. 600 Squadron RAF
CSDIC(MAIN)/X 109: Covertly recorded conversation between *Gefr.* Hoffmann of 40. *Luftnachrichten Regiment* and *Fw.* Kaspar Stuber of 1./NSG 9

Ufficio Storico... Daily Reports (op. cit)

Personal communication from Volkmar von Grone
After The Battle magazine, Number 52, *Anzio* (Plaistow Press, London 1986)
Carlo D'Este: *Fatal Decision, Anzio and the Battle for Rome* (Fontana, London 1992)
Dominick Graham and Shelford Bidwell: *Tug of War, The Battle for Italy 1943–45* (Hodder & Stoughton, London 1986)

CHAPTER 4: "TOO SLOW AND MANOEUVRABLE"

ULTRA KV 2761, KV 2858, KV 3021, KV 3040, KV 3542, KV 3551, KV 3727,KV 3650, KV 3874, KV 3888, KV 4386, KV 4288, KV 5181, KV 5676, KV 5720, KV 5842, KV 6016, KV 5943, KV 6140

AIR26/382: ORB Wing 276, 1944
AIR 23/8566: MATAF operations in support of "Diadem" May 12–18 1944, Vol. I

CSDIC AFHQ report A.406: *Detailed Interrogation Report on Ju 87 Pilot shot down near LORETTO on night of 5 July 1944*

Ufficio Storico… Daily Reports (op. cit)

Karl Gundelach: *Die Deutsche Luftwaffe im Mittelmeer, 1940–45* (Peter D. Lang, 1981)
Percy Ernst Schramm: *Kriegstagebuch des Oberkomandos der Wehrmacht: Band IV, 1. Januar 1944–22. Mai 1945* (Bernard & Graefe Verlag für Wehrwesen, Frankfurt am Main 1961)
Günter Wegmann: *Das Oberkommando der Wehrmacht Gibt Bekannt…* (Biblio Verlag, Osnabrück 1982)
Kriegsberichter Rudolf Bruening: *Nachtschlachtflugzeuge im Ringen der Italienfront — mit Bomben und Bordwaffen gegen den feindlichen Nachschub* (magazine cutting from 12 June 1944, via Nawroth)
E-mails from Dr Joel S. Hayward, 9 and 24 January 1999

CHAPTER 5: "DESPITE MASSIVE LOSS OF BLOOD"

Shooting down of CR.42: This account draws on Horst Greßler's letters to Dirk Bunsen (12 August 1991) and the author (23 April 1997), the former relying on memory and his Wound Badge citation, the latter with help from Allied records. Greßler's initial recollection was that he had been attacked on the night of 31 May–1 June but the citation is dated 1 June, as is the relevant casualty report. A tally kept by No. 600 Squadron puts this victory on 1/2 June as does the Squadron ORB while Rees and Bartlett's RAF Form 441A Sortie Report is headed "2/3 June" (the ANR *Situazione Aeronautica* also listing a CR.42 missing on this night, incidentally). Because the dates differ and the combat report refers to a Fiat shot down into a lake while the *Personalverlustmeldung* mentions only that Greßler crashed on his airfield (nothing about a night fighter), these were treated as separate events in an earlier work. Only after meeting Greßler in 1996 and cross checking with other archive sources was it possible to tie the present account together.

In addition, Rees and Bartlett's sortie report states that they flew Beaufighter V8492, "M" while the ORB says MM905. Unwilling to trust the sortie report — which also misstates Rees's initials — I have listed the aircraft in the "Claims" appendix as MM 905.

ULTRA KV 5971, KV 6257, KV 6293, KV 6340, KV 6385, KV 6508, KV 6555, KV 6588, KV 6610, KV 6640, KV 6687, KV 6987, KV 9317, XL 325, XL 353

AIR24/951: MAAF ORB Intelligence Appendices, June 1944
AIR40/2152: GAF Activities, West Med
AIR40/2161: A.I.2(g) Reports 1613–1750 Incomplete (Captured Enemy Aircraft — Italy. List No. 10)

RL20/311: *Kdo. Flughafenberiech 18/XI KTB Nr. 7, 01.04.44–22.10.44* (also ADI(K) 80/72)

Ufficio Storico… "*Situazione Aeronautica — Aeri da Combattimento Notturno*"

Letter from Hans Nawroth: 16 December 2000

Völkischer Beobachter "from our Luftwaffe Correspondent, Wilhelm Jung": *Nachtschlachtflugzeuge greifen ein, wirkungsvolle Unterstützung des Heeres — Erfolgreiche Angriffe bei Frascati* (newspaper cutting circa 9 June 1944, via Nawroth)

After The Battle magazine, Number 52 (op. cit.)
Jim Bailey, *The Sky Suspended, A Fighter Pilot's Story*, Images Publishing (Malvern, 1995)

Alfons Eck *Ein Schutzengel mit Meisterbrief: die Lebensgeschichte eines Optimisten* (self-published, 1998)

Günter Wegmann: *Das Oberkommando…* (op. cit.)

The Other Side

PRO AIR27/2062 & 2063: Operations Record Book No. 600 Squadron, January 1944–August 1945 and Appendices May 1944–August 1945

Personal communication from Robert A. Rees, 25 June 2000.
Logbook of F/L Stewart Rees (RAAF)

Ufficio Storico… "*Situazione Aeronautica*" (op. cit.)

Roy Cross: *The Fighter Aircraft Pocketbook* (Batsford, London 1962)
William Green: *War Planes of the Second World War — Fighters Volume Two* (Macdonald, London 1961)
Bill Gunston: *Night Fighters, A Development and Combat History* (Patrick Stephens, Cambridge 1976)
James J. Halley: *The Squadrons of the Royal Air Force* (Air Britain (Historians) Ltd, Tonbridge 1980)
Alfred Price: *Word War II Fighter Conflict* (Macdonald and Jane's, London 1975)
John Rawlings: *Fighter Squadrons of the RAF and Their Aircraft* (McDonald and Janes, 1976)
Martin Streetly: *Confound and Destroy — 100 Group and the Bomber Support Campaign* (Macdonald and Jane's, London 1978)

http://www.raf.mod.uk/bob1940/401to601.html

CHAPTER 6: 'HE ENDED UP IN AFRICA"

ULTRA KV 3737, XL 402, XL 607, XL 527, XL 707, XL 632, XL 836, XL 983, XL 1006, XL 1134, XL 1120, XL 1235, XL 1272, XL 1360, XL 1508, XL 1553, XL 1840, XL 2210, XL 2465, XL 2696, XL 2706, XL 3086, XL 3059, XL 3844, XL 3970, XL 3919, XL 4110, XL 4196, XL 4218, XL 4267, XL 4300, XL 4336

AIR20/7710: Translations Vol. XI: Second World War
AIR24/443: ORB Desert Air Force: Equipment, Signals, Adv HQ Unit etc., 1943-44
AIR26/328: ORB Wing 244, 1942-44
AIR26/380: ORB Wing 276
AIR26/383: ORB Wing 276 - Appendices
AIR27/2062: ORB No. 600 Squadron
AIR40/2152: GAF Activities, West Med

CSDIC AFHQ Report A.406 of 16 July 1944

USAFHRA Microfilm Reel K1028Y, Index 1598: Koller material, frame No. 726 "*Tagesverlauf, Datum unbekannt (…nach der Invasion)*"

BA-MA RL2 III/60: *Az. 11b16.18A Nr.11 711/44 g.Kdos.(2.Abt.(IIB)) Betr. Umbenemmung der2./N.S.Gr.2 und Aufstellung des Stabes N.S.Gr.9*
BA-MA RL20/311: *KTB Koflug 18/XI, Cardano al Campo*
BA-MA RL20/230: *Flughafenbereich 2/VI, Bologna — Anlagen zum Kriegstagebuch, April–Oktober 1944*

Ufficio Storico… "*Situazione Aeronautica*" (op. cit.)

Letters Hans Nawroth, 22 November 1993, 21 February 1994 and 22 May 1999
Letter from Harry Fischer, 18 December 2000

Günter Wegmann: *Das Oberkommando der Wehrmacht* (op. cit.)

Events after Nawroth bailed out: as told to Sigrid Leinberger, Linda Pardoe and the author, Bacharach, 14 May 1998.

Müller's hit on ammunition dump: originally stated to author by Rudolf Sablottny as having occurred during a raid on Cattólica and gaining OKW citation. Only corresponding report from OKW is from 6 July attack however and supported by information from Sablottny to Nawroth.

Zimmerman's article: (magazine cuttings, via Nawroth) at least two versons were published, *Kühne Kämpfer der Nacht — Vom Einsatz der Nachtschlachtflieger in Mittelitalien* and *Fliegerische Höchstleistungen — Vom Einsatz der Nachtschlachtflieger — Ueber 1000 Einsätze in einem halben Jahr*. They were the same except for some sentences about the *Oblt.*'s "death" and the closing paragraph and I have synthesized them into one account. The full names of the airmen are as provided by Hans Nawroth. Author's translations.

Mokrus and Wagner: details of Mokrus from *Verlustmeldung* and information from Hans Nawroth. Information on Wagner and aircraft tactical markings from research at *WASt.* by Winfried Bock (*Verlustmeldung* not among those held by Nawroth).

Wolff: CSDIC CMF Report A.412 of 9 August 1944. Postwar quotations combined from two letters to Dirk Bunsen in late September 1988 and January(?) 1989.

Events of 26/27 July: personal communication from Hans Nawroth, 23 September 1944.

Castello di Bardi: http://www.diasprorosso.com

In Their Own Words: Morale and recreation

Personal communications from and made available by Dirk Bunsen, Alfons Eck, Willy Ferling, Harry Fischer, Horst Greßler, Werner Hensel, Alfred Kunzmann, Heinrich Leinberger, Werner Lotsch, Hans Nawroth, Rudi Sablottny, Helmut Schäfer, Paul Sonnenberg and Paul-Ernst Zwarg,

CSDIC reports A.412 of 9 August 1944; A.499 of 4 December 1944; A.520 of 27 December 1944; A.589 of 23 August 1945.

Zimmerman articles (op. cit.)

CHAPTER 7: "WITHOUT LUCK YOU'RE DONE FOR"

ULTRA XL 4336, XL 4468, XL 4700, XL 4712, XL 4827, XL 5558, XL 5564, XL 5890, XL 6103, XL 8007, XL 8460, XL 9083

PRO AIR24/952: MAAF ORB Intelligence Appendices, July–August 1944
PRO AIR40/2152: (op. cit.)
PRO AIR51/94: MAAF microfilmed records
BA-MA RL21/210: *Kriegstagebuch Fl.H.Kdtr. E(v) 228/VI, 07.05.44–19.08.44*

CSDIC CMF Reports A.436 of 15 September 1944 and A.440 of 19 September 1944.

Ufficio Storico… "Situazione Aeronautica" (op. cit.)

Letter, Werner Hensel to Hans Nawroth, 14 April 1996
Letter, Harry Fischer to Dirk Bunsen, 28 December 1992.
Personal communications from Herbert Kehrer.
Conversation with Harry Fischer, Krauschwitz, June 1997.
Conversation with Harry Fischer and Herbert Kehrer, Tengen, 1 June 1999.

Note: Wolfsen and Wilk's aircraft code is from Winfried Bock's *WASt.* research and is not in the *Verlustmeldung* held by the author (sometimes there is a second report on file with either additional or contradictory information). Bock gives the Ju 87's WNr. as 1120, which may have been all that was painted on the aircraft. From known Ju 87 series, I have opted for 131120 as the likely full number.

A life in aviation: Harry Fischer

Personal communications from Harry Fischer.
Letter, Harry Fischer to Dirk Bunsen, 28 December 1992.
Conversation with Harry Fischer and Herbert Kehrer, Tengen, 1 June 1999.

Barry Rosch: *Luftwaffe Codes, Markings and Units 1939-45* (Schiffer, Atglen USA 1995)

CHAPTER 8: "FLY THROUGH THE WRECKAGE"

ULTRA XL 9056, XL 9204, XL 9295, XL 9320, XL 9407, HP 33, HP 736, HP 1310, HP 1371

AIR22/80: Air Ministry Weekly Intelligence Summaries, 1 April–30 September 1944
AIR24/443: Desert Air Force ORB 1943-44
AIR20/7703: Translations vol. IV, Second World War
AIR26/315: Wing 239 ORB
AIR40/2152: (op. cit.)
BA-MA RL20/236: *KTB Nr. 2, (1 August - 31 December 1944) Kommando Flughafenbereich 10/VII*
BA-MA RL21/209: *KTB Nr. 1, Flugplatz Kommando Càmeri*
BA-MA RL2 II/118: *Gen.Nafü (1.Abt.II) Vortragsnotiz betreffend Egon-Führung für Nachtschlachteinsätze auf Brücke und Brückenkopf Remagen*

Letter, Paul Sonnenberg to *Frau* Hug, 2 October 1948
Letter, Dirk Bunsen to Manfred Zundel, 22 June 1989
Letter, Dirk Bunsen to Helmut Schäfer, 13 July 1989
Letter, Dirk Bunsen to Harry Fischer, 24 August 1993
Personal communication from Werner Lotsch, 16 March 2000
Conversations with Willy Ferling, Kestert, 28/29 May 2000

Alfons Eck *Ein Schutzengel* (op. cit.)
Alfred Price: *Blitz on Britain 1939-45* (Purnell Book Services, Abingdon, England 1977)
Ernst Obermaier: *Die Ritterkreuzträger der Luftwaffe, Band II: Stuka- und Schlachtflieger* (Verlag Dieter Hoffmann, Mainz 1988)

In Their own Words: Operations

Personal communications and conversations with Dirk Bunsen, Willy Ferling, Franz Fischer, Harry Fischer, Herbert Kehrer, Alfred Kunzmann, Hans Nawroth, Helmut Schäfer, Rudi Sablottny, Paul-Ernst Zwarg.

PRO AIR50/164 & AIR27/2063: Sortie reports of No. 600 Squadron

USAFHRA: various CSDIC (Air) CMF reports on interrogations of captured NSG 9 aircrew.

Alfred Price: *Focke Wulf 190 at War* (Ian Allan, Shepperton 1977)

CHAPTER 9: "SAUWETTER"

ULTRA HP 1969, HP 2109, HP 2314, HP 2355, HP 5475, HP 5050

AIR24/443: Desert Air Force Operations Record Book and Appendices 1943–44
AIR40/2152: (op. cit.)
AIR 22/81: Air Ministry Weekly Intelligence Summaries, 7 October 1944–24 February 1945

BA-MA RL20/236: "KTB Kdo. Fl.Ber. 10/VII" (this source refers to an operation on 26th by "II. NSG 9": 1./9 from Bovolone; 2./9 from Ghedi and 3./9 from Villafranca. There are however no other indications that anything took place).
RL21/213: *KTB Nr. 3 der Fliegerhorstkommandtur E (v) 205/VII*
RL9/4: Ic monthly report on *Eigener Einsatz*

Dirk Bunsen correspondence

In Their Own Words: "Us and Them"

Pesronal communications from Dirk Bunsen, Willy Ferling, Franz Fischer, Harry Fischer, Alfred Kunzmann, Heinrich Leinberger, Hans Nawroth, Rudi Sablottny, Helmut Schäfer, Paul-Ernst Zwarg.

CSDIC (Air) CMF Report No. A.595.

CHAPTER 10: "UNDER GROUND CONTROL"

ULTRA HP 5288, HP 5362, HP 5556, HP 5593, HP 5875, HP 5637, HP 5654, HP 5801, HP 5887, HP 5947, HP 8050, HP 8118

AIR20/7710: "Translations Vol. XI Second World War"
AIR 22/81: Air Ministry Weekly Intelligence Summaries, 7 October 1944–24 February 1945
AIR23/6511: MATAF Intops Summaries, October-December 1944
AIR23/6791: HQ MAAF Air Intelligence Weekly Summaries 4 Dec 1944–11 May 1945, Nos. 107-129
AIR24/443: (op. cit.)
AIR24/955: FIU "B" Report No. 6
AIR27/2063: ORB No. 600 (City of London) Squadron, RAF
AIR40/1462: M Reports (Report M.82)
AIR40/2867: Summaries (Ref. T.369/19)

ADI(K) report No. 650B/1944
CSDIC (AIR) CMF Reports A. 499. A. 514 & A.520
CSDIC(MAIN)/X 109: (op. cit.)

RL9/4: Ic monthly report on *Eigener Einsatz*
RL20/236: *Kriegstagebuch, Kdo. Flughafenbereich 10/VII*, June 1943–December 1944
RL9/10: *Kdr. General d. Dt. Lw. in Italien, Stellenbesetzungen, Kräfteverteilung, Dislozierung von Kommandobehörden, Verbänden, Einheiten Bereich Italien (Sammelordner mit Übersichten) 1944 –April 1945*

Letter, Dirk Bunsen to Manfred Zundel, 22 June 1989
Letter, Willy Ferling to Dirk Bunsen, 19 July 1989
Conversation with Willy Ferling, Kestert, 29 May 2000
Letter from Dirk Bunsen: 8 August 2000

Ernst Obermaier: *Die Ritterkreuzträger* (op. cit.)

Commanding Officers

Conversations and communications with NSG 9 veterans

CSDIC (Air) CMF prisoner of war interrogation reports
ADI(K) prisoner of war interrogation reports

RL9/10: *Kdr. General d. Dt. Lw. in Italien, Stellenbesetzungen, Kräfteverteilung, Dislozierung von Kommandobehörden, Verbänden, Einheiten Bereich Italien (Sammelordner mit Übersichten) 1944 - April 1945*
RL10/509: (op. cit.)
RL10/507: *Entwicklung der NSGr. 2*

WASt. : personnel loss reports for NSG 9

Ernst Obermaier: *Die Ritterkreuzträger* (op. cit.)

CHAPTER 11: "SIGNS OF AGGRESSIVENESS"

ULTRA HP 8552, BT 272, BT 421, BT 508, BT 620, BT 747, BT 861

AIR23/3479: MAAF Sigint Daily Reports, October 1944–May 1945
AIR23/6511: (op. cit.)
AIR23/6791: (op. cit.) (Summaries Nos. 108, 110 & 111)
AIR24/443: Desert Air Force ORB, 1942-44
AIR27/2062: ORB No. 600 Squadron RAF

CSDIC Report No. A.589, 23 August 1945

RL9/4: Ic monthly report on *Eigener Einsatz*
RL10/509: (op. cit.)
RL20/236: KTB Kdo. Fl.H.Ber. 10/VII

Letters from Hans Nawroth: 19 January 1994, 21 February 1994 and 28 January 1996
Letter from Herbert Kehrer: 6 April 1998
Letter from Werner Lotsch: 16 March 2000
Personal communication from Helmut Schäfer: (undated)

A Life in Aviation: Wolfgang Leo Hugo Holtz

Letter, Dr. Mathilde Holtz to Hans Nawroth, 8 June 1988
Holtz *curriculum vitae* (including citations and *Wehrpass* extracts) and police reports on his death via Dirk Bunsen and Hans Nawroth
Wolfgang Dierich: *Die Verbände* (op. cit.)
Barry Rosch: *Luftwaffe Codes* (op. cit.)

CHAPTER 12: "THE JU BELOW STRUCK US"

ULTRA BT 1446, BT 2713, BT 2758, BT 3088, BT 3205, BT 4079

AIR22/81: (op. cit.)
AIR23/6791: (op. cit.) (Summaries Nos. 114 and 115)
AIR23/8289: Mediterranean Allied Strategic Air Force Intelligence/Operations Summaries Nos. 588–652, 1945
AIR24/955: FIU "B" Report No. 9
AIR27/2062: ORB No. 600 Squadron
AIR29/1181: No. 29 Field Signals Unit, Appendices October 1944–May 1945
AIR40/2232: Egon — ground control of bombing aircraft on to targets, used by German Air Force units in Europe.
AIR55/227: "HQ 2 TAF Disarmament Intelligence Summary No. 2: Operational units of Luftflotte Reich, as at 6th May 1945"

RL9/4: Ic monthly report on *Eigener Einsatz*

Aircraft loss reports of *Luftflotte 6* and records of *General Quartiermeister 6. Abteilung* (E.J. Creek collection)

Letter, Dirk Bunsen to Helmut Schäfer, 13 July 1989
Personal communication from Herbert Kehrer (undated)

Stollwerck's parachute jump: Personal communication from Herbert Kehrer and conversations with NSG 9 veterans in Duisburg (June 1996) and Weißwasser (May 1997).

Alfred Price: *Fw 190 at War* (op. cit.)

The Night Fighter Problem

AIR25/818: ORB Group 205, 1944-May 1945
AIR25/833: Group 205 Operations Record Book Appendices, March 1945
AIR26/380: ORB Wing 276 1942-45
AIR26/385: ORB Wing 276, Appendices
AIR27/2062 & 2063: ORB and Apendices No. 600 Squadron (op. cit.)

BA-MA RL10/419: KTB of 2.(F)/122, 1 January 1944 – 5 April 1945

USAFHRA: Microfilm roll (copy held by Ferdinando D'Amico)

Nick Beale, Ferdinando D'Amico, Gabriele Valentini: *Air War Italy 1944–45, The Axis Air Forces from the Liberation of Rome to the Surrender* (Airlife, Shrewsbury 1996)

CHAPTER 13: "DOWN TO THE DREGS"

ULTRA BT 4423, BT 4485, BT 6044, BT 6621, BT 6733, BT 7402, BT 7569

AIR20/7891: Translated German Documents
AIR22/82: Air Ministry Intelligence Summaries March-June 1945
AIR23/3479: (op. cit.)
AIR23/6512: MATAF Intops Summaries, January-March 1945
AIR24/1035: MATAF ORB April-May 1945, Appendices
AIR25/818: (op. cit)
AIR25/833: (op. cit.)
AIR26/380: (op. cit.)
AIR26/385: (op. cit.)
AIR26/385: Letter, Major Nicholas J. Kasun Jr. (HQ 62 Fighter Wing — White Fighter Control) to OC No, 10 Field Signals Unit, RAF, dated 5 March 1945
AIR27/1121-1125: ORB No. 178 Squadron and Appendices
AIR40/152: Focke-Wulf 190A, F and G
AIR40/1461: "M" Reports
AIR40/2152: (op. cit.)
AIR40/2154: GAF Recce, Western Med

RL9/4: Ic monthly report on *Eigener Einsatz*

Letter, Dirk Bunsen to Manfred Zundel, 22 June 1989
Letter, Dirk Bunsen to Harry Fischer, 24 August 1993
Letter, Harry Fischer to Dirk Bunsen, 12 February 1993
"Wir sahen nichts": conversation with Willy Ferling, Duisburg, 4 July 1996
Letters from Hans Nawroth, 21 February 1994 and 24 May 1999
Personal Communication from Werner Lotsch, 16 March 2000
Letter from Dr. "Deb" Wylder, 25 August 1997
Letter from Neil M. Galloway, 8 January 1998

347th Fighter Squadron newspaper "De-Nuss-ance" for March 1945 (via D'Amico)

Gebhard Aders, *Close-Up 8: Fw 190F* (Monogram Aviation Publications, Boylston, Mass., 1986)
T. Poruba & A. Janda, *Focke-Wulf Fw 190F, G* (JaPO, Czech Republic, undated)

Note: 1/Lt. Asbury (KIA 27 February 1945) was intially identified by cross-referencing information from Dirk Bunsen, files at BA-MA and PRO (see above) and Ferdinando D'Amico's extensive material amassed in correspondence with veterans of the 350th Fighter Group. Final confirmation was supplied by James H. Kitchens III in the form of Missing Air Crew Report 12AF-XAG-P11.

Note: "Deb" Wylder wrote that on 3 March, "Hausner was flying a P-47D-27RE, Serial No. 42-27293, and I was flying a P-47D-20 — or about that vintage. I do remember it was a Razorback."

CHAPTER 14: "THE FIRST MOSQUITO DIDN'T SEE ME"

ULTRA BT 9633, BT 9935 KO 351, KO 453, KO 959, KO 1378

AIR20/8534: CSDIC (Air) CMF Report No. A.596 of 19 October 1945, "The German Air Force in Italy"
AIR23/3460: FIU Party "B" 1944-45 (Technical Reports Nos. 1-43) — Reports No. 17 of 4 May 1945 (Radar Station – Monsélice) and No. 21 of 19 May 1945 (German Radar Stations in Northern Italy).
AIR23/6513: MATAF Int/Ops Summaries, April 1945, Nos. 719 to 748 Complete
AIR23/6788: RAF Mediterranean Review, vol. 2, Nos. 6-10: January 1944 - May 1945
AIR23/7767: MAAF G-2 Intelligence Summaries Nos. 1-10, 1945
AIR25/818: (op. cit.)
AIR25/834: Group 205 Operations Record Book Appendices, April 1945
AIR27/359: ORB No. 31 Squadron SAAF
AIR26/380: (op. cit.)
AIR26/385: (op. cit.)
AIR27/1524: ORB No. 256 Squadron RAF
AIR27/2063: (op. cit.)
AIR40/2373: 2TAF Summaries of GAF Activity, April-May 1945
WO204/6802: Desert Air Force Daily Intsums from 18 Mar 1945 to 3 May 1945

USAFHRA: Microfilm roll K1028Y (Index 1598)
USAFHRA: CSDIC (AIR) CMR Report No. A.555: Interrogation Report on 3 Senior GAF Officers
USAFHRA: CSDIC (AIR) CMR Report No. A.564: The Latter Months of the GAF in Italy as Represented by Captured Documents

BA-MA: RL9/8, Anlage B zu Komm. Gen. Qu/Ib Nr.222/44 g.Kdos — B) Einheiten der Fliegertruppe

Ofw. Horst Rau: *Bericht über den Abschuß einer Ju 87 durch zwei amerikanische Mustang-Jäger* (dated 2 May 1945)

Letter, Peter Stollwerck to Dirk Bunsen, 29 November 1946
Letter, Dirk Bunsen to Manfred Zundel, 22 June 1989
Letter, Harry Fischer to Dirk Bunsen, 28 December 1992
Letter, Dirk Bunsen to Harry Fischer, 24 August 1993
Letter, Werner Hensel to Hans Nawroth, 15 April 1996
Letter from Air Historical Branch 5 (RAF) to NB, 6 September 1996
Letter from Dirk Bunsen, 14 July 1997
Letters from Herbert Kehrer, 5 December 1996, 6 April 1998 and 7 February 2001

Personal communication from Werner Lotsch, 16 March 2000

Note: The quotation about the Mozzecane *Flak* installation draws on Bunsen's letters of June 1989 and August 1993 (see above) and 18 April 2001.

Note: Since his *Flugbuch* and other personal effects were lost, Dirk Bunsen relies on memory for the dates of his last missions. In 1989 he wrote (to Manfred Zundel) of 23/24 and 24/25 April, in 1997 (to the author) of 21/22 and 22/23 April. Given his assigned targets, reference to surviving *Flugbücher* and other sources has led me to amend his dates to those in the text.

Alfons Eck: *Ein Schutzengel…* (op. cit.)
Tom Ivie: *Photographic Reconnaissance* (Aero Publishers Inc., Fallbrook CA, 1981)
Tom Ivie: *Recce's Rowdy Rebel* (Air Classics magazine, September 1986 issue)
Ernest R. McDowell and William N. Hess: *Checkertail Clan: The 325th Fighter Group in North Africa and Italy* (Aero Publishers Inc., 1969)
Capt. John B. Woodruff: *A Short History of the 85th Mountain Infantry Regiment* (www.10thmtndivdesc.org)

CHAPTER 15: "I'D BROUGHT ALONG A BICYCLE"

PRO AIR41/58: The Italian Campaign 1939–45: Vol. II, Operations June 1944–May 1945

CSDIC (Air) CMF Report No. A.564: (op. cit.)

HQ MATAF, Intelligence Section: Notes on the Operations of the Air Liaison Party with the CG, GAF in Italy, Located at Bolzano (dated

24 May 1945)
Letter, Peter Stollwerck to Dirk Bunsen, 29 November 1946
Letter, Herbert Kehrer to Dirk Bunsen, 29 March 1990
Letter, Harry Fischer to Dirk Bunsen, 28 December 1992
Letter, Harry Fischer to Dirk Bunsen, 12 February 1993

Personal communication from Alfred Partzsch, 10 December 1999
Personal communication from Werner Lotsch, 16 March 2000
Conversations with Werner Hensel, Minden 13–14 May 2001

Joachim Brückner: *Kriegsende in Bayern 1945: Der Wehrkreis VII und die Kämpfe zwischen Donau und Alpen* (Verlag Rombach, Freiburg-im-Breisgau 1987)
James Lucas: *Last Days of the Reich — The Collapse of Nazi Germany, May 1945* (Arms and Armour Press, 1986)

APPENDIX 1: MARKINGS AND CAMOUFLAGE OF NACHTSCHLACHTGRUPPE 9

ULTRA KV 1979, KV2089

AIR23/3459: Technical Report No. 14: No. 1 F.I.U., R.A.F., "A" — Villafranca di Verona A/D
AIR23/3460: Party "B", No. 1 Field Intelligence Unit, Report No. 17 — Vicenza Airfield and Report No. 18 — Bovolone airfield
AIR24/951: MAAF ORB, Intelligence Appendices, June 1944 (Report No. 231, "Viterbo Main Aerodrome")
AIR24/1001: MAAF ORB Intelligence Appendices, April–May 1945
AIR40/2161: A.I.2(g) Reports 1613–1750 Incomplete (Captured Enemy Aircraft — Italy. List No. 10)

CSDIC CMF Report A. 406 of 16 July 1944
CSDIC CMF Report A. 440 of 19 September 1944

Letters from Hans Nawroth, 23 September 1994 and 15 January 1995
Conversation with Horst Greßler, Duisburg 1996.
Letter from Horst Greßler, 31 July 1999.

Gebhard Aders: *Monogram Close-Up 8* (op. cit.)

Beale, D'Amico, Valentini: *Air War Italy* (op. cit.)
Kenneth A. Merrick: *German Aircraft Markings 1939-45* (Sky Books Press, New York 1977)
Kenneth A. Merrick and Thomas H. Hitchcock: *The Official Monogram Painting Guide to German Aircraft 1935-45* (Monogram Aviation Publications, Boylston Mass. 1980)
Martin Pegg: *Hs 129: Panzerjäger!* (Classic Publications, Burgess Hill 1997)
J. Richard Smith and John Gallaspy: *Luftwaffe Camouflage and Markings 1935-45 Vol. 3* (Kookaburra, Melbourne 1977)
Karl Ries: *Deutsche Luftwaffe über der Schweiz 1939–45* (Verlag Dieter Hoffmann, Mainz 1978)
Thomas A. Tullis: *A Quick Reference Guide to the Colours & Markings of the Fw 190A/F/G, Part 1* (Cutting Edge Modelworks, Merrifield VA. 1998)

APPENDIX 4: NSG 9 ORDER OF BATTLE

ULTRA VL 7980, XL 3059, BT 3088, BT 6621, BT 7402

CSDIC A.564 (op. cit.)

BA-MA RL2 III/61, 331–332, 728–735, 881–882; KART 40 series disposition maps

USAFHRA K1113.3101, vol. 6, 1944

Data compiled postwar by *Gen.* Hellmuth Felmy

Data researched by J. Richard Smith and Ulf Balke

COMPARATIVE RANKS

	Luftwaffe	RAF	USAAF
Officer Ranks	Reichsmarschall		
	Generalfeldmarschall	Marshal of the RAF	General (Five Star)
	Generaloberst	Air Chief Marshal	General (Four Star)
	General	Air Marshal	Lieutenant-General
	Generalleutnant	Air Vice-Marshal	Major-General
	Generalmajor	Air Commodore	Brigadier-General
	Oberst	Group Captain	Colonel
	Oberstleutnant	Wing Commander	Lieutenant-Colonel
	Major	Squadron Leader	Major
	Hauptmann	Flight Lieutenant	Captain
	Oberleutnant	Flying Officer	First Lieutenant
	Leutnant	Pilot Officer	Second Lieutenant
Non-Commissioned Ranks	Stabsfeldwebel	Warrant Officer	Flight Officer
	Oberfeldwebel	Flight Sergeant	Master Sergeant
	Feldwebel	Sergeant	Technical Sergeant
	Unterfeldwebel		Staff Sergeant
	Unteroffizier	Corporal	Corporal
	Hauptgefreiter		
	Obergefreiter	Leading Aircraftman	
	Gefreiter	Aircraftman 1st Class	Private First Class
	Flieger	Aircraftman 2nd Class	Private Second Class

Notes:

1. Due to the more numerous non-commissioned ranks in the Luftwaffe, equivalences in this area are less precise than among commissioned officers.

2. The Luftwaffe also had three Officer Candidate grades, beginning with *Fahnenjunker* (prefixed to the normal NCO rank, e.g. *Fhj.Uffz.*) and continuing through *Fähnrich* and *Oberfähnrich* (used as rank designations in their own right).

3. In the USAAF only commisioned and warrant officers were pilots; in the RAF sergeants and above; in the Luftwaffe on occasions even a *Flieger* could pilot an aircraft. Other RAF and USAAF aircrew were at least sergeants whereas the Germans observed no lower limit. Also the Luftwaffe tended to entrust command to lower ranks than their opponents did. Whereas a *Major* commanded NSG 9, in an equivalent size of formation in the RAF (a Wing) the CO would probably have been at least a Wing Commander, more likely a Group Captain and for a USAAF Group a Lieutenant Colonel.

4. The abbreviations for ranks used throughout this book are the ones commonly found in the documents of the time.

GERMAN PERSONNEL

ITALIAN PERSONNEL

ALLIED PERSONNEL